THE
MACDESIGNER'S
HANDBOOK

THE
MACDESIGNER'S
HANDBOOK

ALASTAIR CAMPBELL

RUNNING PRESS
PHILADELPHIA, PENNSYLVANIA

A QUARTO BOOK

Copyright © 1992 Quarto Pubishing plc

All rights reserved under the Pan American
and International Copyright Convention.
First published in the United States of America
in 1992 by Running Press Book Publishers.

9 8 7 6 5 4 3 2 1
Digit on the right indicates the number of this
printing

ISBN 1-56138-128-4

Library of Congress Cataloging-in-Publication
Number 91-51058

This book was designed and produced by
Quarto Publishing plc
The Old Brewery
6 Blundell Street
London N7 9BH

Senior Editor Cathy Meeus

Copy Editors Judy Martin, Maggi McCormick

Designer and illustrator Alastair Campbell

Picture Research Manager Sarah Risley

Art Director Moira Clinch

Publishing Director Janet Slingsby

This book contains examples of computer
software and graphic design work. These
examples are included for the purposes of
criticism and review.

Film output in Great Britain by The Alphabet Set
Manufactured in Hong Kong by
Regent Publishing Services Ltd
Printed in Hong Kong by
Excel Printing Company

This book may be ordered by mail from the
publisher. Please include $2.50 for postage
and handling. <u>But try your bookstore first!</u>

Running Press Book Publishers
125 South Twenty-second Street
Philadelphia, Pennsylvania 19103

6 CONTENTS

INTRODUCTION

One day early in 1989, while tearing out what little hair I had left (I'd just bought my first Macintosh computer), I received a telephone call.

"Hello. My name's Jackie and I'm calling on behalf of Leadotype Corporation. We've just released a new typeface family called Jaggie Gothic. It looks really nice and is available in light, medium and bold weights with their respective italic variations. Would you like to buy it?"

My reaction was one of combined bewilderment and shock. Nobody had ever tried to sell me a typeface before, let alone over the telephone. I refused, explaining politely that I, like every other discerning typographer and graphic designer – while one day possibly agreeing that Jaggie Gothic Medium may indeed be "really nice" – might perhaps like to have a little glimpse of this wonderful new contribution to the global typographic arsenal before parting with hard-earned cash. I went on to explain, with diminishing patience, the criteria with which graphic designers choose and use typefaces...before eventually giving up, realizing that my caller really wasn't in the slightest bit interested in hearing why anyone could possibly *not* want to buy Jaggie Gothic, whether they had seen it or not.

The significance of this single, seemingly innocuous, telesales call – and of my reaction to it – was the realization that, by buying a Macintosh, I had left the cosy world of traditional graphic design, and stepped across the threshold of a new era, not just of graphic design, but of the entire graphic arts and printing industries.

Centuries of a craft tradition, years of training and practice, and hundreds of hours of careful and painstaking design are probably embodied in Jaggie Gothic, which was now being offered over the telephone by someone to whom it meant no more than if it had been double-glazing. Typography, the bedrock of all graphic design and several other industries had, like double glazing, become available to the masses. The shock of this realization was immediately

followed by a parallel thought: why not?

The Swiss writer Max Frisch once wrote that technology is "...the knack of so arranging the world that we don't have to experience it." In the context of graphic design, it would seem that the opposite is true – technology, in making everything accessible to all, has subjected us to some horrific graphic design experiences. These all too frequently spew forth from the world of "desktop publishing" (the means of producing printed matter literally from the desktop), the phenomenon of which provided the catalyst for the revolutionary changes now occurring across all the graphic arts industries. Computers are not by any means new to these industries – computerized laser scanners have been around for almost twenty years while computers have been used in typesetting for some thirty years. But desktop publishing, using friendly machines that anyone can operate, has begun a radical redefinition of the graphic arts industry.

Of course, change for the better must be applauded but, in the meantime, the instability it creates also generates the risk of undermining the very core of those industries – the places where design and graphic arts are taught: the schools and colleges. Until recently, typographic instruction was based entirely on a type craft defined by the limitations of movable type and, more recently, photomechanical type. Because the æsthetic aspects of type design were very much the domain of typographers working for, or commissioned by type foundries, the graphic designer's time was more likely to be devoted to other creative tasks. Of course typography and printing have always been evolving crafts, but hitherto at a pace that allowed the technology to be absorbed and understood as much by those teaching it as by those learning it. Unfortunately at present the design industry seems to be faced with a choice between Mac wizards who can't design and competent designers who have no Mac experience, either through choice or through lack of opportunity.

Travesties of graphic design are perpetrated not only by desktop publishers but also by many so-called "designers" who use the computer as a subterfuge for their creative inadequacies. Look around and you see the clichés of computer-generated graphics assaulting you from everywhere – pixelated images, distorted type, every font on the menu, dreadful kerning, appalling justification values – and so on.

On the positive side, the computer is a wonderful means not only of extending and enhancing the creative options available but also of providing the designer with the potential for total control over every stage and aspect of the design process – something that has hitherto not been possible.

It is as well to remember that just as desktop publishing is not graphic design, so graphic design does not necessarily involve computers. Graphic design is the manifestation of a

creative solution to a given problem. A computer may give its owner the means to produce graphics, but then so does a pencil and a piece of paper. A computer enables you to render Times Roman but, as many people have discovered, it doesn't tell you what color and size it should be or how to arrange it. No matter what you use the Mac for — type design, illustration, or whatever — nothing can replace the thought process in your head and your ability to transfer those thoughts into a visual statement.

Never before has the responsibility been bestowed so firmly on the shoulders of the design profession to police the technology and re-establish and uphold standards which have been steadily eroded in the face of a tidal wave of amateurism brought about by the "progress" of technology.

At the core of the desktop publishing revolution is the way in which the user enters instructions into a computer and the way the computer, in turn, displays those instructions – the "user interface." All computers, by virtue of the fact that they must be given instructions, interface with their users. But the *real* change was the way in which the interface of the new computers began to simulate a desktop by using graphic symbols and a "pointer," controlled by means of a "mouse." This concept, pioneered by Xerox Corporation's Palo Alto Research Center (PARC), became known as a "graphical user interface" (GUI) and was adopted by Apple for its unsuccessful Apple Lisa computer, which was the precursor of the Macintosh.

The Macintosh, by using graphics for its interface, allowed the concept of graphic display to be exploited – and desktop publishing was born.

There *are* other computers which utilize a GUI – notably the NeXT computer, the brain child of Steve Jobs, who was one of the founding fathers at Apple. And the introduction of Microsoft's Windows program has given the world of IBM-compatible personal computers (PCs) a GUI. Yet the edge which the Macintosh computer had on its competition enabled it to establish a stronghold in the graphic arts industries. The support for graphics software on the Macintosh is now unparalleled and, if you need any reason for getting a Macintosh it must be – and this will run against the grain of most designers – why be different?

So what, then, will a Macintosh do for you? Its benefits are numerous: it will enable you to transform ideas speedily into a more finished state; further down the line, it will eliminate the quaint part of the design process that required you to stick small bits of paper onto larger ones; and it will give you the opportunity to enhance and control all those tasks which had hitherto either been difficult to control, laborious, time-consuming or costly.

The aim of this book is to give you a complete overview

of every aspect of choosing and using a Macintosh for graphic design. So much of what is written in books and magazines is aimed at the general Macintosh enthusiast, corporate desktop publisher or other business user and thus leans towards all-embracing, highly-detailed technical information, making it extremely difficult for the novice design user to beat a straight path through a jungle of irrelevant information and advice.

In planning the book, I decided that it should fulfill three basic functions: the text serves as general introduction to Macintosh computers for the designer, whether he or she be a novice or a seasoned professional. It is deliberately written to help them overcome any fears they may have of computers. It is also designed to provide instant reference for the experienced computer user – in the form of tracking and justification examples, color correction examples, rule thicknesses and so on. Finally, I hope it provides insights into some aspects of using computers in design that readers may not previously have considered.

Chapter One is a simple explanation of the Macintosh "environment," concerned only with what the graphic designer really needs to know: what "system software" is and what it does; the difference between memory and storage; what "RAM" and "ROM" do; how the "desktop" works; files and folders; and so on.

Chapter Two is concerned with the choice of hardware for graphic design. It explains the different functions of hardware with an explanation of what each element of the set-up does, from the computer itself through to scanners and graphics tablets.

Chapter Three is a survey of suitable software for the graphic designer – what different types of application are for and what they do, rather than how to use them. Applications are grouped according to their function: page-makeup, drawing, painting, etc. Choosing an application is one of the most difficult decisions confronting the Mac graphic designer. Many applications, particularly those for drawing, may offer very similar features and ease-of-use, so final choice may ultimately depend simply on the recommendation of others. I have tried to avoid voicing too many of my own preferences, since your requirements will quite probably be different from mine. The exception is page-makeup, and I refer consistently throughout the book more to QuarkXPress than to any other application. This is not to say that XPress is necessarily *better* than its competitors; it's just that the Mac-based graphic arts industry as a whole has adopted it as its favored layout program on the basis that, as the result of it being seemingly the most geared toward professional output, it is the most widely-used by professionals.

Chapter Four examines what is probably the most important, and also the most difficult aspect of the computer

for the graphic designer to grasp – typography and the Mac.

Chapter Five advises you on appropriate hardware and software configurations and describes the experiences of two design practices which have "gone Mac."

Chapter Six advises you on how to input text and how to handle corrections, how to organize images and your work, back-up strategies and working with service bureaus.

Chapter Seven is concerned with all those pre-press activities – from imagesetter output to color separation and correction – which were previously the preserve of special- ist technicians but which are becoming increasingly within the control of the graphic designer.

Chapter Eight is an anti-panic, quick-reference trouble- shooting guide to all the problems that a designer is most likely to encounter on the Macintosh: system crashes; mem- ory problems; disk management problems; printing prob- lems and fending off viruses. I have also suggested some titles for further reading.

Chapter Nine, a combined Glossary and Index, explains over 2000 terms, many of them already familiar to the graphic designer, but here applied in a Macintosh context.

This book was written, designed, illustrated, typeset, color separated and output to final film on Apple Macintosh com- puters. For hardware I used a Macintosh IIfx with 8Mb RAM and a 185Mb hard disk, an E-Machines T19 color monitor (some screen captures were performed on an Apple 13in RGB monitor – for which many thanks to Roger Pring of Cooper Dale), two 44Mb removable hard disk drives and an Apple LaserWriter IINTX printer. Most of the images in the book were scanned on a LinoColor system and film was output on Linotronic 530 and 630 imagesetters. The images in Chapter Five were scanned conventionally.

As far as the production process is concerned: I started first by writing the glossary. I had originally amassed a database using Dynodex, but when this fell over (the database was just too large) I transferred the material to Microsoft Word. The glossary was output as laser-printed galleys set in 12pt Helvetica Condensed, double-spaced (editing 7½pt text – its final size – would have been impracti- cal). Word was used both because of its sorting feature and so that edits could be made directly to disk in the publish- er's offices. The edited version was then copied and pasted into QuarkXPress, where it was formatted. I wrote the main text directly in QuarkXPress, outputting galleys in its final typeface and size (9pt Walbaum), but with double leading to make the editor's job more comfortable. I laid out the book in QuarkXPress once edited galleys had been returned. I then prepared the illustrations using FreeHand, from which EPS files were exported for incorporating into the QuarkX- Press layouts. I wrote the captions in position and laser page

proofs of the layouts were printed for editing and proof correction. The illustrations of the various applications featured in the book were set up on screen using, of course, the applications themselves, from which screen captures were taken with the utility Capture. The screen captures were saved as TIFF 5 files, which were then separated into process colors using PhotoShop. The resulting EPS files were then taken into QuarkXPress, from which final separated film was output. Scanned images were also saved as TIFF files, separated in PhotoShop and output via QuarkXPress. The files for film output were transported to the bureau on 44Mb removable hard disks (the total combined size of just the files used to output this book was 69Mb). The total time taken to output film was approximately 24 hours.

Many people helped me with information, products, advice and tips during the preparation of this book, and I am eternally grateful to all of them. In particular, I would like to thank the following: Alasdair Scott, John Jolly and Olaf Wendt of ZAPfactor; Trevor and Sheila Bounford of Chapman/Bounford & Associates; Andrew Wakelin and the staff of Thumb Design Partnership; Charles Stirrup, Patrick Brown and the staff of The Alphabet Set; Nick Souter; James Morris of Fingerprint Graphics; Anthea Backwell; Alan Coul of Amtech; Dave Taylor of Letraset; Fiona Cochrane of Adobe Systems; Dan Rampé of Claris; Iain Friar of Aldus; Bill Allen of Gomark; David Broad; Judy Martin; finally my wife and kids for putting up with my hermit-like existence while I worked on this book (beware – the Macintosh does that to you).

Alastair Campbell

Alastair Campbell graduated from London's Chelsea School of Art in 1969. In 1972 he co-founded the design group QED, with which he won a number of awards for design and illustration – among them a Designer's and Art Directors Association Silver Award – and had work exhibited throughout Europe. He went on to help build up one of the world's largest producers of illustrated books where he was creative director responsible for a long list of titles including a wide range of art and design books. Several of his titles received awards, including The Times Educational Supplement's Information Book Award and The Glenfiddich Award. In 1984 Campbell wrote The Designer's Handbook, *which has been adopted as required reading in many design colleges throughout the world. In addition, he has sat on judging panels for various annual design and illustration exhibitions and has lectured extensively throughout Europe on various aspects of design, typography and illustration. Since 1989, when he bought his first Macintosh computer, Campbell has been working as a freelance design consultant with clients both in the United States and in Europe. He lives near Cambridge with his wife and children.*

1
UNDERSTANDING THE MAC
BITS AND BYTES/THE OPERATING SYSTEM/
THE DESKTOP/THE FINDER/ICONS/THE POINTER/
MENUS/WINDOWS/INTERFACE/APPLICATIONS/
FILES/MEMORY/STORAGE

This chapter is an introduction to the Macintosh "environ ment" rather than instruction on how to use a Mac – that is amply covered by the substantial manuals that come with the computer. It's not important that you know exactly how a computer works – a lot of what goes on inside a Mac will seem like magic, and for peace of mind it's probably best left that way. However, there *are* a few basic features of computers – or at least, Macintosh computers – that you will need to know a little about even before you buy one.

As far as physical appearance is concerned, most Macs consist of four items of apparatus, or "hardware" – a tray of what look like typewriter keys, a small plastic box with a rectangular "button" on its top and a rubber ball protruding from its underside, a television set (or what looks very much like one) and a gray box. The first three items are called the "keyboard," "mouse" and "monitor" respectively, and they are all connected to the fourth item, the gray box, which is the Macintosh computer itself.

When you first connect these items together and switch them on – nothing happens. This is because, just as the human brain needs to acquire knowledge (to use the inevitable analogy), so the computer needs to be "pro- gramed" (given instructions) before it can operate.

BITS AND BYTES Like the brain, the computer consists of millions of tiny interconnected circuits and switches which, as with any other kind of switch (a light switch, for instance), need to be moved into a position that contributes toward forming a circuit, or "path," before anything hap- pens. This is achieved by giving a set of instructions to the computer – not in a way that makes sense to you, but in the only way the computer can recognize: in the form of a code which simply instructs the switches to turn "on" or "off." The reason for using such a seemingly basic system of instruction is that the "on" and "off" pairing can be repre- sented in so many ways – it can be a positive (on) or nega- tive (off) electric charge; it can be something or nothing –

an electric current, for instance, which may flow (on) or not (off), or a light, which may shine (on) or be extinguished (off) – it may be something large (on) or small (off); it may be a magnetically charged particle with north (on) or south (off) polarity; or it may even be yes (on) or no (off). When written down, "on" is represented by a "1," and "off" by a "0." (You will find that the power switches on many electrical appliances use the symbols "1" and "0" to denote on and off). This method of coding is known as the "binary" system (binary meaning dual, or in pairs) and a single unit (1 or 0) is called a "binary digit" – or, to use its more common, contracted, form, a "bit."

However, one bit on its own doesn't contain any real information, and it is only when several bits are strung together that the computer can do anything meaningful. Two bits, for instance, can give four instructions – 0 and 1 can be configured to give four separate on/off instructions: 00, 11, 10 and 01). So that you can enter words into the computer, and your computer can show you what it's doing in a way that *you* can understand, all the characters of language must be represented by a code. This means that, by the time lower-case letters, capital letters, numbers, punctuation marks, accents and other symbols have been accounted for, more than two hundred separate pieces of information are required. Thus each character is represented by an 8-bit

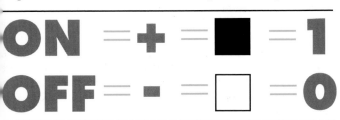

A computer carries out instructions by responding to an electric circuit, which is either complete or broken (on or off). The state of the circuit is represented by a 1 (positive, or on) and a 0 (negative, or off), called binary digits, or bits, each of which signify something or nothing, black or white, etc. (**above**). Two bits can be written in four different combinations and can thus only give four instructions, such as four shades of gray (**above right**). However, eight bits can be written in 256 combinations, each representing a single character. 24 bits can give 16.7 million combinations.

2-bit instructions

00
01
10
11

8-bit instructions

01000001 = A
01100001 = a
01000010 = B
01100010 = b
00110001 = 1
00110010
01000011

"code number," the total number of character codes amounting to 256 (the maximum number of different configurations that eight 0s or 1s can make – the letter "H" is recognized by your computer as "01001000"). These eight bits are called a "byte," and a byte represents a single character.

If this is beginning to sound complex, don't panic – to use a Mac, you don't need to know any more about binary code than this – actually, you don't need to know *anything* about binary code to use a Mac, but it helps if you know what constitutes bits and bytes.

THE OPERATING SYSTEM Computer code takes two forms. The first is the prewritten code that enables you to use the computer and which, when assembled as a complete story, is called a "program" (programs are collectively called "software" – as opposed to "hardware," the apparatus that uses the software). The second type of code represents the work you actually do on the computer: "data" code, or just "data" – but again, don't panic, to you it appears as plain English if you are typing something, or as shapes if you are drawing.

You make your computer work by "feeding" it a string of code – a program called an "operating system" or, in other words, the system of instructions that has been devised to enable the computer to operate. The Macintosh operating system is provided in two forms – part of it is permanently embedded in a microchip inside the computer and is unalterable, the other comes as software which you "load" into the computer from a "floppy disk" (see p.37).

THE DESKTOP When you switch on the Mac, having installed the operating system, the monitor screen presents you with a picture of a large expanse of gray containing two little symbols, or pictures, in the top right and bottom right corners. Along the top of the gray area is a narrow white strip containing a few words and more symbols. This is your first view of the Macintosh working environment, and it displays what is called the "desktop." The picture symbols are called "icons," and the white strip is the "menu bar." The analogy with a desktop is deliberate, and the vernacular follows, as far as is practical, that of your *real* desk, with folders, files and even a trash can for throwing things away.

One of the great advantages of the Macintosh system is that it allows you to customize your desktop so that it suits the way you work – you can choose to have the pointer move fast or slow, you can choose the speaker volume, you can change the desktop background pattern, and so on.

THE FINDER The program that provides the Mac's operating system is called simply the "System." However, the desktop described above is actually provided by another, separate, program called the "Finder." The Finder program provides the icons, menus and windows that are the "tools" on your

Below To operate a computer, you give it instructions ("input") via a keyboard (**1**). The computer (**3**) converts your instructions into data that it can understand (but which you cannot) and which enables it to carry out its tasks. In order that you can see what you are doing and what the computer is doing, your input and the results of anything you have asked the computer to do are converted back into a form that you can understand. This is done by means of displaying characters and

From bits to gigabytes
8 bits = 1 byte
1,024 bytes = 1 kilobyte (K)
1,024 kilobytes = 1 megabyte (Mb) (1,048,576 bytes)
1,024 megabytes = 1 gigabyte (gig) (1,073,741,824 bytes)

Strictly speaking, "kilo" means one thousand, but because computers use a binary system (pairs of numbers) each number is doubled: 2; 4; 8; 16; 32; 64; 128; 256; 512; 1,024.

words on a monitor screen ("output") (**4**). The relationship between your input and computer output is called the "user interface." The Macintosh utilizes a variety of graphic devices which have been designed to make the computer easier to use. These devices, called "WIMPs," comprise "windows" (**5**), "icons" (**6**), "menus" (**7**) and a "pointer" (**8**) which you can move around the screen by means of a device called a "mouse" (**2**). The use of WIMPs is known as a "graphical user interface" (GUI).

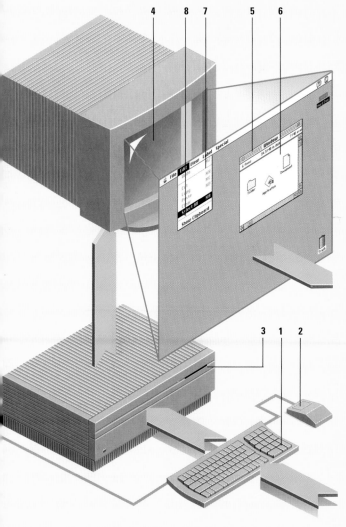

desktop and that enable you to organize your work both on the desktop and in folders. The System and the Finder are inseparable – to use a Macintosh computer, both programs must be present.

ICONS An icon is a pictorial representation of a collection of data such as a file or a disk. As far as is possible, the picture on the icon depicts the type of file it represents – a document is usually represented by a rectangle with a turned-over corner, while an application icon often depicts a hand holding a pen, or an image that symbolizes the purpose of the application. System file icons are sometimes pictures of a Mac.

THE POINTER You will also see on the screen a small, left-leaning arrow, called the "pointer." When you move the mouse on a flat surface, the pointer responds accordingly by moving around the screen. If you position the pointer over an icon and press the button on top of the mouse (this is called "clicking" the mouse), the icon changes color – it becomes highlighted, indicating that it is "selected"; (you cannot achieve anything on a Mac unless you select something first – an icon, a command or a piece of text, for example). The shape of the pointer may change from an arrow to a symbol of something else – an "I-beam," for example, if you are editing text, or a wristwatch if your Mac requires you to wait while it performs some task or other.

MENUS The icon at top right of the desktop represents a "hard disk," the place where all your work and everything else that you work with will be stored – the "drawers" of the desk, if you like. Just as the drawers in your desk can be opened, so can your hard disk. You do this by selecting the icon as described above, then moving the pointer to the word "File" in the menu bar and clicking the mouse. A list will suddenly appear, or "pop down." This list is called a "menu," and the items listed on it are called "commands" - by choosing a command on the menu, you are telling your Mac to do something. On the menu you have chosen are several items, one of which says "Open." Still keeping the mouse button depressed, you move the pointer down the list until it reaches "Open." As you move the pointer down the list, each item it crosses becomes highlighted until the pointer moves to the next item. When the pointer reaches the item "Open," that, too, becomes highlighted. By releasing the mouse button, you select that menu item.

WINDOWS When you have selected "Open" from the "File" menu, a white, framed panel – containing more icons - instantly appears. This panel is called a "window," and the contents of every icon you "open" in the above manner will be displayed in such a window. Icons can also be opened by another, more usual, method: you select the appropriate icon by using the mouse and pointer, as described earlier, and then press ("click") the mouse button twice in rapid

succession, and presto – the window and its contents are displayed! This technique is called "double-clicking."

INTERFACE When you press a key on the keyboard, you enter, or "input," something into the computer – you either type words or tell the computer to do something (a "command"). So that you can keep track of what you are doing, your actions are displayed on the monitor screen. Likewise, if the computer wants to ask or tell *you* something, it will also do so on the screen one way or another, or make an audible sound. This relationship between you and the computer is called the "user interface" ("interface" describing the method by which a computer interacts with a person or some other device). The combination of windows, icons, menus (or mouse) and pointer is sometimes referred to as a "WIMPs" computer interface, but this use of graphic devices which interact with each other is more commonly called a "graphical user interface" (GUI).

APPLICATIONS Using the Finder is fine for moving icons around the desktop, opening folders, organizing your work and so on, but it doesn't enable you to *create* anything. To create and produce something, you must use another set of program instructions, specially written to perform specific tasks and to enable you to do the things you want to do. Programs that do this are variously called "application software," "application programs," or just "applications." When you open an application, you are effectively opening up a box of tools, complete with its own drawing or writing pad, and putting it onto the desktop. With this application you write, draw, paint, or do whatever the application is designed for. Most of the work you do – and certainly everything you actually produce – will be done while working "in" an application (see p.50).

It may seem, then, that the applications you use are more important than the computer. But what gives the Macintosh its unique edge over other computers (even those imitating it) is not just the way that it presents a "user-friendly" environment even without any applications, but the way in which Apple promotes the same user-friendliness within applications written by other developers (the use of consistent vocabulary across applications – commands, and menus, for example). Apple does this by laying down rules and guidelines for software developers to follow when writing their applications and, although these guidelines involve activities which are often invisible ("transparent") to the user, they can determine the effectiveness of the application; or, at least, the way in which that application conforms to the "ease-of-use" ethos of the Mac environment.

FILES A file is a collection of data to which a name has been given so that it can be used or stored either by you or by your computer. Every icon you see on your desktop (even a

When a Macintosh computer is turned on, the monitor displays a gray area, along the top of which runs a white strip containing words and symbols. The gray area is called the "desktop" (**1**), the white strip the "menu bar" (**2**), and the words within it "menu titles" (**3**). Although represented pictorially, the icons in the menu bar are menu titles for the "Apple menu" (**4**), the "Help menu" (**5**) and the "application menu" (**6**). When a menu title is "selected" with the pointer (**7**), a panel, called a "menu," drops down (**8**). The items listed in the menu are called "commands" (**9**). On the desktop are at least two icons: a hard disk icon (**10**), representing the contents of the computer's hard disk, and an icon of a garbage can, called the "trash," where you "throw away" things you no longer need. To see what's "inside" an icon, it must be "opened" by selecting the icon with the pointer (it becomes highlighted) and then choosing the "Open" command from the "File" menu. This produces a panel called a "window" (**11**), which displays the contents

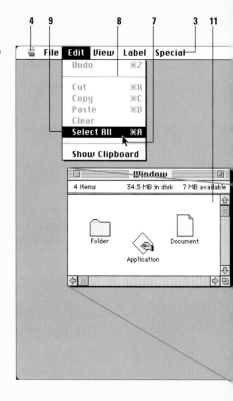

Icons Icons represent disks in, or attached to, a Macintosh computer and the folders and files stored on them. An icon will generally depict, as closely as possible given its small size, the item it represents. The color of the icon indicates its current state, for instance, the icons (**left**) represent an unopen floppy disk (**1**), a selected floppy disk (**2**), an open floppy disk (**3**) and an ejected floppy disk (**4**). The icons (**right**) depict a folder in its unopen (**5**), selected (**6**), and open state (**7**). The trash icon (**8**) is where you delete files you no longer require. The icon bulges when something is placed in the trash (**9**). Just as with a folder, the trash can be opened and its contents viewed.

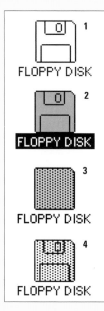

FLOPPY DISK — 1
FLOPPY DISK — 2
FLOPPY DISK — 3
FLOPPY DISK — 4

FOLDER ICON — 5
FOLDER ICON — 6
FOLDER ICON — 7

8   9

of the icon. A window comprises a "Title bar" (**12**), a "Close box" (**13**) for closing the window, a "Zoom box" (**14**) for opening up the window to full size, a "Size box" (**15**) for altering the size of the window, and "Scroll arrows" (**16**) for viewing items hidden beyond the edges of the window. The

relative position of the visible portion of the window is indicated by the "Scroll box" (**17**) in the "Scroll bar" (**18**). The icons displayed in the window represent "Files" (**19**) or "Folders" (**20**). The latter may contain other folders or files.

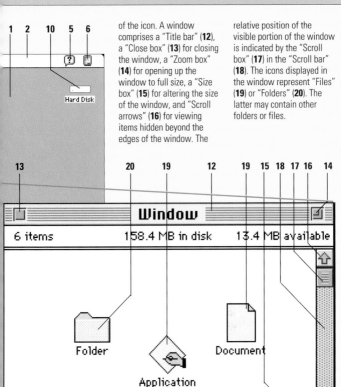

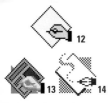

Folders depicting other icons on the front will either be the system folder (**10**) or a folder within it (**11**).

The basic Macintosh application file icon depicts a hand holding a pen over a piece of paper (**12**) to reflect the productive purpose of an application. Other application icons usually

symbolize the purpose of the application, such as page make-up (QuarkXPress, **13**) or drawing (FreeHand, **14**). Documents are the files you generate within an application. The "generic" document icon depicts a piece of paper with a turned-over corner (**15**). Documents created in applications also retain the identity of their application icons (QuarkXPress, **16**, and FreeHand, **17**, **18**). System

files are often represented by a Mac icon, such as with the Finder (**19**) and the System file itself (**20**).

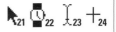

The mouse is represented on screen by the "pointer" icon (**21**) which assumes different shapes for different tasks. The wristwatch (**22**) means "wait," while the "I-beam" (**23**) is used for text and the cross-hair pointer (**24**) for drawing shapes.

hard or floppy disk icon – the place where you *store* files) represents a file of one kind or another. There are also some files that are not represented by icons, and you cannot see them – for example, the desktop itself has an "invisible" file where changes (such as deleting a file) are recorded. Files fall into four main groups: system files, application files, document files, and folders.

System files These are all the files that form part of the Mac's operating system, including the System and Finder files. They also include files that you may have added to enhance the system, such as fonts. The picture depicted by a system file icon will vary depending on the function it performs, but those that form the basis of the operating system generally display a symbol of a Macintosh computer (the System file itself shows a Mac on the side of a suitcase). System files are always kept somewhere in the system folder – either inside other folders or "loose" (not in another folder).

Application files This term refers to all files belonging to an application, including the application itself. Many larger applications come with several files, some of which must be kept in a special place – for example, loose in the same folder as the application file (on the same "level") or, sometimes, in the system folder. It can be quite confusing knowing where to put all the various files belonging to an application, so many applications are supplied with a separate little application called an "installer." When you open ("run") the installer, it places all the files in appropriate places, creating new folders if necessary. "Help," "Data," "Preferences" and "Defaults" are all typical application files. The application itself is usually identifiable by the full name of the application; for example, the application QuarkXPress is called "QuarkXPress®" underneath its icon, whereas other application files belonging to QuarkXPress are given such names as "XPress Help" and "XPress Data" and have their own icons different from that of the application.

Documents A document is any file that you create or modify with an application – a page layout or a letter, for example. The document file is created the first time you "write" ("save") that item to disk, having named it and put it in an appropriate place (you will automatically be asked to do this).

Folders These are easy to identify – their icons look just like a closed folder. Strictly speaking, folders are not data files in themselves, but places where you *keep* data files – you use folders to organize everything on your Mac by putting documents and applications inside them. You can also put folders within other folders. The files which comprise your Mac's operating system have their own folder called, not surprisingly, the "system folder." The system folder is easily identified because it is the only folder icon to bear a picture of a Mac.

MEMORY In order for both you and the computer to manage your work, the computer must be able to remember what you do not only as you do it, but also so that you can retrieve your work in the future.

Using your own memory as an analogy, just as you record your memories by writing them down – in a diary, say – so a computer must transfer data from temporary memory to storage of a more permanent kind.

To achieve both things, the computer uses two kinds of memory – one temporary, the other permanent. Temporary memory is called "random access memory," or "RAM." Confusingly, RAM is also commonly referred to as just "memory." Permanent memory is generally called "storage." Even experienced users sometimes misunderstand the difference between memory and storage. To confuse things even further, there is a third kind of memory called "read-only memory," or "ROM," and I'll deal with that first.

ROM As described earlier in this chapter, the Macintosh operating system is provided in two parts – one as software that you install yourself, the other embedded in a microchip. This microchip stores memory called "read-only memory" (ROM), whose contents can only be read, not added to or altered. ROM chips, as they are called, have their information installed at the time of their manufacture and, once the chip is plugged into the Mac, the information cannot be changed except by replacing the chip. The information in ROM is always available and, unlike RAM, is not erased when you switch your Mac off.

The part of the system software that resides in ROM is called the "Toolbox," and this contains the pre-installed permanent software that provides information, or "routines," about windows, menus, dialog boxes, etc, that programmers use when they create applications to make them consistent with the Mac GUI. Although the ROMs in non-Macintosh computers also contain system software, it is partly the extent to which the Toolbox provides the Mac's GUI that sets it apart from other computers. The Mac's ROM also provides "diagnostic routines" that test certain hardware functions every time the Mac is switched on. The capacity of a ROM chip is not something you need be concerned about, since this is predetermined at manufacture and is unalterable.

RAM Just as your memories are erased forever when you die, so "random access memory" (RAM) is lost when the computer is switched off. This is because, just as you need energy to live, so RAM needs power (in the form of an electric current) to retain the information stored within it. RAM is used by applications to enable you, in turn, to use the application – when you open an application, you are effectively copying part of it, from the place where it is stored, into RAM (although the application remains stored and

Memory and storage

While you work on a computer, you work with data held in its memory, called "random access memory" (RAM). Some of the data may be generated by you, and some put there by the computer's "central processing unit" (CPU) on instructions from you or from the software you are using. The CPU acts as a switch that routes data from one place to another. The CPU retrieves permanently stored data from a medium such as a disk and puts it into the computer's memory

(**1**). From here the data is used for display on a monitor (**2**). Data that you generate is temporarily stored in RAM (**3**) and lasts only for as long as power is supplied to its microchips; thus everything in RAM is lost when you turn the computer off. So that you do not lose your work, it must be "written" to a suitable storage medium (**4**). Another kind of memory, called "read only memory" (ROM), contains permanently stored data that the computer needs in order to operate (**5**).

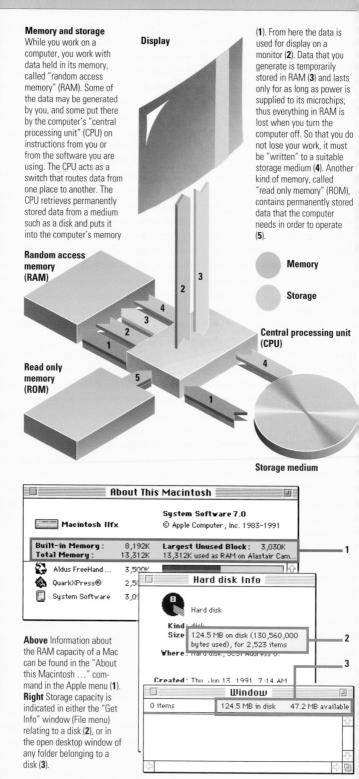

Display

Random access memory (RAM)

Read only memory (ROM)

Central processing unit (CPU)

Storage medium

Memory

Storage

About This Macintosh

Macintosh IIfx

System Software 7.0
© Apple Computer, Inc. 1983–1991

| Built-in Memory : | 8,192K | Largest Unused Block : | 3,030K |
| Total Memory : | 13,312K | 13,312K used as RAM on Alastair Cam… |

Aldus FreeHand …   3,500K

QuarkXPress®   2,5[

System Software   3,0[

Hard disk Info

Hard disk

Kind : disk
Size : 124.5 MB on disk (130,560,000 bytes used), for 2,523 items
Where : Hard disk, SCSI Address 0.

Created : Thu, Jun 13, 1991, 7:14 AM

Window

0 items   124.5 MB in disk   47.2 MB available

Above Information about the RAM capacity of a Mac can be found in the "About this Macintosh …" command in the Apple menu (**1**).
Right Storage capacity is indicated in either the "Get Info" window (File menu) relating to a disk (**2**), or in the open desktop window of any folder belonging to a disk (**3**).

other parts of it may be put into RAM if and when they are required). When you use an application – when you type words or draw shapes, for instance – you are doing so in RAM, and the work that you do on screen has no permanence until you store it somewhere (you "save" it to disk – see below). Consequently, this is the most unstable aspect of using a computer, and it is essential to get into the habit of saving your work at frequent intervals – the more frequent, the better.

Since storage is also memory, you would expect your Mac to use a disk for its RAM. But, because a disk is mechanical (this creates problems of transferring data quickly), the Mac relies, like ROM, on chips for its RAM, these providing the speed that a disk cannot match. RAM uses chips called "single in-line memory modules," or "SIMMs" for short. The greater the capacity of your SIMMs, the more you can achieve in RAM – for example, you can use more fonts (a font only uses RAM when it is placed inside your System file), have more applications open at one time (an application only uses RAM when it is open), and you can work on large, complex layouts or illustrations (as with applications, documents only require RAM when they are open).

Having said that RAM resides in chips rather than on a disk – well, some models of Macintosh are able to supplement their built-in ("installed") RAM by "tricking" the Mac into thinking that part of the hard disk is RAM, thereby increasing the amount of RAM available for you to work with. This type of RAM is called "virtual memory" and is slower than installed RAM. There is another kind of RAM available to the Mac called "parameter RAM," or "PRAM" (pronounced "pee-ram") for short, where certain settings such as the time and date are stored. I say "stored," because, unlike RAM, this information is not erased when you turn off the Mac – for the simple reason that it is powered by its own battery (if you removed the battery, you would lose the settings).

STORAGE To save your work permanently, you copy it from RAM to one of a variety of "storage media." Your storage medium will be a "hard disk" or a "floppy disk," and usually both. Unlike RAM, which you cannot actually "see," storage media are represented on the desktop by icons, each separate storage device having its own icon (you can have several hard disks attached to your Mac – see p.30). Copying your work from RAM to disk is called "saving" it, and you save your work by using the "Save" command from the File menu in the menu bar. This command will only be present in a menu when you are using an application – you cannot save anything in the Finder because you don't create anything, and any changes you make to the desktop are recorded in the invisible desktop file.

2
HARDWARE

THE MACINTOSH/THE MICROPROCESSOR/
COPROCESSOR/SPEED/MEMORY/STORAGE/
CONNECTIVITY/MONITORS/STORAGE MEDIA/
MAGNETIC MEDIA/OPTICAL MEDIA/LASER
PRINTERS/SCANNERS/MODEMS/ACCELERATOR
CARDS/INPUT DEVICES

When you buy an item of furniture or piece of equipment – a telephone, say – for your home or office, while function is obviously paramount among your criteria for selection (isn't it?), design and appearance will rate pretty high on the list, if not at the top. When you buy a computer, however, it will probably be one of the few times you will be required to make a purchasing decision based *entirely* upon what happens inside the object rather than upon the object itself.

The computer world is one which is furnished, in the most part, with bland, ugly boxes, distinguishable, to the novice, only by the number of twinkling colored lights – the more there are (surely?), the more whizzo it must be. So it is, then, that the real criteria for buying a computer system depend entirely upon what you intend using it for. You may be forgiven for thinking that, when it comes to computers, the needs of all graphic designers are more or less the same, regardless of what specific activity they may be engaged in. Fortunately, one of the outstanding features of the Mac is that it seems to be virtually limitless in its adaptability to different design disciplines.

Obviously, cost will rate high on your list of considerations. Don't be under any misapprehension; this is not a once-only capital purchase – you will inevitably find yourself spending money on a more-or-less continuous basis on such things as service agreements, performance enhancements, add-on hardware, new software, upgrades, etc. Of course, the extent to which you continue to shell out depends not only on your relationship with your bank, but also upon your own self-discipline – be warned, you may often find it difficult to resist the many temptations tantalizingly floated in front of you by increasingly hard-nosed marketing techniques.

THE MACINTOSH The Macintosh box is often referred to as the "CPU" (central processing unit), even though this term really applies to the microprocessor within it. Of all the

hardware that you will buy, one of the most straightforward items to choose is probably the Macintosh computer itself, simply because there are a limited number of models available for you to choose from, even though there may be many configurations within each model.

There are two basic types of Macintosh computer: those which incorporate a screen as part of the body of the computer ("compact" Macs) and those which don't ("modular" Macs, although the monitor may be included as part of the package as with the Macintosh LC). A third kind of Mac, a "notebook" type, is also available, but it is less appropriate as a primary machine for doing design work unless you happen to do a lot of traveling as part of your business to sites where Macs are not available – otherwise, you can carry an external disk drive or removable cartridges (see p.38).

The screens of compact Macs are small – 9in diagonally – and, while they are impractical for design work, they can be useful as an additional machine if you require extensive keyboard input or word processing.

THE MICROPROCESSOR This chip, the central processing unit, represents the "brain" of the computer. Macintosh computers are equipped with CPUs of the Motorola 68000 series, and will be either a 68000, 68020, 68030 or 68040 chip (numbers like these are, alas, something we apparently just have to live with). The 68030 and 68040 chips incorporate a "paged memory-management unit" (PMMU) which, among other things, allows you to take advantage of "virtual memory" (see p.25). A separate PMMU chip can be added to the motherboard of computers using a 68020 chip, such as the Macintosh II. Whatever design work you do, it is best to buy a computer with a 68030 or 68040 chip, but it is possible to upgrade a 68020 computer by adding a PMMU chip.

COPROCESSOR This is a chip designed to take the strain off the CPU by undertaking specific computation tasks. The coprocessor used as standard on Macs is the Motorola 68882 math coprocessor (the 68881 was used on earlier Macs). You will be better off with a coprocessor, but, since the Mac that you are likely to buy will probably have one as standard anyway, it is not something you need give much thought to.

SPEED Theoretically, a computer's speed is related to the number of times per second that a quartz crystal inside it pulsates, which, in turn, determines the speed of such things as the time it takes for the screen to redraw or how frequently the CPU needs to access RAM. These pulses are measured in megahertz (MHz), one MHz representing one million cycles, or instructions, per second, and is referred to as "clock-speed." However, advances in computer technology – such as the ability to handle greater amounts of data at once and a CPU with integrated coprocessors and memory – mean that a modern Mac with a clock-speed of 25MHz

(Macintosh Quadra) *actually* runs at more than twice the speed of an older model with a faster clock-speed of 40MHz (Macintosh IIfx).

Of all considerations when buying a Mac for professional use, speed is one of the most important. If you have read any Macintosh magazines, you may have noticed the preponderance of ads for all manner of speed-related enhancements; if you buy a slow machine, you will discover, the hard way, why there *are* so many.

Of course, speed, like so many things, is relative; and for the first few months of learning to use the Mac, it may not seem a priority. However, as you become more proficient, you may also become increasingly frustrated by the time it takes for commands to be implemented, which in many situations could be quite considerable.

Your requirement for speed depends upon what kind of design work you intend using the Mac for; this determines the type of application you will be using (the speeds of different applications vary, even if they are performing similar tasks). If all you require is a paste-up substitute for creating small-format, short documents such as ads, the greater cost of a fast machine may be difficult to justify – after all, you wouldn't use a Ferrari to make deliveries around town. If you intend doing anything more than the most basic kind of design work, you will find increased speed not just useful, but a necessity. Working on long documents which are dripping with graphic devices and tints, working with images and creating complex illustrations are all activities that demand the fastest computing speeds if you don't want your creativity to atrophy during the process.

If you think you may require even greater speed than the fastest Mac can provide, you will need an accelerator board (see p.47).

MEMORY Vying with speed for important-criteria-when-choosing-a-Mac is the amount of random access memory (RAM) your computer has (don't make the all too common mistake of confusing *memory* with *storage* – see p.23).

RAM is less important than it used to be, not only because additional RAM chips (SIMMs) are now both inexpensive and easy to install, but also because the introduction of System 7 has brought with it the facility of virtual memory (see p.25). However, because virtual memory is much slower than installed, or *real* RAM, it makes sense to have as much real RAM installed as you think you'll need – and the answer to that is, as much as will fit into your machine. This normally means around 8Mb (megabytes), although the Macintosh LC will expand up to 10Mb and the IIsi to 65Mb, with the IIci and the IIfx having a capability of a massive 128Mb RAM – although this means installing *very* much more costly high-density RAM chips. 128Mb is really only necessary for image-intensive documents such as

Inside a Macintosh All the components of a typical Macintosh computer are connected to one another via a single circuit board called the motherboard (**1**). This houses the many microchips which process data and switches it from one component to another. At the core of these microchips is the central processing unit (CPU) (**2**). Random access memory (RAM) is held in banks of chips called single in-line memory modules (SIMMs) (**3**), which are plugged into the motherboard. The capabilities of a Mac can be extended by plugging expansion "cards" into sockets called slots, such as NuBus slots (**4**) or a Processor Direct Slot (**5**). The ports (sockets) of NuBus cards are accessed by removing the appropriate expansion cover shield and hole cover on the rear panel of the Mac. The floppy disk drive (**6**) is accessed via the opening on the front of the computer (**7**). Some models of Macintosh have provision for two floppy disk drives. An internal hard disk for data storage is sealed within its own disk drive unit (**8**). The Mac's power supply (**9**) is self-adjusting to any voltage and is cooled by a built-in fan. Power-on is indicated by a green light on the front of the computer (**10**).

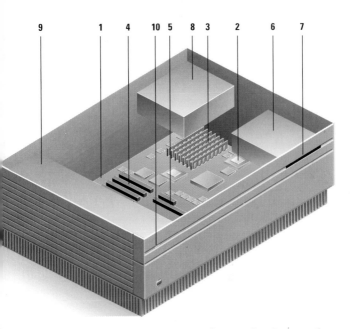

those used at the pre-press stages of reproduction, or for very memory-intensive operations such as those undertaken by some CAD (computer-aided design) and multimedia applications.

Although RAM is used by any applications you have open – the more you have open at one time, the more RAM you occupy (see p.24) – it is also required in certain "invisible," or background, areas. System files, and most particularly fonts, in use eat up RAM, as do large color monitors.

STORAGE All Macs come with an internal floppy disk drive and the facility for an internal hard disk (drive), if not the drive itself. The floppy drive will be a 1.44Mb SuperDrive, or high-density drive, as distinct from earlier, 800K (kilobyte) floppy drives. The standard hard disk drive may have a capacity of 40Mb, 80Mb, 160Mb or 400Mb, although internal hard disk drives are also available with a capacity far in

Right There are usually only a few basic models of Macintosh available at any one time. Most can be configured in a variety of ways, there being several choices of such things as the amount of memory, hard disk capacity and display capabilities. A Floating Point Unit is a coprocessor designed to help the CPU with number processing – essential for complex graphics.

*Monitor and video card must be purchased separately

Macintosh Model	Processor (CPU)	Speed	Floating Point Unit (FPU)	PMMU
Classic	68000	8MHz	No	No
Classic II	68030	16MHz	No	Yes
LC	68020	16MHz	No	No
IIsi	68030	20MHz	Optional	Yes
SE/30	68030	16MHz	Yes	Yes
IIci	68030	25MHz	Yes	Yes
IIfx	68030	40MHz	Yes	Yes
Quadra 700	68040	25MHz	Yes	Yes
Quadra 900	68040	25MHz	Yes	Yes

excess of these.

It may seem obvious that the greater the hard disk capacity, the easier it is to work, but since Parkinson's Law always prevails (in this context, the fact that your work, in the form of data, will always occupy the space available for it), I am convinced that, contrary to media hype which generates ever-increasing pressure for limitless storage, a *smaller* disk capacity is sometimes preferable, simply because it encourages neater housekeeping. However having said that, if you intend working extensively with images (scanned or drawn), large documents or multimedia applications, you really will need the largest capacity disk you can afford; a single image, for example – even scanned at a low resolution – can easily occupy 1Mb of disk space.

CONNECTIVITY The bewildering battery of connector sockets ("ports") at the back of the Mac, and slots inside, will be the hardest part for you to get to grips with when you start out (the IIci has no fewer than nine, with a potential for 12). Mercifully, most are common to all Macs and, with the exception of NuBus slots, shouldn't influence your purchasing decision.

The ports that you will find common to all Macs are:

Apple Desktop Bus (ADB) port This is used for connecting the mouse and keyboard to the Mac, and also for connecting graphics tablets. Most Macs have two ADB ports.

SCSI (small computer system interface) port Pronounced "skuzzy," this port is used for connecting peripheral devices such as external drives and scanners. Although you will find only a single SCSI port on all Macs, several devices (up to seven, including the internal hard drive) can be "daisy-chained" together, using the one port.

Serial port This port is used by LocalTalk, Apple's own cabling system, to connect the Mac to printers, modems, or

Built-in memory (RAM)	Internal Storage	Display capabilities	Macintosh Model
2Mb or 4Mb Expandable to 4Mb	Floppy: 1.44Mb SuperDrive Hard disk: 40Mb	Built-in screen, b/w	**Classic**
2Mb or 4Mb Expandable to 10Mb	Floppy: 1.44Mb SuperDrive Hard disk: 40 or 80Mb	Built-in screen, b/w	**Classic II**
4Mb Expandable to 10Mb	Floppy: 1.44Mb SuperDrive Hard disk: 40 or 80Mb	12in b/w 12,13in color	**LC**
3Mb or 5Mb Expandable to 65Mb	Floppy: 1.44Mb SuperDrive Hard disk: 40 or 80Mb	12in b/w; 15in gray 12,13in color	**IIsi**
2Mb or 4Mb Expandable to 128Mb	Floppy: 1.44Mb SuperDrive Hard disk: 40Mb	Built-in screen, b/w	**SE/30**
5Mb Expandable to 128Mb	Floppy: 1.44Mb SuperDrive Hard disk: 40, 80 or 160Mb	12in b/w; 15in gray 12,13in color	**IIci**
4Mb or 8Mb Expandable to 128Mb	Floppy: 1.44Mb SuperDrive Hard disk: 80 or 160Mb	None*	**IIfx**
4Mb Expandable to 68Mb	Floppy: 1.44Mb SuperDrive Hard disk: 80, 160 or 400Mb	12, 21in b/w; 15in gray 12, 13, 21in color	**Quadra 700**
4Mb Expandable to 256Mb	Floppy: 1.44Mb SuperDrive Hard disk: 160 or 400Mb	12, 21in b/w; 15in gray 12, 13, 21in color	**Quadra 900**

Ports are the "sockets" by which you connect hardware accessories to a Mac. These include (**right**), with their identifying icons, the Apple Desktop Bus (ADB) (**1**), serial ports (**2**, **3**), sound output (**4**), built-in video port (**5**), SCSI port (**6**, **7**), and a floppy disk port (**8**, **9**). The chart (**below**) shows which ports are available on which Macs and how many.

*Optional

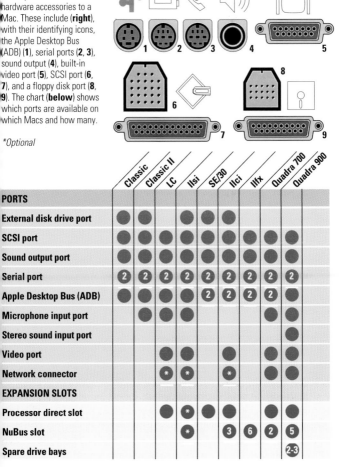

	Classic	Classic II	LC	IIsi	SE/30	IIci	IIfx	Quadra 700	Quadra 900
PORTS									
External disk drive port	●	●		●	●				
SCSI port	●	●	●	●	●	●	●	●	●
Sound output port	●	●	●	●	●	●	●	●	●
Serial port	2	2	2	2	2	2	2	2	2
Apple Desktop Bus (ADB)	●	●	●	●	2	2	2	2	●
Microphone input port		●	●	●				●	●
Stereo sound input port									●
Video port			●	●		●		●	●
Network connector		*	*			*		●	●
EXPANSION SLOTS									
Processor direct slot			●	*	●	●		●	●
NuBus slot			*			3	6	2	5
Spare drive bays									2-3

to a network. Macs come with two serial ports.

Sound, or audio, port This provides a sound-out port to an amplifier or headset.

Other ports that are available on certain Macs are:

External disk drive port For connecting an external floppy disk drive.

Video port The port used to connect a monitor to Macs which feature an "on-board" video facility. Only Apple monitors, whether monochrome or color, can be connected to this port. If you use any other monitor, you will need to connect it via a video card installed in an internal NuBus or Direct slot.

NuBus slot This is a socket found inside the Mac where you can plug in all manner of features and enhancements, such as video cards for connecting a monitor, accelerator cards for enhancing performance, fax cards for connecting to telecommunications lines, cards for connecting to video camera input, etc. The port for a card inserted into one these slots is accessed by removing one of the detachable covers at the rear of the Mac. It is not necessary to remove the cover to insert a card such as an accelerator.

Before you buy a Mac, give serious consideration to what enhancements you may eventually add – if you think you may at some stage add, say, a large color monitor, a fax, an accelerator card (some occupy two slots), and a video camera, you will eventually need five slots. This will seriously reduce your options, since there is only one Mac available with enough slots (Quadra 900), unless you buy a used Mac II, IIx, or IIfx.

Direct Slot: This will be either an 020,030 or an 040 Direct Slot depending on, not surprisingly, which computer it's in. The Direct Slot is for providing services similar to those given by the NuBus slot, although the boards for one slot will not fit the other – this incompatibility also exists between the 020,030 and 040 Direct Slots. You will find only one Direct Slot in Macs which have them.

Microphone input port: For voice recording, should you ever need to.

Cache connector: A connection for adding a memory "cache" card (see p.47) to enhance performance. Only the Mac IIci and the Quadras have one.

MONITORS The item of hardware between you, the computer and the keyboard is the display screen, or monitor. Monitors work in much the same way as ordinary television sets, whereby the screen inside a cathode ray tube (CRT), coated with light-sensitive phosphor, is bombarded by a stream of electrons. The phosphor glows briefly, creating an image. Compact Macs have screens already built in to their cases, so it is not necessary to choose one. However, since it is likely that you will be buying a modular Mac, there are several things about monitors that you should familiarize

yourself with.

Resolution As far as design work is concerned, the most important consideration – even before size and color – is the resolution of the screen. Effectively, this refers to the crispness of the image on the screen – particularly important when you are working with small type sizes. The screen image is represented on screen by dots, or "pixels" (which create a picture by being either on or off). The more pixels there are per inch, the smaller they are and the better the resolution of the screen, thus the sharper the image. Most high-resolution monitors have 72 dots per inch (dpi) or more. If a salesperson tries to seduce you by raving on about the total pixel count of a monitor (and they do), don't listen – 1,920,000 pixels may sound impressive, but you'd expect that kind of number on a 21in screen. It's still only 72dpi, though.

Size Monitor sizes are always described in inches, measured diagonally from corner to corner. This is a tradition perpetuated by cathode tube manufacturers, but is misleading when it comes to establishing the actual dimensions of the total image area of a computer monitor. A 19in screen may *look* huge when it's switched off, showing a potential image area of an adequate 11½ x 15¼in but, when it is switched on may display only 10¾ x 13⅜in – not quite enough height for a letter-size page. To establish the usable image area of a monitor, all you need to know is the number of pixels both horizontally and vertically, plus the resolution, in dpi, of the monitor. You then simply divide each of the horizontal and vertical pixels counts by the resolution – thus a screen described as 19in, with a horizontal pixel count of 1024, a vertical pixel count of 808 and a resolution of 75dpi will produce an image area of 10¾ x 13⅜in. Incidentally, don't be confused by the *appearance* of a monitor – a monitor marketed by one supplier may look identical from the outside to a different product marketed by another. This is because the CRT itself will have been manufactured by a third company, but is used by the two suppliers as a vehicle for displaying their wares – the video card circuitry design and software.

For most design work, a 13in monitor is quite adequate, but if you work extensively with page layouts where you need to see a two-page spread, you will need a larger screen. A useful monitor for designers is Radius' "Pivot" monitor, which you can physically rotate from a portrait format to a landscape one – the screen image remains the right way up all the time.

Color Monitors are either monochrome, "grayscale," or color. Monochrome monitors, as the name suggests, display pixels as either black or white, with no intermediate grays (a semblance of grays is still achievable, by alternating black pixels with white ones). Grayscale monitors,

on the other hand, are able to display pixels in a range of grays, the exact number depending on the "pixel depth" of the monitor, but usually providing 256 grays. Color monitors operate on much the same principle as grayscale monitors, but instead of the pixels being different shades of gray, they are different colors.

Pixel depth becomes important on color monitors since, if you opt for a color monitor, you will be faced with a choice of its being either eight bits or 24 bits per pixel – or perhaps more. The difference is startling – 8-bits produces a mere 256 colors whereas 24-bits produces more than 16 *million*! This doesn't mean that you can only display 256 colors or tints because, as with four-color halftone printing (which, after all, produces a pretty good range with only *four* colors), a group of different colors in close proximity

Resolution Computer monitors, although similar to television screens in that they utilize cathode ray tubes, display images at much higher levels of definition, or "resolution," than televisions. Typical monitors have a resolution of between 72 and 87 dots, or pixels, per inch. Despite this high resolution, small sizes of type can be difficult to read on screen (**right**), thus most applications incorporate a "zoom" feature so that you can work with type at any size by enlarging it on screen.

7pt Univers

7pt Garamond

12pt Univers

12pt Garamond

36pt Univers

36pt Garamond

Below In color monitors, each pixel is made of three phosphors: red, green and blue (RGB) – the additive primaries which, when mixed in pairs, form the subtractive pigment primaries of cyan, magenta and yellow. When all three colors are combined they form white light – as distinct from the subtractive primaries which form black when combined.

Above It is possible to link a large monitor to a compact Mac, which "drives" its own built-in monitor as well as the other one. This enables you to keep "palettes" (featured in most applications) on the small screen, thus leaving the whole of the larger one free for your layout. The relative positions of the screens are configured via the Monitors Control Panel so that the pointer moves smoothly from screen to screen.

optically merges to form a variety of colors adequate for most purposes.

Whether you need color or not in the first place, let alone whether it should be 8- or 24-bit, is debatable. Of course, it's nice to be able to preview any color you may have chosen, but this is a luxury you wouldn't even contemplate were you preparing, say, camera-ready art conventionally – you would specify tints and spot colors from reference charts, quoting either percentages of process colors or reference numbers, or taping color samples to the artwork. With mono or grayscale monitors, the same is possible – you can still *specify* colors (assuming, of course, that the application you are using allows you to) even if you can't *see* them – and you can still produce them as separated film. Large color monitors are expensive and may exceed

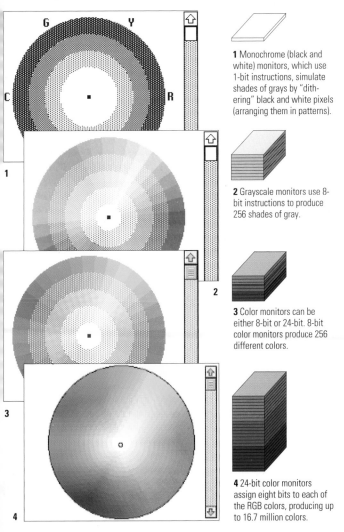

1 Monochrome (black and white) monitors, which use 1-bit instructions, simulate shades of grays by "dithering" black and white pixels (arranging them in patterns).

2 Grayscale monitors use 8-bit instructions to produce 256 shades of gray.

3 Color monitors can be either 8-bit or 24-bit. 8-bit color monitors produce 256 different colors.

4 24-bit color monitors assign eight bits to each of the RGB colors, producing up to 16.7 million colors.

the cost of the most expensive Mac, so make sure you really *need* one for your work before buying.

Several models of Macintosh have video circuitry already built in so that you can plug the monitor straight in. If you do decide to buy a non-Apple monitor, you will need to add a *video* card to one of your Mac's expansion slots – you cannot simply plug the monitor into the back of your Mac. Be warned, though – opening your Mac's case voids the warranty unless done by an Apple-approved engineer. (This is something of an anomaly, since to maximize use of your Mac's expandability, you've *got* to open up your Mac sometime – perhaps Apple figures that by the time you've gathered enough confidence to open up your Mac, the warranty will have run out anyway.)

Refresh rate This is a background, but nonetheless important, consideration when choosing a monitor (it's to do with comfort and, since you will be staring at a screen all day, should not be dismissed lightly). Put simply, it relates to whether or not the screen may flicker – the slower the refresh rate, the more likely it is to do so. Refresh rate is measured in hertz (Hz), referring to the number of times that the electron beam "rakes" the screen from top to bottom – a refresh rate of 67Hz, say, means that the screen is "refreshed" 67 times each second. Do not confuse refresh rate with screen "redraw," since the latter refers to the time it takes for the screen image to redraw itself after you make a change.

The most important thing to do when you buy a monitor is, if you get the chance, to view the screen image for yourself. While other people's opinions are useful, particularly if they are graphic designers, there is no substitute for making a decision based upon your own criteria. For example, I use an E-Machines T19 color monitor which doesn't seem to attract many compliments from some reviews that I've read, but, for my needs, and compared with the many other monitors that I've worked with, it is hard to beat for crispness and fidelity.

STORAGE MEDIA Computer memory (RAM) is erased when the computer is switched off. "Storage" is the computer facility for preserving your data by allowing you to copy data from RAM to one of a variety of storage media so that it is permanently saved.

MAGNETIC MEDIA There are four basic types of media for magnetically storing data; all are made up of a metal or plastic substrate coated with iron oxide particles. When data is "written" to (recorded on) the media, these particles are magnetized and aligned in one of two directions ("north" or "south") by the disk drive's "read/write heads," this polarity corresponding to either a 1 or a 0 according to the data being written (see "bits and bytes," p.14). Because of their sensitivity to magnetic fields, you must always keep disks

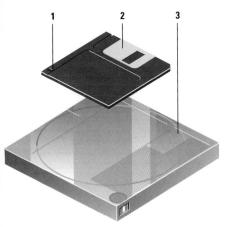

Left The most basic medium for storing computer data is a magnetized disk, which can be either "floppy" or "hard." Floppy disks (**1**) are typically 3½in diameter, consist of a flexible disk contained within a rigid plastic case, and are transportable. The disk is inserted into the computer's floppy disk drive, which gains access to the disk via a protective sliding shield (**2**). Another transportable medium is the "removable" hard disk (**3**), which is considerably more capacious than a floppy disk.

away from magnets such as those found in telephones and audio speakers.

Floppy disks These are the most basic of all forms of storage, magnetic or otherwise. Floppy disks for the Mac comprise a single, circular platter of magnetically coated flexible plastic (thus the term "floppy"), which is housed in a rigid plastic case. You use a floppy by inserting it into the slot on the front of the Mac, this slot being the entrance to the drive mechanism. The drive spins the disk and contains the read/write heads for reading data from, and writing it to, the disk as it spins beneath the heads. All Macs contain at least one floppy disk drive.

Floppy disks for the Mac are 3½in in diameter and are either single-sided (capable of holding 400K of data), double-sided (800K) or high-density (1.44Mb). "Double-sided" means that the disk is magnetically coated on both sides, each side being read and written to by its own head – you don't need to turn it over. High-density disks are called "FDHD" (floppy disk, high density) and can only be used in drives called "SuperDrives" (although SuperDrives can also read and write single- and double-sided disks). Floppy disks are used primarily for software installation, transferring documents between non-networked computers, limited backups and for transporting files to service bureaus.

Hard disks In principle, these are similar to floppy disks. The significant differences are that the disk substrate is rigid; the disk itself may actually consist of several disks (each one called a "platter") stacked one on top of another with a space in between for access by the read/write heads; the disk is housed permanently within a sealed, dustproof unit. Hard disks provide the primary means of storage and can be fitted internally in your computer or connected to your Mac as an external device. In contrast to the limited storage capacity of floppy disks, hard disks can hold 600Mb or more.

Below A typical hard disk drive consists of several disks, called "platters" (**1**), which are sealed within a dust-free box (**2**). This unit may be housed within the computer (internal), or mounted inside a free-standing box which incorporates a separate power supply and suitable ports for connection to the computer (external). The platters consist of a rigid substrate which is coated with magnetized iron oxide particles. These particles are aligned in one of two directions (corresponding to 0 or 1) by a read-write head which changes their polarity by transmitting a magnetic field as the platter spins beneath it (**3**). The magnetic field is generated by the varying voltage of a servo coil (**4**). Each side of a platter (**5**) is served by its own read-write head. Data is written to and read from different parts of the platter by the head as it oscillates rapidly back and forth on its spindle (**6**). For data storage, each platter is divided into concentric rings, called "tracks"(**7**), and each track is divided into segments, called "sectors"(**8**). A single data file may occupy several non-contiguous sectors on different parts of a volume, in which case it is said to be "fragmented."

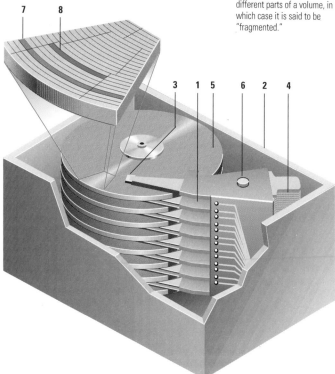

Removable hard disks Because of the limited capacity of floppy disks and the inconvenience of transporting hard drives, external drives with removable hard disks are becoming increasingly popular. There are several makes of removable hard disk drives which, although none are inter-changeable, are broadly similar in that a rigid hard disk, usually measuring 5¼in, is housed within a plastic cartridge. There are only a few manufacturers (known as "original equipment manufacturers," or OEMs) of the basic drive equipment, but there are many companies who combine their own components with drives made by these manufacturers, and who use their own name on the outside of the box. If you buy a removable disk drive, make sure you

know who manufactured the drive mechanism (SyQuest, for example) because that's the name you'll need to use when reordering cartridges.

Storage capacities of removable hard disks range from about 40Mb to 80Mb, which makes them ideal for transporting large files such as scanned images. Although it might seem that this type of storage would be vulnerable to all kinds of hazards, particularly dust, they have generally been found to be extremely reliable.

Tape drives Much the same as audio and video tapes, these consist of a reel of magnetic tape housed in a removable cartridge. Unlike disks, on which data can be accessed from any random point on the disk, data on a tape can only be accessed as the tape runs from one reel to the other. This makes them slow in comparison to disks, and they are thus used only for backing up hard disks.

OPTICAL MEDIA Generally, these are expensive, capacious media, usually used only for high-volume data storage. An optical disk is similar to an audio compact disk (CD) in that data is stored by means of tiny pits burned into the disk's surface, the size of which determines a 1 or a 0. The physical nature of writing data in this way has presented problems in erasing it, and, until recently, optical media have only been available in a form in which the data is either factory written and can only be read (CD-ROM, meaning compact disk read-only memory), or which can have data written to it only once (WORM, meaning write once, read many). Optical disks are also relatively slow, having an access time of up to 650 milliseconds (ms) compared with around 25ms of a typical hard disk.

CD-ROMs tend to be used for mass reference data such as encyclopedias, but some type foundries also supply their complete font library on CD-ROMs (not that you necessarily need to buy a whole font library – in some cases, you are supplied with a disk containing a whole library, but are only given access codes to "unlock" those you have purchased).

Because of the ability to store digitized audio data, optical media are particularly important in multimedia and music activities, with most drives providing standard hi-fi output jacks.

Other optical media include magneto-optical, or "erasable optical" (EO) drives. These get around the problem of unalterable CD-ROMs in a variety of ways. One kind has tiny magnetic particles imbedded into its surface; the polarity of these particles is determined by a combined laser and electromagnet which enable you to read and write to the disk. Another kind – "phase-change" drives – turns the surface of the disk opaque (on) or transparent (off), using either two laser beams or one beam with variable intensity.

There is also a drive that will hold up to six CD-ROM disks and audio CDs at the same time, giving a total com-

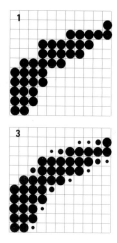

Laser printers transfer an image to paper by means of a laser light which exposes the image onto a light-sensitive surface to which toner ink is attracted or repelled by an electrical charge. The toner is then fused onto plain paper by heat. The fineness of print, or "resolution," is determined by the number of dots per inch, typically 300. Usually, these dots are all of equal size (**1**), but because 300dpi is relatively low resolution (imagesetters use 2540 dpi), stepping is often visible,

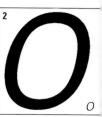

particularly on type (**2**). To compensate for this coarseness, some laser printers smooth out the edges of black areas by interspersing smaller dots in appropriate places to give an optically smooth result (**3**).

bined capacity of three gigabytes. It is also capable of using both EO and WORM disks.

Faster (around 60ms), less expensive, but also less capacious EO drives, using 3½in disks, are also now available.

LASER PRINTERS As an intermediate stage to producing high-quality output in a form acceptable for commercial printing, such as bromide or film, you will need to see what your work looks like on paper. To achieve this you will need a printer – which almost certainly means a "laser" printer. Screen quality, although supposedly "WYSIWYG" (pronounced "wizzywig," an acronym for "what you see is what you get"), does not render an image with anything like the accuracy that you need to assess the finer subtleties of a design. Even a proof printed on a laser printer will not produce the subtleties of high resolution imagesetter output (you should never rely on laser printer output to make typographic judgments – always have a sample run out on an imagesetter). This is not to under-value the role of laser printers in electronic design, since it was their ability to produce excellent results that contributed at the outset to the widespread acceptance of the computer as a professional design tool.

There *are* other kinds of printers, such as "dot matrix" and "ink-jet" printers, but, as far as professional graphic design is concerned, laser printers head the list of those producing better quality output at an affordable price. And, more importantly, PostScript (see below) is available only on laser printers.

Laser printers work by means of a pulsating laser light beam exposing a bitmap pattern (the image) onto the light-sensitive surface of a cylindrical drum. The printing (or, sometimes, nonprinting) areas of the drum are electrically charged to attract particles of "toner," a fine, black, magnetic powder, to its surface. The image is then transferred to paper by means of an electrically charged wire which,

again, attracts the toner. Finally, the toner is fused to the paper by heat. These mechanical components of a printer are called its "engine."

PostScript or non-PostScript? When you "send" a page design to a printer, it is intercepted by a kind of "mini" computer called a "controller." The controller uses a program to "interpret" the computer code comprising your design, which it then "describes" to the printer engine in a language that the engine can use to re-create your design on paper. This language is known as a "page description language" (PDL). PostScript is one such language and is licensed by Adobe Systems Inc. to various manufacturers of laser printers who use it with their printers' own, internally-built controllers.

With the Macintosh, the alternative to printers using PostScript interpreters are so-called "non-PostScript" printers, which use Apple's "QuickDraw" routines. This means that instead of having a controller built into the printer, some QuickDraw printers are able to use the Mac itself as the controller, the advantage being cost.

TrueType fonts can be printed by any printer that uses QuickDraw as well as by PostScript printers, whereas PostScript fonts can only be used on PostScript printers unless you use a utility program called Adobe Type Manager (ATM). However, the advantages of PostScript printers outweigh those of any other type, not least because so many graphic design-related applications utilize PostScript as a file format. There are, however, software packages called PostScript emulation programs which enable you to print PostScript files at an acceptable standard on QuickDraw printers, although because they have difficulty handling complex images, PostScript emulators cannot replace the real thing.

Printer resolution Like monitor screens, printers use bitmaps (see p.60) for creating images, thus outline fonts and object-oriented images must be converted to bitmaps by the interpreter before they can be printed. And, again like screens, because bitmaps are made up of dots, the more dots per inch (dpi) that a printer can handle, the better resolution, or quality, of the printed image. However, resolution of laser printers is less of a consideration since the majority of them output images at only 300–600dpi, compared with the 1270–2540dpi output of imagesetters. 1000dpi laser printers are also available, but at more than twice the price of most 300dpi printers.

Paper size Most laser printers will only print pages up to a maximum of size 8½ x 14in although the actual image area may be smaller than that – for instance, the image area of a letter-size page (8½ x 11in) printed on Apple's LaserWriter IINTX measures only 8 x 10¹³⁄₁₆in. If you need larger printed pages, many applications support "tiled" printing whereby

Right Pixels are used to display images on screen, for low-resolution laser printing, scanning input, and high-resolution imagesetting, all with varying degrees of resolution. Conventional halftone screens are also measured in dots (expressed as lines per inch). "Pixel depth" refers to the number of bits used to define each pixel – 8 bits enables 256 values to be assigned to each pixel (**below**).

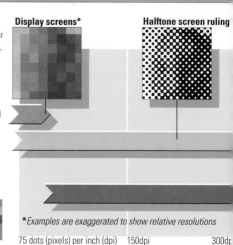

Display screens*

Halftone screen ruling

Pixel

*Examples are exaggerated to show relative resolutions

75 dots (pixels) per inch (dpi)   150dpi   300dpi

the image is printed onto several sheets of paper – the number depending on the size of the image – which you then join together. Laser printers that will print on B-size (11 x 17in) paper are also available – but at more than three times the cost of most smaller printers. In most circumstances, you will find it acceptable to simply reduce the printing size of your page so that it will fit onto the smaller paper size.

Color printers If a large proportion of your work involves color presentations, you may consider buying a color printer – if not, don't bother, since the cost will probably be disproportionate to your needs; and the quality, although improving all the time, is not good enough for any other design purpose. Better to take your work to a service bureau. However, if you do opt for color, you should consider those printers that combine color copying, scanning (even from transparencies) and printing all in one unit, such as Canon's CLC laser copier.

SCANNERS The rapid technological advances made in desktop scanning equipment may create something of a dilemma for you as a graphic designer. Up until now, you have probably been sending your color transparencies to a color origination house for separation on sophisticated scanning equipment, operated by highly skilled and experienced technicians. But now you've been told that, with a scanner attached to your Mac, you can *actually do it yourself*. Well, you can't – or, at least, you shouldn't. Yes, the equipment exists that enables you, in theory, to achieve passable results, and, yes, your favorite color separation house is now using Macs (probably not entirely, but somewhere along the line), but the reality is that if you start spending your time getting embroiled in the intricacies of quality color separation (and by that I mean the *high* quality you have hitherto been used to), you will find that your chosen profession is rapidly displaced by another. However, a scan-

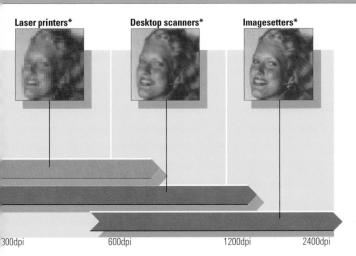

Laser printers* | **Desktop scanners*** | **Imagesetters***

300dpi | 600dpi | 1200dpi | 2400dpi

ner *can* be a substantial aid to your graphic design activities if you don't expect too much of it.

There are four main uses that designers have for scanners: scanning in line artwork, even to an acceptable reproduction standard; scanning in images to be used as positional guides (particularly useful for cutout images); inputting text copy by means of optical character recognition (OCR) software; and scanning images for subsequent manipulation with special effects. In time, and if you choose an appropriate scanner, you will probably find that you are able to scan in black-and-white continuous tone originals to produce halftones to an acceptable reproduction standard.

Not only is there a wide variety of makes of scanner, but of *types* of scanner, too: a scanner may be monochrome, grayscale or color, it may be flatbed, sheetfed, handheld, overhead, a video digitizer or a transparency scanner. Each type is designed for a specific purpose, but, frustratingly, none combines all of those purposes.

Scanners work by employing a light-sensitive scanning head, called a "charge-coupled device" (CCD), which responds to the various intensities of light being reflected from an original by generating an electric charge – black reflects little light, thus producing a low charge, whereas white is very reflective and generates higher voltages. This electric charge is then converted into a series of 1s and 0s, each one representing a single pixel (in 1-bit mode) which corresponds to the original image. A 1-bit scan will respond to the tones on both sides of a mid-tone threshold, reducing the image to pixels which are either on or off – black or white, thus producing a line image. An 8-bit scan offers 256 combinations of 1s and 0s per pixel, thus being capable of 256 grays or colors.

Resolution Just as with monitor screens and printers, the quality of a scanned image depends upon the resolution of the scanner – the more dots per inch, the sharper the result.

However, the final appearance of an image depends entirely upon how it is to be output – there is no point in scanning a continuous tone original at a high resolution if you only need it as a positional guide and thus will be printing it on a 300dpi laser printer (the default halftone screen applied to the image will probably be around only 60 lines per inch, so it's much more sensible to scan images at lower resolution if you only need them for reference). Conversely, images for halftone reproduction will always stand a better chance of fidelity if scanned at higher resolutions than the halftone screen ruling. High resolution scanning is, surprisingly important when scanning line artwork, since an image scanned at the typical resolution of 300dpi may display noticeable lack of smoothness when printed at a higher resolution on an imagesetter.

File sizes Before even considering buying a scanner, you should be aware of the voracious appetite of scanned image files in terms of both RAM space and disk storage space. An 8 x 10 inch image scanned with 256 gray levels at a low, but typical, resolution of 300dpi will demand around 7Mb of both disk and RAM space. This rises to more than 20Mb if you scan with 24-bit color. Unless you intend using a scanner for extensive image manipulation and special effects or for multimedia work, stick to a grayscale scanner – for those occasions when you need to work with a scanned color image, you can always have it scanned by a service bureau or, better still, a color separation house.

Hand-held scanners These are the most basic type of scanner, being small, plastic devices which you drag across an original by hand, the scan head "sucking" up the image as it goes, almost like a vacuum cleaner. The two drawbacks of hand-held scanners are that, being hand-held, they make it difficult to scan images without the inevitable distortion associated with the problem of moving the instrument in a straight line, and most can only scan images up to 4in or 5in wide. Neither can they scan transparencies. However, if you think you will only very occasionally have need for a scanner, consider one of these – it is cheap, small and portable, but you won't be able to use it for anything more serious than rough reference scans and the odd bit of OCR text scanning.

Flatbed scanners These work much like photocopiers inasmuch as you place your original face down on a glass screen and a scan head then passes across the original, scanning it as it goes. Flatbed scanners are probably the most useful for design purposes, being easy to use, capable of reasonably faithful line artwork scans and grayscale scanning, and very good for OCR work. Most flatbed scanners have a scanning resolution of 300dpi, but some will scan at higher resolutions.

Sheetfed, or edge-feed, scanners These are similar to

Bits per pixel (pixel depth)	1	4	6	8	24
Colors or gray shades	1 (b/w line)	16 grays	64 grays	256 grays or colors	16.7 million colors
File size of 4 x 5in image	300K	900K	1.3Mb	1.7Mb	5.2Mb
File size of 8 x 10in image	900K	3.5Mb	5.2Mb	6.9Mb	21Mb

Images scanned by desktop scanners demand large amounts of disk storage space, the amount occupied increasing with image size, pixel depth (the number of bits assigned to each pixel) and scan resolution. The chart (**above**) is based on images scanned at 300dpi, and the file sizes are approximate. The problem of file size can be partially alleviated by using file compression software or, if you intend working extensively with scanned images, a special file compression card which is installed inside the computer.

Line art, 72dpi, 1-bit

Line art, 300dpi, 1-bit

Line art, 800dpi, 1-bit

Halftone, 72dpi, 8-bit

Halftone, 300dpi, 8-bit

Halftone, conventional repro

File size notwithstanding, desktop scanning of halftone and color images is only acceptable for reproduction when scanned at a high pixel depth. Many designers prefer to use images scanned at low resolutions for positional guides; final reproduction is carried out conventionally. Line artwork, however, when scanned at 600dpi or more, generally achieves adequate quality.

Color, 300dpi, 24-bit

Color, conventional repro

flatbed scanners, but, instead of the scan head moving across the original, the original is passed under a fixed scan head. Sheetfed scanners don't really offer the designer any advantages over other types of scanner, being aimed primarily at high-volume work. Furthermore, because the original artwork is fed beneath a stationary scan head, there are limitations on the thickness of material you can pass through it.

Overhead scanners These usually consist of a scanning camera mounted above a copy board on which the original is placed. The advantage of these scanners is that you can scan transparencies (by placing a lightbox on the copy board), three-dimensional and, sometimes, large originals, although they can occasionally be difficult to focus. By using an "image-grabber" board in a NuBus slot, you can also rig up a specially-made video camera (or even your own camcorder, if you feel really adventurous) for scanning 3-D setups or for capturing frames from prerecorded video sequences.

Slide scanners These are effectively scanning cameras housed inside a box, the slide original being placed between the scan head and a light source. At the lower end of the quality-for-price scale, slide scanners offer little for designers; the scan quality is poor considering the high price of even the cheapest slide scanner. The higher end can provide quality approaching that of conventional professional color separation, but to get the best results, you really need considerable experience and thus the job of scanning for color separation is best left to those with that experience. You will otherwise need, as well as experience, a fat wallet.

MODEMS A modem is a device which enables you to use telephone lines (by converting outgoing data from digital to analog signals and vice versa for incoming data) to connect your Mac to other computers. By doing so, you can send and receive files directly to and from another computer, and you can also connect up to the central computer ("file server") of one of many commercial information services.

Although the efficacy of telecommunications depends as much upon the software as on the hardware, there are two main points to bear in mind when you set out to purchase a modem: speed and compatibility.

Speed You will find the speed of modems described in either "bauds" or "bits per second" (bps). Essentially, these descriptions equate to the same thing although, because the meaning of a "baud" (one unit per second) can be somewhat imprecise in this context (two or more bits can be contained in a single event), "bits per second" has become more widely favored. Inside your Mac, the eight bits of data comprising a character (eight bits = one character, or "byte") travel together side-by-side along paths, each bit on its own path, these paths being called "parallel" communi-

cation paths. A modem, on the other hand, uses what is called a "serial" communications path – that is, the bits travel along a single wire one after the other: since eight bits are needed to make up a single character, two additional bits – the "start bit" and the "stop bit" – are required to indicate the beginning and end of each byte, expanding each character to ten bits. (The use of start and stop bits when transmitting data is, incidentally, known as "asynchronous" communication). Thus modem speed is important since transmitting 10 bits one after the other takes a lot longer than sending eight bits all at once. Modems are available with switchable speeds from 300bps up to 9600bps, with 2400bps the norm, although fax modems are usually 9600bps.

Compatibility In the absence of an organized standard for modem design, it fell by default to one of the earliest manufacturers of modems, Hayes Microcomputer Products. You will see modems advertised as being "Hayes-compatible," meaning that they understand that manufacturer's communications commands, as do the modems used by all information services. Make sure your modem is Hayes-compatible. Compatibility of speed is another consideration, since the modem yours is connecting *to* must be at least the same speed, or faster, and likewise, yours must at least match the speed of incoming data.

Will you need a modem? That depends very much on the sort of data you think you may be transmitting. Transmitted data is only as good as the line it is being sent along and, just as you encounter line interference in a telephone conversation, so your data will also be confused by the same kind of line "noise." While some "garbage" data may be acceptable if all you are transmitting is, say, text for editing, if you are considering sending page layouts to a service bureau for imagesetter output, don't – the effect of such noise on your design will be catastrophic. To reduce the effects of line interference, many modems are equipped with noise filters. Although these are by no means totally effective, they may clean up transmission well enough for you to use a modem to send material for, say, urgent approval or proofreading.

It is quite likely that you will be generating sizeable files containing extensive graphic devices (tints, rules, illustrations, etc.), so you should bear in mind the economics of sending data over telephone lines – a file-size of 1Mb will take about four minutes to transmit at 2400bps, and many people use data compression software to speed things up, thus reducing transmission costs.

ACCELERATOR CARDS When you start out looking for the "right" Mac to buy, the last thing you'd think about is ways of speeding it up – why not just buy a fast Mac at the outset?

At first, while you find your way around your Mac and the applications you have chosen, you won't even notice its speed, or lack of it. It could also be the case that your Mac will operate at a pace that you will always feel comfortable with – probably meaning that you made the right decision in the first place.

However, it is also quite likely that you will become increasingly frustrated by even the briefest pause while your Mac computes some complex task or other – especially if you use one of the slower machines to carry out memory-intensive tasks such as those generated when you create color illustrations with a drawing application, or when your own dexterity outstrips the pace of even the fastest Mac.

Fortunately, you can enhance the speed of your Mac by installing one of many add-on "accelerator" cards available. The means by which they achieve extra speed is complex and falls firmly into the category of "magic that we don't really need to know about." Actually, accelerator cards may employ CPU's with a faster "clock" speed, more RAM, wider data paths, NuBus "block transfer" when two cards are used, "application-specific integrated circuits" (ASICs), "reduced instruction set computing" (RISC) processors, hardware programs (called "hardwired" programs) as distinct from software programs, task-specific enhancements such as QuickDraw acceleration ... need I go on? Suffice to say that the way a card achieves performance depends upon the tasks it is required to do – there are general-purpose accelerators for all-round speed, graphics accelerators for speeding up large color files, accelerators for speeding up memory-intensive CAD applications, and so on.

INPUT DEVICES When you buy a Mac, you will be offered a choice of two Apple keyboards and no choice at all of mouse – what you get is what they deliver. There are, however, several alternative devices for keying-in text and moving the pointer around the screen.

Keyboards The two keyboards on offer from Apple are the Apple Keyboard and the Extended Keyboard II. The Extended Keyboard II scores over the standard Keyboard by sporting a cluster of six additional dedicated keys, 15 very useful "function" keys (enabling you to assign keys to frequently used commands) and a few twinkling lights. However, you will probably find that the standard Keyboard is perfectly adequate for most purposes. If you decide to go beyond the standard Apple Keyboard, you should look at some non-Apple keyboards, most of which provide at least the same features as the Extended Keyboard II for less money and, or many of them, more features – for instance, modular key clusters which enable you to configure each group of keys in whatever way you want.

Mice Apart from the Apple standard-issue mouse which

like the Apple Keyboard, you will probably find perfectly adequate, there are several alternative non-Apple pointing devices. These include mice with additional buttons which allow you to assign frequently-used commands to each button. Others, called "trackballs," take the form of upturned mice, with which you move the pointer by rotating the ball rather than by moving the mouse, thus allowing the mouse to remain in one place on your desk while you use it. There is also a "cordless" mouse, which does away with interfering connecting wires by using an infrared light connection.

Tablets Variously called "graphics" tablets or "digitizing" tablets, these devices enable you to draw on screen as you would on paper – if your application offers the appropriate drawing tools and will respond to the features offered by the tablet. There is, needless to say, a variety of tablets; in its most basic form, a tablet consists of a rectangular pad (the tablet) on which you draw with a stylus, a pen-like device attached to your Mac by a wire. One step up from this is a stylus that does away with the wire, making it less cumbersome to use. The most sophisticated tablets are those that feature pressure-sensitive styli, enabling you to simulate the marks that a pen or brush would make if you pressed it harder onto paper – an essential property if you intend using your Mac extensively for illustration. Even though some tablets incorporate all the functions (and more) of a keyboard, you should not regard one as a replacement.

Most input devices connect to the Mac's Apple Desktop Bus (ADB) port, of which there are two on some models, and several devices can be "daisy-chained" together to a single port – you can, for instance, link together a keyboard, mouse and graphics tablet.

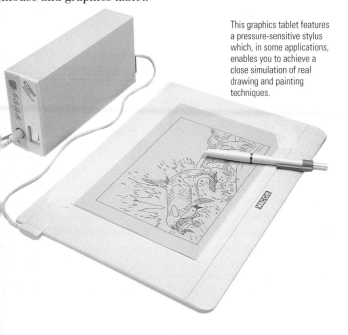

This graphics tablet features a pressure-sensitive stylus which, in some applications, enables you to achieve a close simulation of real drawing and painting techniques.

3

SOFTWARE

CHOOSING SOFTWARE/TRAINING/UPGRADING
SOFTWARE/COPYRIGHT/PAGE MAKEUP
APPLICATIONS/DRAWING APPLICATIONS/PAINTING
AND IMAGE-EDITING/SPECIAL EFFECTS/
ADVERTISING/TYPE DESIGN AND MANIPULATION/
MULTIMEDIA/WORD PROCESSING/OTHER
APPLICATIONS/UTILITIES

When you start exploring the available options for application software, you will understand why I suggested earlier that buying a Mac will seem relatively easy.

Your choice of application depends largely on which main area of design you work in and on how you envisage a Mac helping you in that discipline. Avoid the temptation to go too far, too fast. The Mac is an easy machine to learn how to use, but many applications are very powerful and complex, particularly at the professional end, and take considerable time and practice to master. It takes a while before your new tool becomes productive (revenue-earning, that is) and it will pay you to ease your new knowledge gently into your traditional way of working.

One of the first things to be aware of is that a Macintosh will not take over the job of *design*, nor will it make you a better designer, no matter how powerful your software or technically sophisticated your output. Your prime tools are and always will be, your imagination, a piece of paper and markers.

So what, then, can a Mac do? Suppose that you have done several pages of thumbnail sketches of ideas on paper – now you want to have a clearer idea of what a few of your thumbnails may look like in reality. Traditionally, you might first make a more accurate drawing of it – choose a typeface for a heading, roughly trace off a few dummy words, indicate lines of text with a gray marker and quickly sketch in an illustration. Or you may decide to take an idea a bit further – create a heading with rub-downs, paste down some body copy, cut out a picture and paste it down. Perhaps you may go as far as to type out the heading and text, copyfit it, mark it up, send it off for setting, proof read it, send it back for corrections, make further amendments to the typeset copy, and so on.

With a Macintosh you can accomplish this last procedure at more or less the same speed as you would the first (less probably). This sounds an attractive prospect, but even if all

you produce is comps, or rough visuals, you will need some high-end equipment to achieve output that matches your more traditional production methods. This includes a very fast Mac, every font available (to give you the freedom of choice you have hitherto had), lashings of RAM, a high-capacity hard disk, a color monitor, a color PostScript laser printer and a color scanner. Does the end justify the cost? It's unlikely. In reality, most designers are happy with a compromise – they maximize the advantage of being able to produce real typography very rapidly and mix that output with more traditional methods of preparing visuals.

There are, however, other significant activities under-taken on the Mac in which output is provided by the Mac itself or by something attached to it – areas such as presen-tation graphics and multimedia, for example, in which graphic design has no small part to play. These activities demand the best that technology can provide.

Virtually every activity involving graphic design has a piece of software specially written to help you. But, putting aside those uses where the computer plays an integral part in the end-product, it is in the preparation of design for reproduction that a Mac really comes into its own.

CHOOSING SOFTWARE Agonizing over a final decision between several applications that apparently do the same job is something you will get used to – the simple fact is that, quite often, there is very little to choose between appli-cations. If you research each application in some depth, you will become aware, the more questions you ask, that an application currently leading the herd in a particular area may soon be left behind by an "upgrade" to one of its rivals (an upgrade is a rewrite of an application, varying from eliminating minor problems found in the earlier version to completely reassessing its features or interface).

"Test driving" possible applications may seem the obvi-ous route, and most software developers will provide a demonstration, or "demo" disk. But, since the application you test first will also be providing your learning platform for the Mac generally, it's quite likely that you will warm to that one, selecting it over another, possibly more appropri-ate application purely for reasons of familiarity. That doesn't really matter if your first choice can do all the things that you require of it at that time. However, you'll find that, as you gain confidence, you will demand more and more out of an application and you may discover that there is another offering more powerful features of the kind you need.

One of the most accurate, and reassuring, ways to make a decision about software is to follow your instincts – ask a friend. At least then you will be able to assess the suitability of the application your friend uses to the kind of work that you do. If you don't know of anyone using a Mac in the same design field as you, do some research – read as many maga-

zine reviews as you can (although these are sometimes over-technical for novices) and talk to as many people as possible, even if they are not themselves designers. There are several "Macintosh User Groups" ("Mugs" for short) whose members are always willing to share their knowledge and experience and among whom will invariably be a few designers.

Be very wary of advice on software from people selling you hardware – it's not that they necessarily lack knowledge, but their prime concern is to shift hardware, and you may not receive the most objective and practical advice from this quarter.

If you are thinking in terms of equipping several designers with Macs, you should consider employing the services of a consultant. Such a person will study the kind of work that you do, and your methods of producing it, and also establish the attitudes of your personnel toward the introduction of new technology. The consultant will then advise on the level at which you can integrate the technology into your practice and suggest the most appropriate hardware and software for your kind of work. He or she may then provide on-site training, which should be geared to achieving an acceptable standard of competence and productivity with minimum disruption to schedules.

Having made your selection of software, make sure that you are buying the latest *versions* of the various applications (see the paragraph on upgrading software, below).

TRAINING There are three levels of expertise for using the Mac. First, you must learn how to use the Mac itself or, more specifically, the Finder (which is itself an application) and certain items of system software. This involves learning the basic functions of the Finder – how to move things around the desktop, how to use menus, create and open folders, organize files, install vital system enhancements (such as fonts), and so on. A useful explanation of the most elementary of these is provided, in the form of a guided tour, on a disk called *Macintosh Basics* supplied with your Macintosh computer. Further instructions are contained in the accompanying manuals: *Setting Up Your Macintosh, Learning Macintosh* and *Macintosh Reference*. With this library of clear and concise instruction, you will quickly teach yourself how to use a Mac, thus confirming its reputation as an "easy to learn" computer.

The second stage of the learning process involves the applications that you are going to use. This is a more complex proposition since, in order to produce work of a professional level, you need some of the most powerful and sophisticated applications available. This may require a monumental learning effort – not to mention the time which that learning soaks up. Here again, the Macintosh GUI contributes greatly toward saving the day, with some software

developers exploiting the benefits of the interface to great advantage. To the novice, the user-friendliness of the manual(s) accompanying the applications is very important – the problem here is that often you won't know what the manual has to offer until you've bought the whole application package.

In many cases it should be possible to teach yourself the application, but at first you may want to consider buying some professional instruction from a training service. Make absolutely certain that the person doing the training is expert with the Mac and is familiar with the particular version (update) of the software that you have just bought – try to find someone who is recommended. If you do decide to go it alone, help is nearly always offered by developers of the software or by their distributors; many have dedicated "helpline" telephone numbers.

The third level of expertise is optional. It involves the exploration of your system folder and beyond into a software "black hole." Lurking behind your favorite application and, especially the system software, is a whole battery of "little" applications, from utility programs for helping you with your desktop "housekeeping," right down to that scourge of deadlines – games. While many such programs are useful (these are discussed later in the chapter), there is a risk with all those shareware and freeware programs of endless "crashes" and untold damage to your System file if they are not compatible with your version of system software. Many designers work very efficiently with their Macs without feeling the need to investigate all of these options.

UPGRADING SOFTWARE If you are thinking of "borrowing" an application or two from a colleague, think twice. Apart from committing an illegal act (see the paragraph on copyright, below) you will be missing out on one of the most important aspects of buying an application – that of keeping up with the developer's constant "tweaking" of the product.

Upgrades are made for two reasons: the addition of new features (most software can be improved one way or another, not least to gain the edge over competition) and to "debug" the application (the fixing of problems which have been identified after its release). The addition of new features may simply involve minor enhancements, or it may involve a complete rewrite of the application. The first versions of major rewrites are usually identified by the use of a whole number (e.g. 3.0), as distinct from minor upgrades which employ a decimal figure (e.g. 3.1). Some version numbers are more complicated (e.g. 1.2.5E), but the principle is the same. As a general rule, be wary of the first versions of major rewrites since they will invariably be "buggy" – most developers quickly identify the problems and rapidly issue debugging upgrades.

When you buy an application, the package includes a

registration card, the return of which will entitle you to various benefits such as free minor upgrades, reduced prices for major upgrades, use of a toll-free helpline for technical support and newsletters.

COPYRIGHT The copyright in software is an extremely sensitive issue among developers, which is not surprising considering how easy it is to copy software. In the past, most software was "copy protected," meaning that an application would require some kind of "key" to enable it to be run – usually in the form of an encoded, non-copyable disk to be inserted every time the application was opened. Although the practice of copy protecting products has largely died out, due mainly to consumer resistance and impracticality, some software (usually expensive and of a specialist nature) is still copy protected.

When you purchase an application these days, the package is usually fastened by a seal, with the warning that by breaking the seal you are accepting the terms and conditions of the license agreement printed on the outside of the pack. Effectively, this means that the price you pay for an item of software is a license fee, and if you fail to comply with any of the conditions specified, you are in breach of the license agreement. When you read the small print of a license agreement, you will find the restrictions quite extensive – you cannot, for example, copy the program (except for backup purposes), or lend it to anyone. It's easy to dismiss the legalese as just being saber-rattling by the software developers, but when software is pirated or misused, it is the end-users who will ultimately suffer – dwindling revenues are bound to erode a software developer's commitment to a product.

PAGE MAKEUP APPLICATIONS Also called "page layout" or "desktop publishing" applications, these are the real workhorses of virtually all graphic design work done on the Mac.

All page makeup applications at the professional end of the scale, of which there are few – there are many more at the so-called "entry-level" – use only slightly varying means to achieve the same end. All allow you to enter text either directly (word-processing features tend to be fairly divergent between applications, and some are quite limited) or by importing it from another application. All allow you to make fine typographic adjustments (some to within .001 pt) to kerning, tracking and scaling. They all provide a limited selection of drawing tools, enabling you to create boxes, circles and ellipses, rules and, in some cases, polygons and freeform shapes. Most provide a facility to lay percentage tints either as spot or process colors which can then be output into separated film.

All applications come with preset default values (selected settings), many of which (particularly kerning) may not be acceptable to you. However, most defaults can be over-

ridden relatively easily by the user.

As with much other specialist software, selecting a suitable page makeup application is not easy – there is little to choose between the most popular applications: Design Studio (Letraset), PageMaker (Aldus) and QuarkXPress. The problem of choice is further exacerbated by the constant upgrading of each product, whereby each leapfrogs the others in turn. Since most offer more or less the same features at more or less the same time, your criteria for choosing one revolve around fewer and fewer differences. Nonetheless, you should consider the following features: the degree of accuracy with which you can specify certain attributes such as the positions of pictures and blocks of text; typographic flexibilities such as kerning, editing and rotatable text; document length – the maximum number of pages you can create in a document varies considerably and, depending on their complexity, can slow down the application quite dramatically; file-importing features, both of text and pictures – although applications are becoming increasingly catholic in this respect; color separation features – although all applications will provide separations of colors and tints created within the application, not all will separate imported picture files without additional software; and finally, the extent to which additional features are available, either from the developer or from third parties.

PageMaker (Aldus Corporation) Effectively the first serious page makeup application for the Mac, PageMaker is well-established as the leading makeup program among desktop publishers and has for some years provided the benchmark which its competitors have striven to surpass. However, despite – or, perhaps, because of – the easy-to-use nature of the product, it has concentrated its sights more upon DTP users than on professional designers, presumably because the former constitute a much larger market. It now seems to have left the high end to its competitors – its features for positioning items and rotating text, for example, are not as powerful as those of either QuarkXPress or Design Studio.

PageMaker championed the concept of a "pasteboard" – a nonprinting area around the page on which items of text or pictures can be kept, much like the bromide repro proofs of a mechanical pasteup. The pasteboard can also be used for experimenting on designs without interfering with what's already positioned on the page. However, both Xpress and Design Studio now feature pasteboards.

QuarkXPress (Quark, Inc.) Comparisons between Pagemaker and XPress seem to appear endlessly. Without getting into a detailed review of the two, I believe, without detriment to either, that such comparisons are odious – if you're a professional designer, you're more likely to prefer the power and precision of XPress; and if you're not, you'll like the easy-to-use features of PageMaker. It really is as cut

Anatomy of a page makeup application A typical professional page makeup application allows you to combine all the functions of layout, typesetting and camera-ready art so that it can be output as color-separated film. The ways in which these applications work vary, depending on such things as their "power" – the extent to which the features that they offer are controllable. Some applications, notably PageMaker, offer an intuitive and easy-to-use interface together with many features, while others, such as QuarkXPress and DesignStudio, are geared to more professional users, both providing customizable features to very fine tolerances.

The illustrations (**below**) are of QuarkXPress and show a few of its features, many of which can also be found in other applications. A feature which XPress shares with PageMaker and DesignStudio is a pasteboard (**1**) where you can play around with ideas, outside the page area. XPress, like DesignStudio, is a frame-based application, meaning that you create boxes (**2**), or frames, into which text is entered. These boxes can be linked together in any order so that text flows automatically from one to the other.

The File menu (**3**) allows you to create, open, save and print documents (common to *all* applications, page makeup or otherwise). The Edit menu (**4**) allows you to, among other things, set the way the application behaves, such as the unit of measurement; you can edit colors, style sheets (consistently used styles for fonts, leading, indents, etc.) which can be applied by a single keystroke) and hyphenation and justification parameters. The Edit Color

14 3 4 7 8 9 2 10 11 13

15 18

feature enables you to define process colors for tints (**5**) or to specify PANTONE and spot colors, or to select a PANTONE color (**6**) which can be automatically output in the correct percentages of process color tints. The Style menu (**7**) is where you select such things as typeface, type size, leading, scaling, kerning, etc. The Item menu (**8**) allows you to apply specific measurements to such items as text and picture boxes, rules, runarounds, etc. The Page menu (**9**) enables you to add, move or delete pages within a document and to set automatic page numbering.

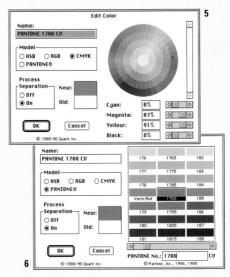

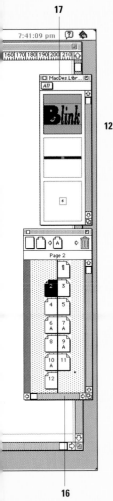

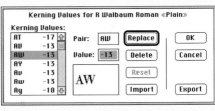

The View menu (**10**) is where you choose the size at which your document appears on your monitor while you work on it (it doesn't affect the size at which it is finally printed) and also enables you to display such things as guides or floating palettes.

Utilities (**11**) are facilities for checking spelling, making hyphenation exceptions, identifying fonts and pictures used within a document, and editing tracking and kerning values – you can customize any kerning pair of any font in the Kerning Table Edit (**12**). In XPress, this is also where extra features, called Quark-XTensions, appear (**13**).

There are a variety of "floating palettes" which you can choose to display and position anywhere on the screen: the Toolbox (**14**) is where you select various tools which enable you to undertake tasks such as

creating, modifying and moving boxes, drawing rules and shapes, and linking text; the Measurements palette (**15**) duplicates some of the commands in the Style and Item menus and displays the attributes of the currently selected item; the Document Layout palette (**16**) allows you to rearrange the pages in your document and design master pages; the Library palette (**17**) enables you to store frequently used items, such as a logo, and retrieve it in any document; the Value Converter (**18**) is a useful feature for making instant conversions of measurements.

and dried as that. XPress dominates the professional end of makeup applications, not only because it offers very powerful features, but because of the ability to add customized features (called "XTensions") written by third-party developers. Perhaps more importantly, it has been widely adopted by the design industry as a whole – a significant consideration when choosing *any* software. Its popularity extends into the prepress areas of the production process where, for example, XPress has been developed, in the form of an application called Visionary, to interface directly with the Scitex scanner.

DesignStudio (Letraset) A relative newcomer to the page makeup arena, DesignStudio is a development from Letraset's earlier entry-level application, ReadySetGo! There is not much that XPress offers that DesignStudio cannot match – it will even provide color separations of imported picture files without additional software, unlike XPress or PageMaker. However, despite being powerful *and* easy to learn, DesignStudio has not achieved the popularity of XPress or PageMaker.

Ventura Publisher (Xerox Corporation) This application, like PageMaker, was originally written for the PC world where it is, with PageMaker, dominant. Unlike PageMaker, it has made a rather uncomfortable transition to the Mac. Ventura is best suited to longer, more complicated documents than those discussed previously and, as such, is not really suitable as a multipurpose design tool. It is also quite difficult to learn.

FrameMaker (Frame Technology) Another application for preparing lengthy and complicated documents, FrameMaker possesses extensive word-processing features and drawing tools. With features such as an equation editor, it is specially appropriate for preparing scientific and technical documents.

Interleaf (Interleaf Corporation) Like FrameMaker, Interleaf is a fully integrated word-processing, drawing and page makeup application and possesses similar features for much the same kind of work.

Quoin (Interset) A hugely expensive and powerful application, this veers uncomfortably toward traditional typesetting in its extensive use of codes, which produces the potential for some very precise typographic control – more, for instance, than in XPress. Quoin is most suitable for newspaper typesetting and makeup, but, due to its complexity and lack of sympathy with the Mac ethos, it is wholly inappropriate as a designer's tool.

Lightspeed CLS (Crosfield Electronics) Crosfield's own page makeup application, designed to complement their StudioLink system, a software/hardware configuration that acts as a prepress "gateway" (here, a link between a Mac-based application and a high-end color repro scanner).

DRAWING APPLICATIONS Just as you sometimes need to create illustration artwork when preparing conventional pasteup, so you will need a facility for doing the same on your Mac. The obvious answer to this problem may be to buy a fully integrated application that includes drawing tools, but such a program will not provide the power and flexibility of separate page makeup and drawing applications. With the exception of some of the more expensive applications, such as FrameMaker and Interleaf, the drawing tools offered by page makeup applications are extremely limited and are unsuitable for preparing anything but the simplest illustrations.

Drawing applications are "object-oriented" programs (the shape and characteristics of a drawn line are stored as data in a single point, or "vector"), as distinct from painting and image-manipulation applications (see p.64) that produce "bitmapped" images. Object-oriented applications allow lines, shapes and text to be altered and edited at any time, whereas bitmapped shapes must be erased and then redrawn or edited by a painstaking process of turning pixels on and off.

The object-oriented nature of drawing applications has two other distinct advantages over bitmap applications. First, because they store the instructions for drawing a line, rather than the line itself, an object-oriented illustration can be output at any resolution. Quality is determined wholly by the resolution of the output device – the higher the resolution, the finer the end result. In bitmapped images, the input resolution determines the output quality. Second, object-oriented files are smaller (regardless of physical dimensions) than bitmap equivalents and thus occupy less storage space.

The best drawing applications offer a full range of PANTONE colors which can be output as spot color film or fully separated film for four-color process printing. Whichever application you choose, accurate screen rendering of PANTONE colors is impossible to achieve – even with 24-bit color and some kind of color calibration device – so always check colors against a sample from PANTONE's color specifier.

Other features offered by drawing applications include "auto tracing" (an ability of the program to trace an outline of, say, a bitmapped image – useful if you want to create an editable version of a scanned design), "graduated fills" for creating smooth, graduated tints and "blending," which allows you to create graduated tones – around the side of a curved object, say. Drawing applications also allow you to import most types of picture file format, although you may not be able to edit them.

Because of their facility to allow the alteration of previously drawn shapes, drawing programs are extremely ver-

satile and can be used for a wide variety of purposes, such as technical illustration, diagrams and charts, maps and all manner of graphic decoration, as well as for general purpose illustration of a more mechanical nature. Being object-oriented, drawing applications also offer the valuable feature of being able to alter and manipulate outline fonts, thus providing an invaluable aid to logo design and also the means for extensive typographic variations. Some drawing applications also provide powerful typographic features, giving them the ability to be used, within limits, for page makeup.

There is justification for making comparisons between the two leading drawing applications, **Illustrator** (Adobe Systems, Inc.) and **FreeHand** (Aldus Corporation), since the differences between the two are subtle and those differ-

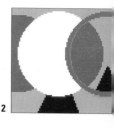

Bitmapped graphics
When you use a paint application to create an image, marks are made by switching pixels on and off (**1**) – a line comprises a series of linked pixels and a solid shape consists of a block of pixels. The color of each pixel depends on how many bits are assigned to each pixel – a one-bit

program only renders black (when the pixel is on) or white (when the pixel is off), whereas an 8-bit program can render 256 grays or colors. This is called a bitmapped graphic. Although the use of pixels permits a wide variety of effects, it can also make editing shapes difficult – when a shape is created (**2**),

the pixels used to render the shape replace any existing pixels such as those forming part of a background. Thus, if a shape is moved, a white space is left (**3**). Likewise, because the shape consists of a solid block of pixels, it can only be modified by adding and/or removing pixels.

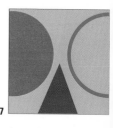

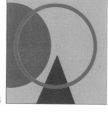

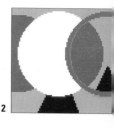

Object-oriented graphics
A drawing application stores information about a drawn line at each end of the line (**6**) or at points along its length. This means that only the data for a section of line between two points need be stored, as distinct from the need of a bitmapped graphic to store

data relating to each individual pixel. Consequently, the file size of an object-oriented illustration depends on its complexity rather than the area it occupies, unlike a bitmapped graphic, the file size of which increases proportionally to the area – thus the number of pixels –

it uses. A line can be edited by selecting it and making alterations as necessary – changes affecting only the data relating to that line (**7**, **8**), not any other element of the illustration. Some paint applications incorporate object-oriented drawing features.

ences are constantly being diminished by the continual upgrade leapfrogging between the two. I use FreeHand, but only because I prefer to make adjustments to an illustration in "preview" mode – the view that allows you to preview tints, colors, etc., as distinct from the keyline view – which is something you cannot do in Illustrator. Probably the most objective advice is, if you can't decide which to get, toss a coin or, if your budget permits, get both.

Hot on the heels of Illustrator and FreeHand comes **Canvas** (Deneba Software, Inc.) which, as well as offering powerful drawing and text features, allows you to import and export files in just about every format available.

The other major player in this field is **MacDraw Pro** (Claris Corporation), which in its first guise as MacDraw was the first object-oriented drawing application. Many

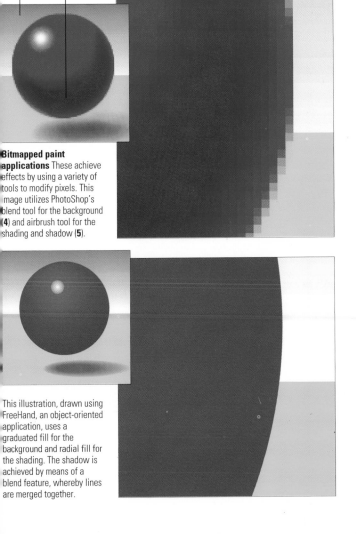

4   **5**

Bitmapped paint applications These achieve effects by using a variety of tools to modify pixels. This image utilizes PhotoShop's blend tool for the background (**4**) and airbrush tool for the shading and shadow (**5**).

This illustration, drawn using FreeHand, an object-oriented application, uses a graduated fill for the background and radial fill for the shading. The shadow is achieved by means of a blend feature, whereby lines are merged together.

Anatomy of a drawing application Graphic designers may need to complement their page-makeup application with one that provides extensive features for creating drawn artwork. Although page-makeup applications offer drawing tools, none achieves the power of a dedicated drawing application. Likewise, no drawing application provides the power of a dedicated page-makeup application, although both Illustrator and MacDraw Pro come close, the latter even providing a spell-checking feature. Designers of information

graphics will find the "graphing" feature of Illustrator useful, whereby statistical data is entered into a spreadsheet that automatically configures the graph, which you can customize to your liking.

Typically, a drawing application (**below**, from FreeHand) provides the standard File and Edit menus (**1**, **2**) for opening, closing, saving, copying, pasting, etc. In the View menu (**3**) you can select various display options such as floating palettes, magnification of the page view, rulers (**4**), grid (**5**), guides (**6**) and "snapping," which enables

accurate drawing by attracting an element to the nearest point, guide, or grid.

The Element menu (**7**) enables you to modify the different elements of your drawing, such as which part is on top of another, add and delete points to a line (**8**), blend elements to give a graded effect (**opposite**), and join together or split apart separate elements. The Type menu (**11**) allows you to attribute typographic styles and also to convert letterforms to "paths" (see below). In the Attributes menu (**12**), you can set the style, color and thickness of lines, the style and color of

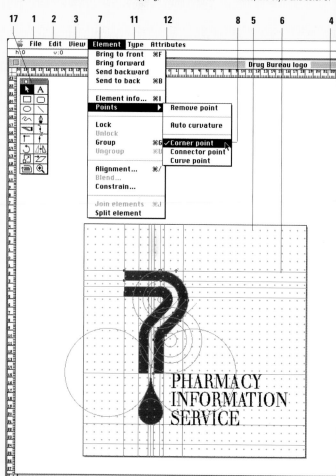

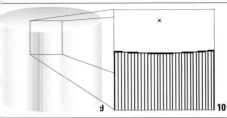

This illustration is drawn using the blend feature in the Elements menu of FreeHand. The gradation is formed (**9**) by blends of cyan and black tinted lines, seen enlarged in keyline mode (**10**).

...lled elements, and specify ...alftone screen ...equirements.

Drawing applications ...ffer the choice of process or ...ANTONE color selection, ...nd each has its own way of ...nabling you to specify ...olors. MacDraw Pro offers a ...eature enabling you to

identify intermediate colors between two tints. FreeHand displays colors on a floating palette (**13**) from which you can copy and edit existing colors or define new ones. Color "libraries," which enable you to store frequently used colors (such as the corporate colors of one of your clients), are also a feature of some drawing applications.

A Style palette (**14**) enables you to define frequently used styles such as lines and fills, and apply them to different elements of your drawing. The Layers palette (**15**) enables you to assign elements of a drawing to different layers, so that you can work on one element without affecting another – you can, if desired, "hide" other

elements. Elements on background layers (below the dotted line, **16**) appear dimmed and do not print. The Toolbox (**17**), as well as offering several standard drawing tools, also offers tools that enable you to rotate, reflect, scale, skew, and trace elements.

Object-oriented applications employ mathematically defined lines, or paths, which allow accurate manipulation of a shape which project from a point on a curve (sometimes referred to as "Bezier" curves). This means that fonts, which use the same method of describing a line, can be manipulated within a drawing application.

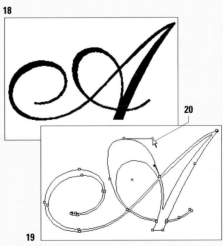

Several object-oriented applications enable you to customize any PostScript font you have installed on your Mac by converting a word or character into paths

(above, **18**, from Illustrator). This generates points along the path (**19**) which can be moved or from which curves can be modified via a "direction point" (**20**).

people prefer MacDraw Pro because of its ease of use, but it lacks some of the power of its competitors.

PAINTING AND IMAGE-EDITING For many people, their first glimpse of a Mac will have been at the receiving end of an entrancing demonstration of a painting, or "paint," application – it's impressive to see a computer achieve myriad paint effects so cleanly. But it is disappointing that the media has bombarded us with a stream of ill-conceived computer "painted" images, most of which look more like an attempt to exploit every trick an application has to offer than to devise a suitably considered graphic solution to a given problem. Yet a paint application is an innovatory graphic tool that, in the right hands, can provide the means of producing appropriate, original and stimulating work. If you produce a lot of illustration work, the computer offers great potential as an alternative illustration medium. However, the seductive effects obtainable with a paint application can easily turn out to be something of a professional irrelevance, so it's important to establish at the outset whether you'll need one at all, never mind which one.

The first consideration for selecting a paint application relates more to hardware than to software and catapults the relative cheapness of the software onto another economic plane altogether. For instance, you will need a large capacity hard disk, since the graphic files produced by these applications can be huge. To take advantage of the application's sophisticated color capabilities, you should really be thinking in terms of a 24-bit color card and monitor. You will need plenty of installed RAM to cope with these memory-intensive tasks – 8Mb should be enough as long as you also use the Mac's virtual memory feature. To simulate the way you would normally work with a pencil or paintbrush, you should also equip yourself with a graphics tablet that has a pressure-sensitive stylus, enabling you to vary the thickness of your line just as you would with a brush (you must be sure that the application you choose takes advantage of this feature).

The different software packages offer similar painting features, but with varying degrees of sophistication in their additional features. They all have adjustable airbrush tools, most allow you to control the opacity of paint, most possess limited image-editing tools, allowing you at least to blur or sharpen a scanned image, and some allow you to draw Bezier curves. Although all paint applications produce images as bitmaps, some also feature object-oriented drawing tools or at least object-oriented text capabilities, both of which you will probably find useful, whatever type of work you do. Other criteria relate to whether or not the application permits you to make direct process color separations and, if so, whether it allows you to adjust halftone screen resolution (although this is not too much of a problem since

you can always save the file in a format that can be separated by another application); and whether the application supports PANTONE colors.

Paint applications providing features at a professional level include **PixelPaint Professional** (SuperMac Software), **Studio/32** (Electronic Arts), and **VideoPaint** (Oldu-vai).

Other important paint applications are **Painter** (Letra-set) and **Oasis** (TimeArts, Inc.), which, as well as fulfilling many of the criteria mentioned above, also offer facilities for simulating traditional artists' media such as pencil, charcoal, pastel, watercolor and oil paint – you can even control, via the pressure-sensitive pen of a graphics tablet, the "wetness" of the "paint" loaded onto a "brush" and the rate at which it "dries."

The alternative to a paint application may be a so-called "image-editing," or retouching, application. This offers, as well as a comprehensive set of paint tools, extensive editing tools for use with directly scanned images. It also supports files that come from, or can be used directly by, some high-resolution color scanners. The leading image-editing applications are **ColorStudio** (Letraset) and **Photoshop** (Adobe Systems, Inc.).

Two other useful image-editing applications are **Digital Darkroom** (Aldus Corp.) and **ImageStudio** (Letraset), but these cater to scanned grayscale images only and thus do not offer such a comprehensive array of features as those mentioned above.

SPECIAL EFFECTS Drawing and painting applications succeed admirably in emulating conventional methods of preparing illustration, but there are applications peripheral to illustration and graphic design that have more exciting possibilities. There are two techniques by which designers and illustrators can *really* utilize computer technology: three-dimensional modelling (3D) and "rendering" (applying a texture to a surface or shape).

Many of the 3D applications are aimed primarily at professional architects, product designers and designers who work in CAD (computer-aided design), and are consequently highly sophisticated, complex and expensive, but mainly irrelevant to graphic designers. However, many others are both easy to use and less expensive, while at the same time offering some quite sophisticated features – the ability to create fully-rotatable 3D letterforms from installed fonts, for instance (although they don't all offer this feature, so be selective if 3D lettering is what you are after). Many 3D applications also provide animation capabilities and limited rendering effects. Popular 3D applications among designers are **ModelShop** (Paracomp), **StrataVision 3d** (Strata, Inc.), **Super 3D** (Silicon Beach Software), and **Swivel 3D Professional** (Paracomp).

Anatomy of a paint application The increasing sophistication of paint applications and the development of hardware that enhances their use has made it essential for many graphic designers to employ this type of software, if only as a means of simulating painterly effects – watercolour washes for backgrounds, for example. Many paint applications, such as Studio/32, Oasis, PixelPaint Professional and Painter support graphics tablets with pressure-sensitive styli, making them increasingly attractive to illustrators too. Paint applications achieve a wide variety of effects (**right**), by modifying the character-istics of groups of pixels and the way in which they behave in relation to their neighbors.

The illustration below shows a document open in Painter, which, typical of many paint applications, allows you to add a wide variety of paint effects to scanned images (**1**) as well as create paintings from scratch. Although potentially very powerful, Painter's interface is simple, the menu commands (**2**) being few, most of them contained on

floating palettes. These include a Toolbox (**3**) supported by a separate Brush Palette (**4**) which

offers many options for drawing and painting media. The shape and size of brushes can be controlled via the Brush Size palette (**5**) and their actions via the Brush Behavior palette (**6**). Brush characteristics can also be modified via the Expression Palette (**7**), which allows you to customize brush thickness, number of dots, opacity and color density according to how you use your mouse or stylus. The Color Palette (**8**) is where you select colors (paint opacity can be set in the Brush Palette), and the Paper Palette (**9**) offers a range of surface textures on

which you can draw – even the direction from which the light falls on the surface can be controlled. In the Correction Window (**10**), you can alter the contrast and brightness of an image. The Frisket Palette (**11**) offers a range of masking features.

Another paint application, PixelPaint Professional, is full of features and makes the differences between a paint and an image-manipulation application difficult to define. It offers a wide range of tools on a palette which can be "toggled" (switched from one view to another via the Precision and Paint buttons) to show different tools (**12**,

13) or displayed together on a single palette. It features a "Path Selector" (**14**) which enables you to create an editable shape in much the same way that an object-oriented drawing application does – by providing adjustable control points with which you can alter the shape or line before it is "painted" (applied) to your artwork. The Continuous Path option (**15**) allows you to paint directly.

PixelPaint Professional, unlike Painter, provides extensive features for duotone, tritone and process color separation and features a novel PANTONE Color Picker in which color selections can be rapidly accessed via a color spectrum slide control. Another useful feature is its "Mesh Warp," which enables you to manipulate portions of an illustration via a grid (**16**).

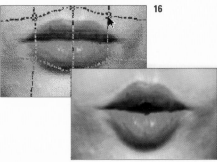

Studio 32, which supports 32-bit color, features a helpful method of defining perspective planes (**right**).

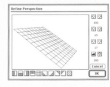

Anatomy of an image-editing application These applications are available in two forms: those which are used for scanning and retouching grayscale images, such as ImageStudio and Digital Darkroom – the latter also featuring a "colorizer" which adds color to monochrome images – and those which are complete color-image processing packages, offering a full range of features from paint tools to sophisticated pre-press color separation.

It is arguable whether a designer will have a need for both a paint application

and an image-editing application, since there is little that the former does that the latter can't do better, but with many more appropriate features for professional output.

Two applications lead this field: PhotoShop and ColorStudio. Both are expensive and powerful; to get full use out of them, you

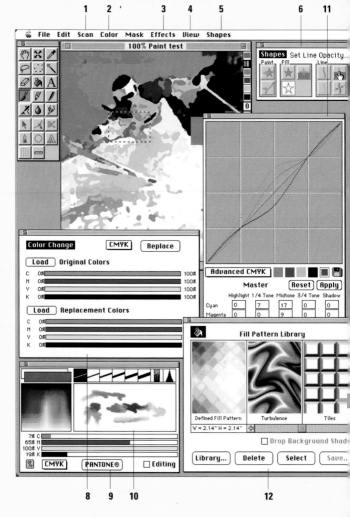

must have some knowledge and experience of prepress activities. However, even without this knowledge, many graphic designers will find either one of these applications useful both for effects that they can render (**left**, using PhotoShop) and for retouching and manipulating images (**right**, also PhotoShop). **Below right**, PhotoShop provides choices of color models in several modes of PANTONE as well as other brandname color systems.

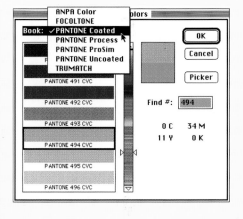

7

6:07:48 pm

Paintbrush Preferences

Shading Changes

○ ● ○ ○

essure   4

Using   Current Color

icture   Normally

Every   1   Pixel(s)

● Mask Off
○ Mask Black
○ Mask White

ustom   Default

Save   Delete

Dynamic Effects

↗Move   ↻Rotate
ch   ⊞Scale

Mask Options

Image   Copy
● Mask off   ●
○ Mask black   ○
○ Mask white   ○

Opacity Slider

48%

13   14

ANPA Color
FOCOLTONE
Book: ✓PANTONE Coated
PANTONE Process
PANTONE ProSim
PANTONE Uncoated
TRUMATCH

PANTONE 491 CVC
PANTONE 492 CVC
PANTONE 493 CVC
PANTONE 494 CVC
PANTONE 495 CVC
PANTONE 496 CVC

OK
Cancel
Picker

Find #:   494

0 C   34 M
11 Y   0 K

The screen capture (**left**) shows some of the features of ColorStudio. Among its menus are: Scan (**1**), for selecting and using a scanner; Color (**2**), for color modifications; Effects (**3**), for special effects and fill pattern commands; View (**4**), where you create new views; Shapes (**5**), with its floating palette (**6**), a facility for incorporating PostScript graphics files and creating object-oriented drawings (image-editing applications primarily use bitmaps to create images).

The floating palettes show: Paintbrush Preferences (**7**); Color Change (**8**), to modify existing colors; Color

Palette (**9**), where you can select a color, color model (RGB, CMYK, PANTONE, etc.) and points for the pen tools – the palette also features a "scratch pad" (**10**) where you can experiment with different pen tools and colors; Color Correction (**11**), for fine-tuning color; Fill Pattern Library (**12**), where you can choose an existing fill pattern or define a new one based on a selected part of an image; Dynamic Effects (**13**), controlling effects such as rotation, skewing and scaling; Mask Options (**14**), for controlling masking functions.

Rendering applications enable you to apply the surface effects of materials such as wood, metal, or marble to an object, and to manipulate the intensity, color and direction of the light source illuminating the object. Be warned, though – rendering can be very slow. Two leading applications are **Ray Dream Designer** (Ray Dream), which is also a 3D modelling application, and **Mac RenderMan** (Pixar).

ADVERTISING If you work in advertising, you will find very little software tailored to your design needs. The leading application is **Multi-Ad Creator** (Multi-Ad Services, Inc.), which offers sophisticated page makeup, drawing and painting features, and quite powerful typographic control in a single package. Nonetheless, it is quite common for advertising studios to use a page makeup application such as XPress in preference, despite acknowledgement that Multi-

Applications for special effects 3-dimensional (3D) and rendering applications now combine high power with ease of use, although some, such as StrataVision 3d, are so powerful that they require a considerable learning effort – but perseverance will be hugely rewarding. Generally speaking, 3D applications follow the same basic principles in the way that they create images, and the illustrations (**right**) show how an image is rendered using Swivel 3D Professional: an object is constructed by first drawing a cross section, plan and/or elevation of your image. The object may be either "extruded," in which case the cross section can be thought of as a sort of die through which material is forced, or "lathed," whereby a profile of your image is rotated along an axis just as if you were carving it on a lathe. The program then creates a 3-dimensional "wireframe" or "mesh" of the object (**1**), the facets of which are filled in to render the object with shading

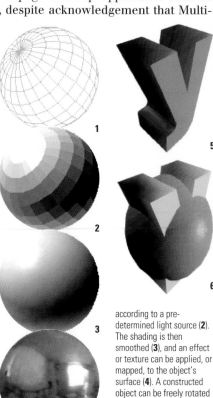

according to a predetermined light source (**2**). The shading is then smoothed (**3**), and an effect or texture can be applied, or mapped, to the object's surface (**4**). A constructed object can be freely rotated around various axes (**5**), and can be combined with other objects (**6**).

Ad Creator may be more appropriate, although more particularly for esthetically less demanding small ads.

TYPE DESIGN AND MANIPULATION Font technology for the Macintosh is a complex subject and is discussed in greater detail in Chapter 5 (p.84). But the computer is a godsend to the typographic designer when it comes to typeface design – even if it is also frequently a scourge as far as some other typographic activities are concerned. Using a suitable application, it is a relatively straightforward matter to create an entire typeface from scratch and then use it as you would any other font. It is also easy to modify every character of any existing font installed on your Mac and then use it as a new typeface. **Fontographer** (Altsys Corp.) and **FontStudio** (Letraset) are applications which are both capable of either generating new faces or modifying exist-

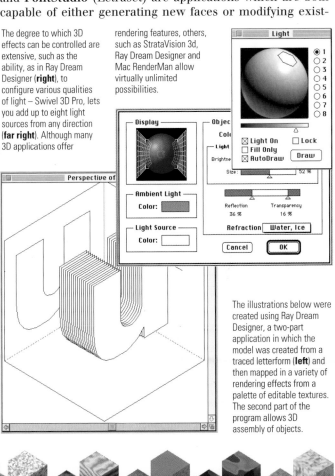

The degree to which 3D effects can be controlled are extensive, such as the ability, as in Ray Dream Designer (**right**), to configure various qualities of light – Swivel 3D Pro, lets you add up to eight light sources from any direction (**far right**). Although many 3D applications offer rendering features, others, such as StrataVision 3d, Ray Dream Designer and Mac RenderMan allow virtually unlimited possibilities.

The illustrations below were created using Ray Dream Designer, a two-part application in which the model was created from a traced letterform (**left**) and then mapped in a variety of rendering effects from a palette of editable textures. The second part of the program allows 3D assembly of objects.

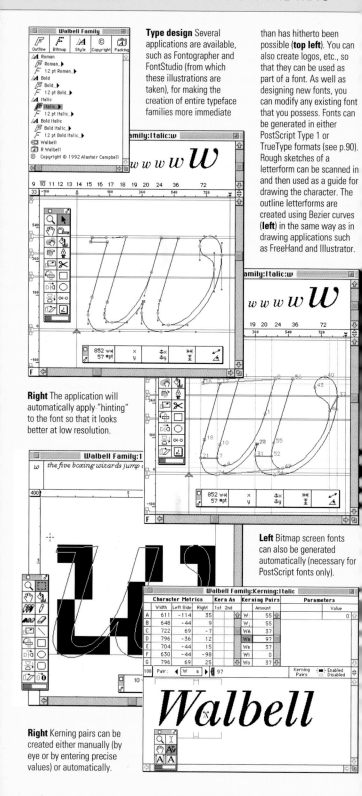

Type design Several applications are available, such as Fontographer and FontStudio (from which these illustrations are taken), for making the creation of entire typeface families more immediate than has hitherto been possible (**top left**). You can also create logos, etc., so that they can be used as part of a font. As well as designing new fonts, you can modify any existing font that you possess. Fonts can be generated in either PostScript Type 1 or TrueType formats (see p.90). Rough sketches of a letterform can be scanned in and then used as a guide for drawing the character. The outline letterforms are created using Bezier curves (**left**) in the same way as in drawing applications such as FreeHand and Illustrator.

Right The application will automatically apply "hinting" to the font so that it looks better at low resolution.

Left Bitmap screen fonts can also be generated automatically (necessary for PostScript fonts only).

Right Kerning pairs can be created either manually (by eye or by entering precise values) or automatically.

Font effects Applications such as Illustrator and FreeHand provide features for manipulating fonts, but there are several dedicated to rendering a wide variety of effects – ideal for logos and display lettering. These include TypeStyler, TypeAlign and LetraStudio, from which these illustrations are taken. In addition to providing a palette of predetermined distortions for LetraFont or Type 1 fonts (**below**), effects can be freely achieved by manipulating Bezier curves (**right**).

ing ones. Both applications are also very useful for drawing up logo designs, particularly if you intend to incorporate the logo into typeset copy.

Unfortunately, because there are so many font formats – PostScript Type 1 (with "hinting"), PostScript Type 3 and, more recently, Apple's answer to PostScript Type 1, True-Type – it may be necessary to convert a font in one format to that of another so that your font creation or manipulation program is able to handle it. Although both Fontographer and FontStudio will undertake this task, there are a few applications written specifically to convert fonts, notably **Metamorphosis** (Altsys Corp.) and **FontMonger** (Letraset). However, fonts converted from one format to another may be degraded because they are converted at a resolution much lower than that of the original font format, which may have been generated from a master font with a resolution of around 900dpi.

You may find a font manipulation program useful, even though drawing applications such as FreeHand and Illustrator are capable of enabling you to produce extensive typographic effects. **TypeStyler** (Brøderbund, Inc.) and **Effects Specialist** (Postcraft International) are two such applications which, as well as offering powerful effects features, incorporate a library of ready-made effects which you can alter to suit your needs. Other recommended dedicated type-manipulation applications are **LetraStudio** (Letraset) and **TypeAlign** (Adobe Systems Inc.).

MULTIMEDIA This is a hugely complex area for any professional graphic designer to get to grips with, let alone a novice Mac user. At its inception, multimedia appeared to be the net result of someone having taken virtually everything it is possible to do on a Mac – painting, text, scanned images, sound, live video, etc. – and thrown it all haphazardly into a single pot, the apparent intention being to wow the viewer with a flashy and seductive experience, and an interactive one at that. Of course, such a scenario presented both the hardware and software marketing men with a dream, but euphoria soon gave way to embarrassment when it was realized that end-users of this new medium were as much bewildered as they were excited by it. To sustain interest from software producers and hardware manufacturers, the hype eventually had to be channeled to a purposeful and commercially productive end. Several potential uses soon became apparent – for instance, educational materials, disk-based reference, museum guides, sophisticated business presentations, and so on.

For the designer's part, the multimedia medium presents both a creative challenge and a nightmare – the technical nightmare of putting the parts together and the dilemma of who generates the creative parts that make up the whole. You can provide the graphics, but who, for instance, writes

he words, composes the music, records the sound, takes
the photographs and directs the video sequences? And if you
decide to simplify matters by using existing material, who
owns the copyrights of each individual element; and, when
you've eventually hunted the owners down, will they let you
use it – and if so, for how much? While multimedia may
serve the original ethos of the Macintosh computer by
enabling anybody to do it, when it comes to professional
output, the parameters change considerably. Another
important factor to bear in mind before embarking on the
multimedia odyssey is the level of hardware you will
require – a color scanner, recording equipment, video
equipment, vast storage media and so on.

Software for multimedia comes in the guise of "authoring" programs which allow you to write or modify program
"scripts" (a simplified form of program language) depending on the complexity of the multimedia task. Many applications include extensions to the scripting language in the
form of "external commands" (XCMDs) and "external functions" (XFCNs) which enable the application to perform
specialized commands or functions, such as in an extra
menu or controlling a hardware device. Multimedia applications range from Apple's own **Hypercard**, through powerful animation packages such as **MacMind Director**
(MacroMind, Inc.), which also has built-in painting tools, to
the hugely expensive **Authorware Professional** and
Authorware Animator (Papillon Publishing).

WORD PROCESSING You may wonder why you would need
a word-processing application when applications such as
XPress and PageMaker provide adequate text-editing
features, but you may have to work with text provided by a
client from a dedicated word-processing application, possibly produced on a PC running, for instance, the MS DOS
operating system. Even though it is possible for most page
makeup applications to directly import text originated in
one of a variety of formats, it is quite likely that you will be
required to provide text in a format that your client can
work with. For this reason, it is best to equip yourself with
one of the most widely used applications. Among these are
MacWrite II (Claris Corp.), **Nisus** (Paragon Concepts, Inc.),
WordPerfect (WordPerfect Corp.), **WriteNow** (T/Maker
Co.), and the most widely used of all, **Microsoft Word**
(Microsoft Corp.).

OTHER APPLICATIONS I have discussed only a few applications of particular significance in those areas which cater
specifically for the graphic designer. Yet there are hundreds
of other items of software, most of little design relevance or
of insufficient power, catering more for the needs of the
non-designer. However, do not dismiss all seemingly unre-
lated applications, since a great many of them can be of
considerable use to designers. Take **Wingz** (Informix), for

This chart summarizes those items of software of particular relevance to professional graphic designers. It also lists some peripheral software such as utilities, selected from many similar packages, which will also be useful.

	A Animation	**B** B/W image retouching	**C** Color image manipulation	**D** Color retouching	**E** Color separations	**F** Drawing	**G** 3D & Effect rendering	**H** Font design	**J** Font effects	**K** Multimedia	**L** Page layout/makeup	**M** Painting	**N** Utility	**O** Word processing
Adobe Separator Adobe Sys., Inc.					●									
ATM Adobe Systems, Inc.													⑤	
Canvas Deneba Software						●								
ColorStudio Letraset			●	●	●							◦		
Compactor Shareware													⑨	
Complete Undelete Microcom, Inc.													②	
DesignStudio Letraset											●			◦
Digital Darkroom Aldus Corp.		①												
Disinfectant Shareware													⑧	
DiskDoubler Salient Software													⑨	
DiskExpress II ALSoft, Inc.													⑩	
Evolution Image Club Graphics, Inc.													③	
FilmMaker Paracomp, Inc.	●													
Fontina Eastgate Systems													④	
FontMonger Ares Software								●					③	
Fontographer Altsys Corp.								●						
FontSizer II MicroLabs, Inc.													⑤	
FontStudio Letraset								●						
FrameMaker Frame Technology											●			◦
FreeHand Aldus Corp.						●			●					
Illustrator Adobe Systems, Inc.						●								
ImageStudio Letraset		●												
Interleaf Publisher Interleaf, Inc.											●			
LetraStudio Letraset														
Lightspeed CLS Crosfield														
MacDraw Claris Corp.						●								
MacRenderMan Pixar							●							
MacroMind Director MacroMind	●									●				
MacWrite II Claris Corp.														●
Metamorphosis Altsys Corp.													③	
ModelShop II ParaComp, Inc.							●							
Multi-Ad Creator Multi-Ad Service											●	●		◦
Nisus Paragon Concepts												◦		●
Norton Utilities Symantec Corp.													⑥	
Oasis TimeArts, Inc.												●		
OmniPage Caere Corp.													⑦	
PageMaker Aldus Corp.											●			●
Painter Fractal Design												●		
PhotoMac Data Translation				●										
PhotoShop Adobe Systems, Inc.			●	●	●							◦		

- ● Primary features
- ◦ Secondary features

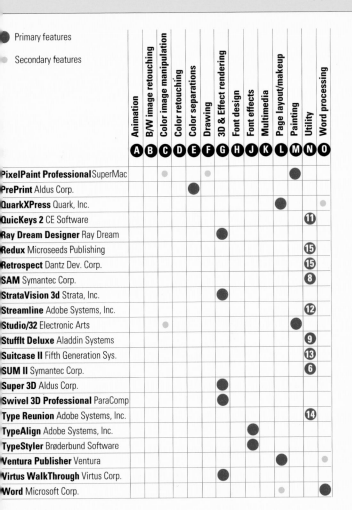

	A Animation	B B/W image retouching	C Color image manipulation	D Color retouching	E Color separations	F Drawing	G 3D & Effect rendering	H Font design	J Font effects	K Multimedia	L Page layout/makeup	M Painting	N Utility	O Word processing
PixelPaint Professional SuperMac			◦		◦							●		
PrePrint Aldus Corp.					●									
QuarkXPress Quark, Inc.											●			◦
QuicKeys 2 CE Software													⓫	
Ray Dream Designer Ray Dream							●							
Redux Microseeds Publishing													⓯	
Retrospect Dantz Dev. Corp.													⓯	
SAM Symantec Corp.													⑧	
StrataVision 3d Strata, Inc.							●							
Streamline Adobe Systems, Inc.													⑫	
Studio/32 Electronic Arts			◦									●		
StuffIt Deluxe Aladdin Systems													⑨	
Suitcase II Fifth Generation Sys.													⑬	
SUM II Symantec Corp.													⑥	
Super 3D Aldus Corp.							●							
Swivel 3D Professional ParaComp							●							
Type Reunion Adobe Systems, Inc.													⑭	
TypeAlign Adobe Systems, Inc.									●					
TypeStyler Brøderbund Software									●					
Ventura Publisher Ventura											●			◦
Virtus WalkThrough Virtus Corp.							●							
Word Microsoft Corp.												◦		●

A Some 3D applications offer animation features.

B Grayscale manipulation and retouching.

C Some paint applications offer limited image manipulation.

D Requires 24-bit color monitor for accurate color rendering.

E For producing color separations and correction from most file formats for separated output within other applications. Some page makeup and drawing applications will generate separations.

F Predominantly object-oriented applications.

G Excludes high-end CAD applications.

H Applications which generate outline printer fonts and bitmap screen fonts for normal keyboard input and printer output.

J Some drawing and painting applications offer features for font effects.

K Requires audio equipment for best results.

M Mostly bitmapped image applications.

N Generally items for work enhancement.

Notes:

1 Includes a colorizer feature for adding tints to grayscale images.

2 Restores accidently deleted files.

3 Converts PostScript Type 3 fonts to Type 1 or TrueType, and vice versa.

4 Lists fonts without the need for scrolling.

5 Creates high-quality PostScript screen fonts.

6 Contains many utilities for disk protection, optimizing and backup.

7 Optical character recognition – requires a scanner.

8 Virus detection and protection.

9 File compression.

10 Disk optimizer (see p.138).

11 Provides keyboard shortcuts to frequently used actions.

12 Autotraces line art.

13 Font management – opens font suitcases.

14 Organizes font lists logically.

15 Disk and file backup.

instance, which is a spreadsheet application aimed primarily at the business user, but which also enables the designer to create sophisticated statistical illustrations. **Persuasion** (Aldus Corp.) and **PowerPoint** (Microsoft Corp.) both provide the means to create customized slide presentations. Some CAD (computer-aided design) and architecture applications such as **Walkthrough** (Virtus) go way beyond what mere modeling programs can achieve.

There are many other peripheral applications, including those for essential tasks such as optical character recognition which allows you to use a scanner to input typewritten text into your Mac. **OmniPage** (Caere, Inc.) is one such application. Since you have a computer, it makes sense to put your accounts onto it; of the many applications available some are quite powerful, such as **MacMoney/InvoicIt** (Survivor Software Ltd), but **Quicken** (Intuit) is perhaps more suitable for the freelance designer, being very easy to use. You may also find a database such as **Dynodex** (Portfolio Systems Inc.) useful for keeping a record of all your business contacts.

UTILITIES There are literally thousands of little applications, called utilities, available either as commercial items, "shareware" (meaning you get it from a friend or user group and pay the author only if you like it and use it), or "freeware," which is software in the public domain and you are not required to pay anything. Some of the more useful are listed here:

Adobe Type Manager (ATM) (Adobe Systems, Inc.) This is a "transparent" utility (it works without you having to do anything with it) that renders PostScript Type 1 fonts smoothly on screen (by using the outline printer font file), replacing the awful "jaggies" of the bitmapped screen fonts that you would otherwise get (see p.91). This utility is absolutely essential unless you are going to use TrueType fonts exclusively.

Adobe Type Reunion (Adobe Systems, Inc.) This essential utility organizes your font menus by family, with submenus for font variations such as italic or bold, thus eliminating the tendency for font menus which would otherwise drop through the floor because every variation of every typeface is listed.

Suitcase II (Fifth Generation Systems, Inc.) This is a useful font-management utility that enables you easily to add fonts to or remove them from your system without the need for dragging them in and out of your System file.

QuicKeys (CE Software) This utility enables you to assign keyboard shortcuts to menu items or to repetitive actions.

Virus protection A virus is a mischievously written program that copies itself from computer to computer (usually via floppy disks, but also over networks) where it can wreak havoc by, for instance, causing repeated crashes or files to

vanish. Fortunately, there are many utilities available for detecting and eliminating such viruses, among them **Disinfectant** (Northwestern University) and **SAM** (Symantec Corp.).

Screen savers If you leave your monitor unattended for any length of time, an image (particularly the menu bar at the top of the screen) will begin to burn itself in over a long period. To prevent this, there are several inexpensive utilities such as **After Dark** (Berkeley Systems, Inc.) and **Pyro** (Fifth Generation Systems, Inc.) which dim the screen or display a constantly changing image after a period of time designated by you.

Disk recovery At some time or other your hard disk will get damaged – files may disappear, or the disk may not appear on the desktop at all. In such circumstances, you may be able to save the day by using a recovery utility such as **Norton Utilities** or SUM II (both Symantec Corp.).

Disk optimizers The more a disk is used, the more it becomes "fragmented" – that is, as the disk gets full, the files get broken up and distributed over different parts of the disk, thus slowing down the time it takes for the computer to access the data. A disk-optimizing utility will find all the parts of a file, join them together to make them contiguous, and rearrange them on the disk, thus speeding up access time. Among several other utilities, both **Norton Utilities** and SUM II offer optimizing features.

File compression One way of economizing on disk space is to use a file-compression utility. In addition to creating space on your hard disk, such a utility is useful for archiving files (for instance, storing old jobs that you need to keep but are unlikely to require regular access to) and transporting large files, to a service bureau, say. If you are mailing disks to an unfamiliar destination, you would be advised to use a compression utility that is used universally, such as **DiskDoubler** (Salient Software) or **StuffIt Deluxe (**Aladdin Systems). There are many other compression utilities, though, some of which may be more appropriate for compressing certain types of image file.

Backup utilities The golden rule in computing is: back up your files. Regularly, and without question. A computer is a complex machine, but even simple machines break down. To make the chore of backing up as painless as possible, there are several specially designed backup utilities, the appropriate one depending upon what media you are backing up to (hard disk, removable disks, tape streamers, or floppy disks, etc). It is possible to back up your hard disk simply by copying the files to another disk, but this means that every time you back up, you must copy the *entire* disk, a time-consuming chore. A backup utility, on the other hand, will only back-up changes made to files since the last time you backed up.

TOOLBOX ICONS

Part of the ethos of the Macintosh GUI is its use of tools to perform tasks, and the consistency in the design and behavior of those tools from one application to another. The tools shown here are a selection of those performing the most commonly found tasks in graphic applications. When a tool is selected, the pointer often assumes the shape of the tool icon, but more often assumes a different shape – a cross-hair cursor, for example.

Tools for pointing

The pointer. Also called the *arrow* tool and the *selection* tool, the pointer is the basic tool for selecting menu commands, tools and other items displayed on your monitor.

A pointing finger is called the *browsing tool* and performs similar functions to the pointer. The *I-beam* positions the text cursor and selects text. A hand means it also moves the contents of a box (*content tool*).

Tools for moving items

Hand tool. Also called the *grabber hand*, the hand tool moves selected items or all the contents of a window.

Mover tool, or *item* tool. Moves selected items.

These mover tools move items in 3D applications.

Tools for viewing work

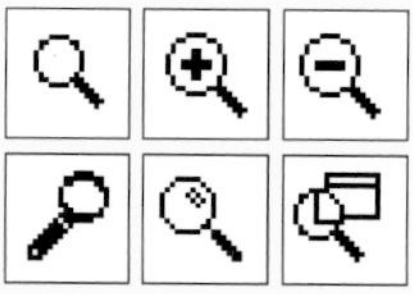

Magnifier tool. Also called the *zoom* tool, this increases or decreases the size of the image displayed on screen to assist accurate working (this does not affect its final size). The place where you click on the image usually becomes the center of the screen. Sometimes you can zoom in on an area by clicking and dragging the tool.

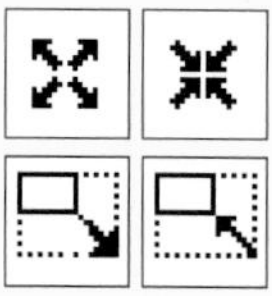

These tools "zoom in" (enlarge, left) and "zoom out" (reduce, right).

More zoom tools, plus a *fractional zoom* tool with which you select the area you want to enlarge.

Tools for selecting areas and shapes

Multiple items, shapes and areas are selected by using one of a variety of *selection* tools. Areas that you select are indicated on screen by a moving broken line, called the "selection marquee."

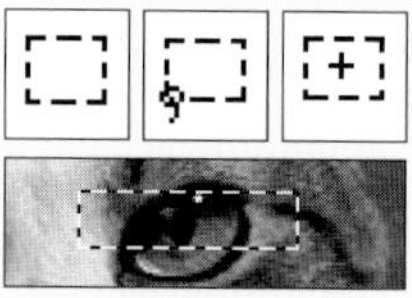

These tools select rectangular areas or, with the *Shift* key, squares. The + symbol indicates that the area will be drawn from the center outward.

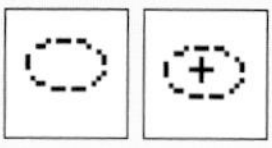

Oval selection tool. Makes an oval-shaped selection or, with the *Shift* key, a circle.

Polygon selection tool. Provides a many-sided selection, whereas the *polyline selection* tool (right) selects lines.

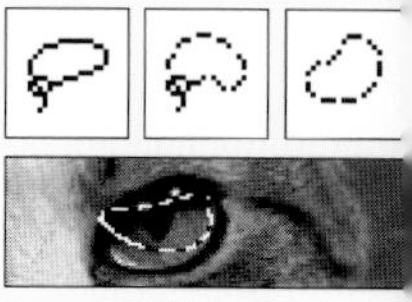

Lasso tool. Makes freeform selections.

Paint selection tool. Selects areas "painted" by the cursor.

Magic wand. Selects all adjacent pixels of a similar or predefined value in a bitmapped image.

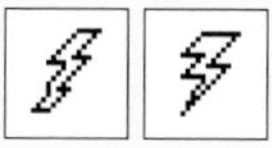

Deselection tool. Also called the *lightning bolt* tool, this deselects individual selections where there are many. Areas can usually be "deselected" by clicking outside the selected area with a selection tool, but this may deselect all other areas.

Tools for selecting colors and tones

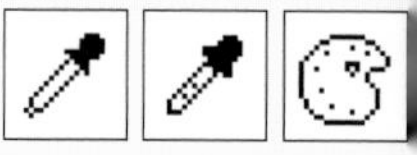

The *eyedropper* or *color pickup* tool selects the color on an image or palette at the point where the mouse is clicked. The *palette* tool applies a defined color to the currently selected item.

Tools for drawing shapes

Almost every application offers tools for drawing shapes of one kind or another. The shapes may contain patterned or colored fills, pictures or text. The *Shift* key often constrains a rectangle to a square or an oval to a circle. Using the *Option* key with a shape tool often makes the shape draw from its center.

Corner/center control tool. Controls the method that drawing tools use – whether they draw from the corner or from the center.

Rectangle tool. The shaded rectangle indicates that the shape will be drawn with a specified fill, and the half-shaded tool means it will be empty or filled depending on which side you select. The icon with an "X" indicates a picture box tool whereas the "A" identifies a text box tool.

Round-corner rectangle tool. The corner radius is sometimes definable via a dialog box.

Oval tool. For drawing ellipses and circles.

Angled ellipse tool.

Freeform shape tool.

Irregular polygon tool.

Regular polygon tool. The number of sides of the polygon shape may be definable.

Bezier shape tool. Also called the *spline* tool, this draws shapes that contain bezier control handles which, when dragged, provide smooth curves.

Tools for drawing lines

Lines may be either object-oriented, in which case they contain control points that can be manipulated to modify the shape of the line, or they may be bitmapped, in which case they are "painted" lines. However, some paint applications provide tools for drawing lines and altering their shape in the same way that object-oriented drawing applications do, before "painting" them to the image.

Perpendicular line tool. Draws horizontal or vertical straight lines.

Angled line tool. Draws angled straight lines. The line may be constrained horizontally or vertically with the *Shift* key.

Polygon line tool. Draws connected straight lines. The intersection of each segment may contain a point which can be manipulated or replaced with a different point.

Bezier line tool. Draws curved lines with bezier control points. *Connector* tool makes smooth connections between straight and curved lines.

Arc tool. Draws arcs.

Freeform line tool. Draws lines along which control points are positioned.

Tools for inserting and deleting new control points along drawn lines.

Freeform path control tool. Controls whether paint tools draw lines as continuous, broken or scattered paths.

Spline tool. Draws bitmapped lines with controllable Bezier curves.

Tools for painting

Painting tools are those that produce marks comprised of pixels. Lines and shapes produced by such tools can only be edited by altering individual pixels or groups of pixels. In some applications, use of these tools is enhanced by a graphics tablet with a pressure-sensitive stylus. Paint tools imitate the effects of conventional drawing and painting media – painted lines may be of varying size and shape, pressure, repeat-rate, fade-out and opacity.

Pencil, chalk and *charcoal* tools.

Paintbrush tool.

Airbrush tool. Also called the *spraycan* tool.

Blur/sharpen tool. Also called the *waterdrop* or *blend* tool, this softens, or blurs, the parts of an image where it is used. The waterdrop tool often toggles to a *sharpen* tool (unless this is displayed as a separate tool) which hardens, or

Finger tool. Also called the *smudge* or *smear* tool, this smudges parts of an image in the same way that running your finger through wet paint would.

Tools for copying

Tools are sometimes available for duplicating items or for copying parts of images (*cloning*).

Rubber stamp tool. Used for copying part of an image and then placing the copied area, or stamping it, in another part of the image.

Copy brush tool. For copying and painting adjacent parts of an image.

Duplicate tool. For duplicating selected items.

Tools for adding large areas of color

Paintbucket tool. For filling selected areas with a color or tint.

Blend tool. Used to define the area to which a graduated fill is applied.

Tools for adding text

The *text* tool, for incorporating type into a

document, invariably takes the form of a capital letter. Double-clicking the icon will sometimes open a type specification dialog box.

Tools for rotating items

Rotation tool. For rotating selected items. Items may be freely rotated, or it may be possible to specify a value. A dialog box can sometimes be called up by double-clicking on or with the tool or by using the tool with a modifier key.

Pitch, roll, yaw and *view rotate* tools. For rotating 3D objects.

Tools for slanting items

Skew tool. Sometimes called the *shear* or *slanting* tool, this slants an item to the left or right.

Tools for flipping items

Reflection tool. Sometimes called the *mirror* tool or *flip horizontal* tool, this makes a mirror-image transformation of an item along a vertical axis, which may be defined in a dialog box.

Flip vertical tool. Reflects an object along a horizontal axis.

Tools for resizing items

Scale. Although the size of an item can usually be altered by entering values in a dialog box, many applications provide a tool for making size alterations to items visually.

Tools for tracing

Tracing tool. Sometimes called the *autotrace* tool, this tool is used to select an area of an image, the edges of which are to be traced automatically. This feature works most effectively with images of a single solid color.

Tools for cutting

Scissors tool. This is used to select and cut areas or lines in an image.

Knife tool. Used to cut a line into segments.

Papercutter tool. Used to make cuts in a straight line.

Tools for erasing

Eraser tool. This tool is used to erase parts of an image. Double-clicking on or with the tool often erases the whole image.

Tools for generating 3D shapes

Lathe shape tool. For generating lathed 3D objects.

Extrude shape tool. For generating extruded 3D objects.

Tools for positioning light sources

Point light source tool. Used for positioning local, non-directional light sources in a 3D environment.

Spot light source tool. Used for positioning localized directional light sources in a 3D environment.

Tools for measuring

Measure tool. Used for establishing the precise linear distance, in a predefined scale, between two points.

Angle measure tool. Used for measuring the angle (in degrees) of an item.

Tools for cropping

Cropping tool. Used for removing unwanted edges from an image.

Tools for linking items

Text linking and *unlinking* tools. These link (or unlink) two or more text boxes so that text flows from one to the other.

Freelinking tool. For linking (and unlinking) objects in 3D applications.

Tools for controlling image density

Brightness tool. For controlling the brightness of a scanned image.

Contrast tool. For controlling the contrast of an image.

Page tools

Note tool. For attaching comments to a document.

Page tool. Used to adjust the page grid area.

Page insertion tool. For inserting new master pages.

4

TYPOGRAPHY

TYPE MEASUREMENT/TYPE CHARACTERISTICS/
POSTSCRIPT/TRUETYPE/FONT CONFLICTS/
FONT ORGANIZATION/DIGITIZING FONTS/
BUYING FONTS

When you select a typeface for a job, you probably spend a little time flicking through type sample books from a few of your preferred typesetting houses. If you don't see what you want in one book, you reach for another, and then another ... until you find what you're looking for. You then mark up your text with type specifications and send it to the typesetter, who gets to work implementing your instructions. Meanwhile, you get on with something else, never giving a moment's thought to the technicalities involved in turning your marked-up copy into high-quality typesetting.

A few hours, days or weeks later you receive beautifully set galleys back from your typesetter.

Now that you are the proud owner of a Macintosh computer system, a whole new world has opened up in front of you – and one that may force you to question the wisdom of your decision to get a Mac at all. The printer that you have bought, along with the Mac, comes with a few (*very* few) built-in fonts, most of which represent a completely inappropriate selection for professional graphic design. Hence your first realization – that you need more typefaces. So, you do as you used to; you reach for a type sample book. But now you find that you're faced with a choice based not just on esthetic criteria but on a whole new set of considerations, many technical, and none of which would ever have concerned you in the past.

Just as you once had to choose between typesetting houses, you now have to choose between font *vendors* – some of whom appear to be offering some fonts which are exactly the same as those offered by another. And having made your choice of typeface, you find that you are also offered a choice of font *format* – TrueType or PostScript (and even, although less likely these days, a choice between PostScript Type 1 and Type 3). Then comes the crunch – a typeface in a set of about eight styles (light, roman, semibold and bold, with their respective italic variations, for example) is *very* expensive – it may even cost more than

your fee for the job. And, to cap it all, you discover that to get the full mix of styles and weights, you must purchase not one, but two font sets (or more – an entire typeface, Helvetica 25 through to Helvetica 95 for example, may be split into *three* sets).

Once you've made your decision, ordered the font, and waited a couple of days for it to arrive, the next dilemma occurs: how do you get all those 20,000 words of typewritten manuscript into your machine? (See p.116 for the answer.) Having input the text into your Mac, formatted it to your desired specifications and printed out a proof, you discover that there is something not quite right about the kerning, or about the character or word spacing on justified text; but now you can't go back to your typesetter to get it fixed – you've actually got to do it yourself. By now you may be forgiven for wondering whether you are a designer or a typesetter.

The problems don't stop there – more begin to unfold the further you get into using your Mac. One of the most acute is the rapidity with which font technology evolves, or rather mutates, meaning that entire new learning processes must often be undertaken within unacceptably short periods of time.

However, typography on the Mac is far from a negative experience. If you discipline yourself to stay within certain parameters – always using the same font format, for instance, or always buying fonts from the same foundry, or always using the same application to output text to your printer or to an imagesetter – you will encounter few problems and will come to rejoice at the typographic control you now have over your work.

TYPE MEASUREMENT The earliest type consisted of solid blocks ("body") upon which the area to be printed ("face") was "punched." Thus measurements of all type relate to these three-dimensional objects – even the digitized type used today.

In the past, printing was an inexact science, and no two printers could agree on a standard system of type measurement, which meant that type cast in different foundries were incompatible. Eventually, in the mid 18th century, the French typographer Pierre Simon Fournier proposed a standard unit which he called a "point." This was further developed by Firmin Didot into a European standard which, although their systems were based upon it, was not adopted by Britain or the U.S.

The Anglo-American system is based on the division of one inch into 72 parts, called points and, mathematically, one point should equal 0.013889in – but, in fact, it equals 0.013837in, meaning that 72 points only make 0.996264in. The European point equals 0.0148in and 12 of these form a unit measuring 0.1776in. This 12-point unit is called a

Much of the nomenclature and measuring systems of traditional typography remain standard language on the Macintosh. Traditional type measurement on the Mac derives from the body size of a non-printing piece of metal, and even though computer type has no physical basis, this idea has been extended for measuring computer-generated letterforms – instead of being based on the physical body size of metal type, computer type is based on an imaginary em square. The unit of measurement used to describe type is still the point. However, PostScript defines one point as being 0.013889in. (exactly ½in.) as distinct from the traditional Anglo-American point size measuring 0.013837in. (72 of which make slightly less than an inch). The terminology relating to different parts of typeset characters is extensive, but the terms most commonly retained by Macintosh parlance are listed here.

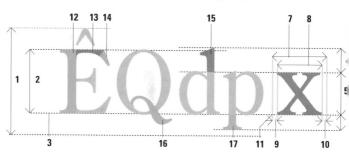

"cicero" in France and Germany, a "riga tipografica" ("riga") in Italy and an "augustijn" ("aug") in the Netherlands. There is no relationship between the Anglo-American point and the Didot point, and neither of them relates to metric measurement.

While it was thought that there would be a gradual move toward the metrification of typographic measurements (virtually every allied trade uses metric measurements), the advent of the Mac as a design tool has probably established a new international standard of measurement (or, at least, it may have delayed metrification in some countries) based on the Anglo-American system. On the Mac, however, one point measures 0.013889in, and 72 points really do equal one inch. It is no coincidence that the basic Mac screen resolution is 72dpi.

TYPE CHARACTERISTICS Among the many basic considerations of typographic design, perhaps the most important are the varying widths of type characters and the spaces between them. An understanding of these elements is essential in order to achieve the twin aim of esthetic appeal and legibility.

The width of characters, or the space allotted to them, depends largely on the equipment used to produce them. For instance, a manual typewriter, in order to maintain consistent letter spacing, uses exaggeratedly wide serifs on letters such as "i" and "l" (*viz* i and l). This gives a string of characters an even appearance by reducing the amount of white around them. On the Mac, however, the number of character widths can be infinite, thus providing the potential for perfect optical spacing between characters.

1 Body height, or em height
2 Cap height
3 Base line
4 Ascender height
5 x height
6 Descender depth
7 Character width
8 Body width
9 Left sidebearing
10 Right side-bearing
11 Character origin
12 Stem
13 Arm
14 Beak
15 Ascender
16 Tail
17 Descender
18 Apex
19 Spine
20 Stroke
21 Serif
22 Bowl
23 Link
24 Ear
25 Counter
26 Cross-stroke
27 Horizontal stem or crossbar
28 Spur
29 Bracket
30 Loop
31 Finial

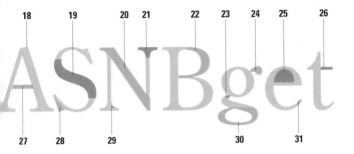

The spacing of words in a line of text owes as much to a convention employed by scribes in medieval times as it does to the evolution of typographic design – because they wanted to make facing pages in books symmetrical, scribes insisted that both the left- and right-hand edges of text should be vertically aligned. This could only be achieved by abbreviating words, which led to the introduction of additional symbols, called contractions, being used to fill the spaces which had been left by abbreviated words or short lines.

This convention was sustained by Johann Gutenberg (*c*.1397–1468), who came up with the idea of printing from movable (and thus reusable) type as long ago as 1436, although more by mechanical requirements than by esthetic considerations. In order to make an impression from a group of pieces of type, all the pieces had to be locked together under tension in a metal frame called a forme. This meant that all the lines of type, including spaces, had to be of the same length; otherwise, all the pieces of type would fall out of the forme as soon as it was lifted. In other words, the whole area between each edge of the forme had to be filled with wood or metal – either type or spaces. The convention of vertically aligning edges of blocks of text was made possible by distributing approximately equal spaces between each of the words along a line of text. This is what we know today as "justified" text, and the technique of achieving it remained more or less unchanged until the advent of alternative methods of setting type in the latter half of the 20th century.

After the introduction of movable type, the next

SCREEN AND PRINTER FONTS

To use fonts successfully, you will find it necessary to familiarize yourself with the distinction between font files which are used to display the font on your monitor and font files which are used by a printing device for output. For monitor display, letterforms are made up of pixels and are called "bitmapped," or "screen" fonts. The printer, on the other hand, uses an object-oriented version of the font, an outline capable of output at any size and at any resolution. These fonts are called "printer," or "outline" fonts. Some PostScript printer font icons are shown below.

Font formats There are two formats from which to choose when you buy a font: PostScript or TrueType. If you opt for PostScript, you will find files on the disk for both screen fonts and printer fonts. TrueType fonts, however, are supplied with only one file – an outline font file which is used both for printing and for generating bitmapped screen fonts.

Screen fonts To render a PostScript font on screen with a semblance of what it

will look like when printed ("WYSIWYG" – what you see is what you get), a screen font must be installed in several sizes. If not, the font is drawn from the nearest available size and results in "aliasing," a jagged appearance ("jaggies"), making it impossible to fine-tune typographic design.

ATM The introduction of Adobe's Type Manager (ATM) resolved this problem by using the "hinting" information stored in the PostScript printer outline font to render more accurate bitmapped letterforms on screen. With ATM installed, only one size of bitmapped screen font is required (so that the font name appears in menus).

Hinting Hints modify character shapes to look better at low resolutions (both monitor and printer). Normally, a screen font will instruct a pixel to turn on if more than half the area of

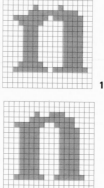

the pixel is covered by the font, resulting in anomalies (**1**). A hinted character, on the other hand, knows how the character should *look* – that the two stems of an "n" should be the same width, for example (**2**).

Font installation

Screen font files are contained within "suitcases" (**3**) – although so are TrueType outline font files

which are also used for printing. PostScript printer font files (**4**) must be placed within the System Folder (**5**, see opposite) in order that they will be automatically downloaded to the printer.

System 7 The PostScript screen font files (**6**) or TrueType outline font files (**7**) must be placed inside the System suitcase file (**8**) before they will work.

Double-clicking a PostScript screen font icon or a TrueType outline font icon will produce a sample of that font (**13**). To use ATM, the

How razorback-jumping frogs can level six piqued gymnasts!

13

ATM program driver file (**9**) must be placed in the System Folder (**5**) and the

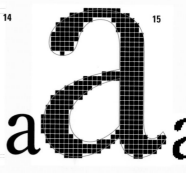

ATM application file (**10**) in the Control Panels folder (**11**). Theoretically, PostScript outline font files (**4**) should be placed in the Extensions folder (**12**), but for ATM to work, they must be loose in the System Folder instead.

System 6.0.X Screen fonts must be installed in the system file by using the Apple utility Font/DA Mover (in System 6.0.X suitcases cannot be opened by double-clicking). Printer fonts must be loose in the System folder instead.

Alternative installation As a designer, you will use a lot of fonts; thus font menus may become very lengthy, and fonts can absorb a great deal of RAM. A utility such as *Suitcase II* allows you to easily open and close suitcase files of screen fonts. You do this by creating font suitcases (using Font/DA Mover if you are using System 6.0.X) for, say, individual jobs, which can be opened and closed as you need them (**below**). The printer fonts can be stored in the same folder as the suitcases, thus reducing clutter in your System Folder.

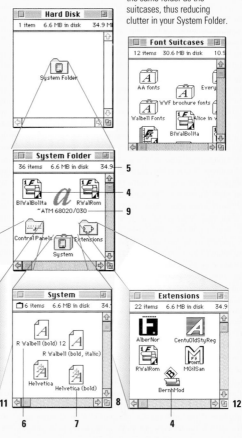

Below The outline font construction (**14**) is shown next to its 60pt imageset character. The hinted bitmapped screen character generated from the outline font by ATM (**15**) and what the 60pt character looks like on screen. Without ATM, the 60pt character is constructed (**16**) from the installed bitmapped font of the closest size, in this case 24pt. Using an application such as FontStudio, bitmapped fonts can be "anti-aliased" – the edges can be smoothed out by adding grayscale pixels in appropriate places (**17**).

significant change came with the invention, patented in 1884, of the Linotype machine by the German-born American engineer Ottmar Mergenthaler. This was the first keyboard-operated composing machine to employ the principle of a "matrix" – a single master containing a complete character set, one for every size and style of a typeface – from which molten metal was used to cast type. Each line of type was cast as a single, solid piece (hence the name "Linotype"), called a "slug."

One year after the patenting of the Linotype machine came the Monotype process, invented in 1885 by Tolbert Lanston of Ohio. This process comprised a keyboard-operated composing machine which cast type as individual letters, using large numbers of matrices (which was only feasible due to the invention of a mechanical punch cutter by L.B. Benton).

In the 1950s, photomechanical typesetting machines were introduced, and they employed matrices stored as negatives on glass disks or strips. Output was produced photographically onto bromide paper.

The first digital typesetting machines appeared in the early 1970s. Letterforms made up of digitized data were generated on the screen of a cathode ray tube (CRT), from which an image was projected onto photographic film or paper. This method of generating digitized type has gradually been replaced by the laser imagesetter, which was first introduced in the mid-1970s.

The Macintosh computer arrived in 1984, but it wasn't until 1988 that it began to be taken seriously by the various graphic arts industries. On the Mac, the amount of control the user has over word and letter spacing is almost limitless. An application such as QuarkXPress offers numerous alternative hyphenation and justification permutations which means that, just as the medieval scribe determined his own criteria for spacing out lines of text, so the modern graphic designer must also be well-versed in the parameters of esthetic acceptability of word and character spacing instead of relying, as we have done for many years, on the skill of the typesetter and the sophistication of his machines.

The first fonts on the Mac were bitmapped fonts which were designed to be both displayed on screen and printed. Unfortunately, the printing quality of bitmapped fonts left a lot to be desired, but it was not long before the introduction of PostScript made a vital contribution to the success of the Mac as a graphic arts tool.

POSTSCRIPT PostScript is the proprietary "page description language" (PDL) of Adobe Systems Inc. A page description language is the program that the printer uses to interpret data from the computer into a form that the printer can use to print from. The PostScript PDL is used to describe graphic images, such as tone images, tints, rules, etc., as

well as fonts, to a printer, so a PostScript printer is still a necessary part of your equipment even if you use non-PostScript fonts (TrueType, for example).

When you buy a PostScript font, you get three items in the package – a "suitcase" file containing screen fonts, individual printer font files (one for each style – italic, bold, etc.) and a folder containing Adobe "font metrics" files (AFMs).

The screen fonts are the bitmapped fonts that are designed to display the font on-screen at a variety of fixed sizes (as well as being called bitmapped fonts, PostScript screen fonts are also occasionally referred to as "fixed-size" fonts – especially by Apple). Screen fonts reside in the System file in the system folder on your hard disk. The problem with bitmapped screen fonts is that, when rendered on-screen, they give an ugly, stepped appearance, called "jaggies." The problem of jaggies is further exacerbated when you specify a size that is not one of the fixed sizes that you installed in the System file.

Printer font files are the "outline" fonts containing data that describes the outline shapes of type characters, from which any size can be drawn and filled in by the output device (printer fonts may also be called "scalable" fonts). The advantage of outline fonts is that, as well as providing a single set of data for any size, they can be output at any resolution whether it be the 300dpi of a laser printer or the 2540dpi of an imagesetter.

The third part of the package, the AFM files, are only required by very few applications such as Scitex Visionary and Interset's Quoin.

Type 1 and Type 3 fonts Originally, Adobe protected their PostScript font technology by reserving a font format for their own type designs. This format, called PostScript Type 1, was encrypted (locked), and the fonts were thus unalterable. Type 1 fonts employed a technique known as "hinting," which was designed to enhance the display of fonts at small sizes – it also improved the appearance of small sizes of type when printed on low-resolution printers.

Type 3, on the other hand (there was no Type 2), was the PostScript format that other (non-Adobe) foundries used for their fonts – unless they were prepared to pay a license fee to Adobe for their Type 1 format, which very few did. Although Type 3 fonts did not contain hinting, they were alterable, which meant that by using applications such as Fontographer, you could change the design of any character, or even of an entire font. But the real drawback of Type 3 fonts was that ATM (see below) only worked with Type 1 fonts.

Adobe Type Manager When Apple announced that they were to offer an alternative font format to PostScript, Adobe responded by releasing a font utility called "Type Manager" (ATM). This little utility made a huge impact on the

KEYBOARD CHARACTERS

Keyboard layout is generally standard, but some fonts may use different keys, such as "expert sets," with additional characters. To view the character set of any of your installed fonts, use the Apple-supplied Key Caps (**below**) utility in the Apple Menu which displays all available characters for the various modifier keys.

Shift + character keys	Option + Shift + character keys
Character key only	Option + character keys

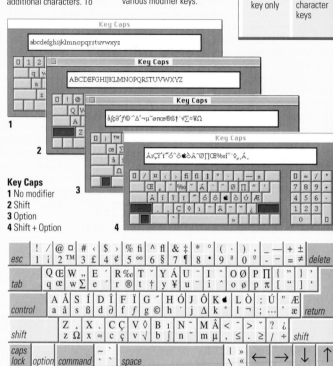

Key Caps
1 No modifier
2 Shift
3 Option
4 Shift + Option

Above All the characters accessible by using combinations of the Shift and Option modifier keys.
Below The commonly available characters and the modifier key combinations for generating that character (where appropriate). There may be slight variations depending on the version of the system software that you use. For example, the # and £ characters are transposed on the U.S. and U.K. systems. The following abbreviations are used for the modifier keys, followed by the character to be pressed.
S = Shift key
O = Option key
SO = Shift + Option keys
/ = two keystrokes

Sym.	Character	Key
´	Acute	**O**e/**O**e
Á	Acute cap A	**SO**y
Í	Acute cap I	**SO**s
Ó	Acute cap O	**SO**h
Ú	Acute cap U	**SO**;
&	Ampersand	&
	Apple	**SO**k
≈	Approximately equal to	**O**x
*	Asterisk	*
{	Brace, open	{
}	Brace, close	}
˘	Breve	**SO**.
•	Bullet	**O**8

Sym.	Character	Key
˘	Carib diacritic	**SO**t
Ç	Cedilla, cap	**SO**c
ç	Cedilla, l/c	**O**c
¢	Cent	**O**4
ˆ	Circumflex	**SO**n
^	Circumflex, ASCII	^
Â	Circumflex, cap A	**SO**m
Î	Circumflex, cap I	**SO**d
Ô	Circumflex, cap O	**SO**j
:	Colon	:
,	Comma	,
@	Commercial "at"	@
©	Copyright	**O**g

Sym.	Character	Key
†	Dagger	**O**t
Ø	Danish cap O	**SO**o
‡	Double dagger,	**SO**7
·	Decimal	**SO**9
°	Degree	**SO**8
Δ	Delta	**O**j
¨	Diaeresis/umlaut	**O**u/**O**u
Ï	Diaeresis, cap I	**SO**f
Œ	Diphthong, cap OE	**SO**q
œ	Diphthong, l/c oe	**O**q
Æ	Diphthong, cap AE	**SO**'
æ	Diphthong, l/c ae	**O**'
÷	Divide	**O**/
$	Dollar	$
˙	Dot accent	**O**h
ı	Dotless i	**SO**b
…	Ellipsis	**O**;
—	Em rule	**SO**-
–	En rule	**O**-
=	Equals	=
ß	Eszett	**O**s
!	Exclamation	!
ƒ	Florin	**O**f
⁄	Fraction bar	**SO**1
`	Grave, ASCII	`
Ò	Grave, cap O	**SO**l
>	Greater than	>
≥	Greater than or equal	**O**.
«	Guillemot, open double	**O**\
»	Guillemot, close double	**SO**\
‹	Guillemot, open single	**SO**3
›	Guillemot, close single	**SO**4
#	Hash	**O**3
˝	Hungarian umlaut	**SO**g
-	Hyphen	-
∞	Infinity	**O**5
∫	Integral	**O**b
¤	International currency	**SO**2
<	Less than	<
≤	Less than or equal	**O**,
fi	Ligature, fi	**SO**5
fl	Ligature, fl	**SO**6
¬	Logical not	**O**l
◊	Lozenge	**SO**v
¯	Macron	**SO**,
µ	Mu	**O**m

Sym.	Character	Key
≠	Not equal to	**O**=
˛	Ogonek diacritic	**SO**x
Ω	Omega	**O**z
ª	Ordfeminine	**O**9
º	Ordmasculine	**O**0
¶	Paragraph	**O**7
(	Parentheses, open	(
)	Parentheses, close	)
∂	Partial differential	**O**d
‰	Per thousand	**SO**e
%	Percent	%
.	Period	.
π	Pi	**O**p
+	Plus	+
±	Plus or minus	**SO**=
"	Prime, double	"
'	Prime, single	'
∏	Product	**SO**p
?	Query	?
"	Quote, open double	**O**[
"	Quote, close double	**SO**[
'	Quote, open single	**O**]
'	Quote, close single	**SO**]
„	Quote, double baseline	**SO**w
‚	Quote, single baseline	**SO**0
√	Radical	**O**v
®	Registered	**O**r
°	Ring	**O**k
§	Section	**O**6
;	Semicolon	;
/	Solidus	/
¡	Spanish exclamation	**O**1
¿	Spanish query	**SO**/
[	Square bracket, open	[
]	Square bracket, close	]
£	Sterling	**O**3
Σ	Summation	**O**w
Å	Swedish cap A	**SO**a
å	Swedish l/c a	**O**a
~	Tilde	**SO**m
~	Tilde, ASCII	~
™	Trademark	**O**2
_	Underline	_
		Vertical bar		
¥	Yen	**O**y

Right Some accented characters are only accessible by two keyboard operations (an o acute is generated by first pressing Option + e together, then o). Some accented caps also have their own key(s).

Accent	Characters	Key
Acute	Á É Í Ó Ú á é í ó ú	**O**e/character
Grave	À È Ì Ò Ù à è ì ò ù	**O**`/character
Diaeresis	Ä Ë Ï Ö Ü Ÿ ä ë ï ö ü ÿ	**O**u/character
Tilde	Ã Ñ Õ ã ñ õ	**O**n/character
Circumflex	Â Ê Î Ô Û â ê î ô û	**O**i/character

Macintosh world generally, but more particularly on its use by designers as a typographic tool. So far as the user is concerned, all ATM does is to draw a font on-screen by using the data contained in the printer outline font file, the result being a smooth screen-rendering of the type design. This did away with the need for bitmap screen fonts (although not entirely – one bitmapped font is still required to be in the System file so that the font name appears in font menus).

However, the differences between Type 1 and Type 3 fonts were to all but disappear when Adobe, in response to the imminent release of Apple's new font format "unlocked" their Type 1 format and made it available to all developers. This means that, by using a suitable font conversion program, any Type 3 font can now be converted to a Type 1 font. It also means that you can create your own Type 1 typeface, with the advantage of rendering it on screen with ATM. Type 1 fonts can be edited using all manner of applications such as FreeHand and Illustrator.

Rules Page makeup and object-oriented drawing applications offer a wide variety of rule styles at virtually any size. While useful, rule styles supplied with applications do not normally allow a great deal of flexibility, particularly in controlling the relative thickness and spacing of different lines which make up the same rule. It is important, when attributing a size to a rule, not to rely on laser proofs for esthetic decision making. In most circumstances, a laser printer will print a hairline rule (0.25pt) at 0.5pt, and thus you would be advised to run out an imageset sample before committing to a size.

300dpi	2400dpi	300dpi	2400dpi		
				0.25pt	0.0882mm
				0.3pt	0.1058mm
				0.4pt	0.1411mm
				0.5pt	0.1764mm
				0.6pt	0.2117mm
				0.7pt	0.2469mm
				0.8pt	0.2822mm
				0.9pt	0.3175mm
				1.0pt	0.3528mm
				1.25pt	0.4410mm
				1.5pt	0.5292mm
				1.75pt	0.6174mm
				2.0pt	0.7055mm
				2.25pt	0.7937mm
				2.5pt	0.8819mm
				2.75pt	0.9701mm
				3.0pt	1.0583mm
				3.25pt	1.1465mm
				3.5pt	1.2347mm
				3.75pt	1.3229mm
				4.0pt	1.4111mm

TRUETYPE For a variety of reasons, not least to avoid paying licensing fees to Adobe for the use of PostScript, Apple deemed it necessary to develop their own outline font technology, which they named "TrueType."

There are two main distinctions between TrueType and PostScript. The first is that TrueType fonts are rendered both on screen and by the printer from a single set of outline data, thus using up less space on your hard disk than an equivalent PostScript version of a font. There is no need for a separate bitmapped screen version, not even for font menu purposes – unlike ATM, which requires a screen font in order to display the name of the font. The second is that TrueType fonts can be printed on any printer, whether PostScript or not – although TrueType is not a PDL, so you still need a PostScript printer to output graphics.

The use of a single file, whether in TrueType or PostScript formats, for screen and printer rendering reduces the possibilities for error – for example, the number of characters in a line of text displayed on screen using a bitmapped version may not be the same as that output by a printer using the outline version.

Traditionally, each size of metal type was cast from its own matrix, and because of this, changes could be made to the design of a face at different sizes in order to adjust optical aberrations that may occur when a face is enlarged or reduced. The problem with outline fonts on the Mac,

2400dpi	2400dpi	2400dpi	2400dpi
0.25pt	2.0pt		2.5pt
0.3pt	2.25pt		3.0pt
0.4pt	2.5pt		3.5pt
0.5pt	2.75pt		4.0pt
0.6pt	3.0pt		4.5pt
0.7pt	3.25pt		5.0pt
0.8pt	3.5pt		5.5pt
0.9pt	3.75pt		6.0pt
1.0pt	4.0pt		6.5pt
1.25pt	4.25pt		7.0pt
1.5pt	4.5pt		
1.75pt	4.75pt		2.5pt
2.0pt	5.0pt		3.0pt
2.25pt	5.25pt		3.5pt
2.5pt	5.5pt		4.0pt
2.75pt	5.75pt		4.5pt
3.0pt	6.0pt		5.0pt
3.25pt	6.25pt		5.5pt
3.5pt	6.5pt		6.0pt
3.75pt	6.75pt		6.5pt
4.0pt	7.0pt		7.0pt

Fractions Few fonts provide fractions as part of their standard character set. However, variations on fonts called "expert sets" provide, among other things, a range of "true" fractions (a single keystroke composite) plus a facility for setting "piece" fractions (**below**) from numerators (**1**), separators (**2**) and denominators (**3**). The selection of fonts for which expert sets are available is limited.

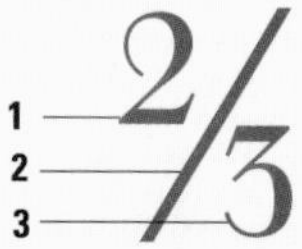

QuarkXPress provides an editable "make fraction" feature, but if you require extensive fraction setting, this can be laborious. An alternative is to create your own fraction font using an application such as FontMonger whereby you can copy any of your fonts, create fractions any way you like, and assign each one any keystroke (**right**).

1/8 1/4 1/3 3/8 1/2 5/8 2/3 3/4 7/8

Expert set true fraction

1/8 1/4 1/3 3/8 1/2 5/8 2/3 3/4 7/8

QuarkXPress fraction with virgule (fraction bar) separator

1/8 1/4 1/3 3/8 1/2 5/8 2/3 3/4 7/8

QuarkXPress fraction with solidus separator

1/32 3/32 5/32 3/16 5/16 7/16

Expert set piece fraction

1/32 3/32 5/32 3/16 5/16 7/16

QuarkXPress fraction with virgule (fraction bar) separator

1/32 3/32 5/32 3/16 5/16 7/16

QuarkXPress fraction with solidus separator

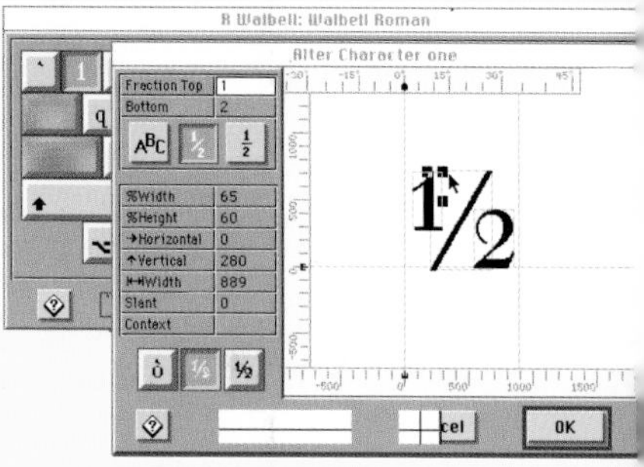

Numerals Traditionally, fonts were often cast with options for numerals both as aligning and non-aligning choices. Standard fonts offer only one choice, but expert character sets provide another.

1 2 3 4 5 6 7 8 9 0

Expert set non-aligning numerals

1 2 3 4 5 6 7 8 9 0

Aligning numerals

Ligatures Standard character sets provide two ligatures – fi and fl. Expert character sets, however, provide more choices. A Quark XTension is available for converting appropriate characters. Ligatures should not be used on small sizes where tracking is tight.

fi ffi fl ffl ff

Expert set roman ligatures

fi ffi fl ffl ff

Expert set italic ligatures

Small caps Expert sets provide specially designed small caps which give a more even weight relative to the capitals of that font, as distinct from the reduced caps of standard fonts.

A A B B C C D D

Expert set small capitals

A A B B C C D D

Small capitals generated via Small Caps command

whether they are TrueType or PostScript, is that each size of a font is scaled from a single set of data, ignoring the fact that, to achieve optimum results, it may be necessary to make changes to the design of a font at different sizes. However, this inadequacy of the current font formats may be redressed by the introduction of TrueType Optical Scaling, which offers a choice of design for different sizes of the same font. Adobe's Multiple Master font format, which generates several weights from a single set of font data, does not offer a choice of design for different sizes.

As for deciding between TrueType or PostScript – it doesn't really matter, since neither format is better than the other and you can mix both formats within the same document. If you are just starting out, you will have received some TrueType fonts with your Mac, so you may want to stick with TrueType as a preferred format – at least you can then take advantage of any special display designs of a typeface. However, for some time yet, you will find that foundries offer a wider choice of PostScript fonts, although the selection of PostScript as against TrueType will eventually balance out. Whichever you decide upon – TrueType or PostScript – if you can't find the font that you need in one format, don't hesitate to get it in the other (if you adopt a TrueType-only policy, but need a PostScript font, just make sure you have ATM installed on your Mac).

FONT CONFLICTS Every font is given an identity number (ID) so that it can be identified by your Mac. Originally, the Mac only made provision for 255, half of which were reserved for use by Apple, the remainder by other foundries. When they were used up and it became apparent that typography was to play an important part in the future of the Mac, the range of ID numbers was increased, but not enough to meet the rapidly growing number of fonts being made available for use on the Mac. This led to an anomaly where different fonts sometimes bore the same ID number (occasionally, even from the same foundry), resulting in a situation where a font selected from a menu produced a screen rendering of an entirely different font, or where the font printed was different from the one displayed on screen.

Fortunately, a number of utility programs, such as **Font Harmony** (Fifth Generation Systems, Inc.), are available that will check the IDs of your fonts and reassign any that clash.

FONT ORGANIZATION It is quite certain that you will accumulate a large number of fonts, most of which you would like permanently on call. If you use PostScript fonts, you will find that they have been given names such as "Sbl 1 Stone Serif SemibdItal" for Stone Serif Semibold Italic, which is extremely unhelpful, because fonts are listed alphabetically in menus, so different weights of the same face appear all over the place rather than all together. However, just as

with many other Macintosh anomalies, programs have been written to save the day. One such program, **Type Reunion** (Adobe Systems, Inc.), renames fonts in menus with names you would expect to see, listing all their variations in sub-menus.

Even by rationalizing your vast number of fonts using a utility such as Type Reunion, you could still end up with an impractically long list in your font menu. Although it is a simple matter to install and de-install fonts (you simply drag them in and out of the System file as necessary – be aware, though, that PostScript outline printer fonts must reside in the first, or "root," level of the system folder for ATM to work), it is sometimes more practical to create a separate font suitcase for each job that you are working on and, using a utility such as **Suitcase II** (Fifth Generation Systems, Inc.) or **MasterJuggler** (Altsys Corp.), open and close the suitcase as you need the fonts. You could even have a separate suitcase to hold the fonts you use regularly, regardless of the job you may be working on.

DIGITIZING FONTS With a suitable application such as **ATF Type Designer** (Kingsley/ATF Type Corp.), **Fontographer** (Altsys Corp.), **FontStudio** (Letraset), or **Ikarus-M** (URW), it is possible to scan in (or draw) any font – for instance, one from an extinct foundry or an old woodcut face – fine-tune it, assign kerning values, etc, and then produce it either as a PostScript Type 1 font with hinting or as a TrueType font. Even existing fonts can be regenerated in this way and without infringing copyright (curiously and, to my mind, outrageously, copyright only exists in the *name* of a font and not in its *design*, enabling you to copy a typeface and reissue it under another name – something that you may have noticed is prevalent among some foundries).

BUYING FONTS Fonts are generally supplied on floppy disks. Buying fonts like this, one at a time as you need them, is what most designers tend to do. However, most foundries offer their entire font libraries on a single CD-ROM disk which, although hugely expensive, is probably more economical than buying fonts individually if you need the ultimate in choice. Some foundries will supply CD-ROMs with all the fonts in encrypted form. The advantage of this is that, although the disk contains the entire library, you only pay for the fonts as you need them – you simply telephone the foundry, which will give you the appropriate code to "unlock" the font that you need.

Of course, you will still need to buy fonts on floppies if you select a newly released font that wasn't included on your CD-ROM of a font library.

Font names The relative ease with which typefaces can be copied, modified or created from scratch on a computer has brought about a proliferation of fonts from various suppliers. Curiously, copyright in a font exists not in the *design* of the font, as you might expect, but in its *name*. This has resulted in many foundries producing, as well as their own new designs, the same fonts as other foundries, but with different names. Listed here are some common typefaces and their alternative names.

Numbering fonts If you create your own typeface using a font design application such as FontStudio, it is important that you assign to it a "font family number," since many applications identify fonts by their number rather than by their name. Certain ranges of font family numbers have been reserved by Apple for specific purposes, such as foreign language scripts. If you intend to distribute the font commercially, you must register it with Apple: Font Registration Program Developer Technical Support Apple Computer Inc. 20525 Mariana Avenue M/S 75-3A Cupertino, CA 95014

If you only intend using the font on your own system, its font family number must fall between 1024 and 3071, which Apple has reserved for non-commercial fonts. These do not need to be registered.

Antique Olive
Alphavanti
Berry Roman
Incised 901
Oliva
Olive
Olive Antique
Oliver
Olivette
Olivette Antique
Olivia
Provence

Avant Garde
AG
ITC Avant Garde
Avanti
Suave

Baskerville
Basque
Baskerline
Beaumont
BK

Fry's Baskerville
Baskerville Display
Baskerville Old Face

Bembo
Aldine 401
Aldine Roman
Ambo
Bem
Griffo
Latinesque

Bodoni
BO
Bodoni No. 2
Brunswick

Bauer Bodoni
Bodoni B
Euro Bodoni
Headline Bodoni

Caslon Bold
Caslon No. 3
Caslon 74 Bold
Caslon Bold 482, 483
New Caslon

Caslon
Caslon Old Face
Caslon Old Style
Caslon 76
Caslon 128

Caslon 471

Caslon 540
Caslon 2
Caslon 74
Caslon 484, 485

Century Expanded
Cambridge
Expanded
CE
Century
Century Light/II
Century X

Century Oldstyle
Cambridge Oldstyle

Century Schoolbook
Cambridge
Schoolbook
Century Medium
Century Modern
Century Text
Century Textbook
CS
Schoolbook

Cheltenham
Cheltenham Old
Style
Cheltonian
Chesterfield
Gloucester
Kenilworth
Nordhoff
Sorbonne
Winchester

Franklin Gothic
Gothic No. 16
Pittsburgh

Futura
Alphatura
Atlantis
FU
Future
Photura
Sirius
Utica

Garamond
American Garamond
Garamond No. 2
Garamond No. 3
Garamond No. 49
Garamont

GD
Grenada

ITC Garamond
Garamet

Stempel Garamond
Garamond
Garamond Antiqua
Garamond Royale
Euro Garamond
Original Garamond

Gill Sans
Eric
Gillies
Glib
Graphic Gothic
Hammersmith
Humanist 521
Sans Serif 2

Goudy
Goudy Old Style
Grecian
Number 11

Helvetica
Aristocrat
Claro
Corvus
Europa Grotesk
Geneva/2
Hamilton
HE
Helios
Helv
Helvette
Holsatia
Megaron
Newton
Spectra
Swiss 721
CG Triumvirate
Vega
Video Spectra

Palatino
Andover
Compano
Elegante
Malibu
CG Palacio
Paladium
Palatine
Palermo

Parliament
Patina
Pontiac
Zapf Calligraphic

Perpetua
Felicity
Lapidary 333
Percepta
Perpetual

Rockwell
Geometric Slabserif
712
Rockland
Slate

Times Roman
Claritas
Dutch 801
English
English Times
Euro Times
London Roman
Pegasus
Press Roman
Sonoran Serif
Tempora
Tiempo
Timeless
Times New Roman
TmsRmn
TR
Varitimes

Trump Mediaeval
Activa
Ascot
Continental
Knight
Kuenstler 480
Olympus
Renaissance
Saul

Univers
Alphavers
Aries
Boston
Eterna
Galaxy
Kosmos
UN
Versatile
Zurich

JUSTIFICATION SETTINGS

Most page makeup applications offer features for controlling the way space is apportioned between words and characters in justified and unjustified text. In justified text the program will attempt to insert spaces according to an optimum value, but failing that will space out a line according to a defined minimum and maximum value. In unjustified text, only the optimum value is used. Usually, the optimum word space represents the normal space width of a font. Using default values in justified text with a short column measure may result in dramatically inconsistent spacing from line to line (see **7**), and the values should be modified (**8, 9**). Among these examples are the default values of QuarkXPress (**1, 5**), Pagemaker (**4**), and DesignStudio, "Professional" option (**6**).

---

1 Unjustified, flush left
Auto hyphenation off
Word spacing
Minimum: 100%
Optimum: 100%
Maximum: 150%
Character spacing
Minimum: 0%
Optimum: 0%
Maximum: 15%

Lorem ipsum dolor sit amet, consectetuer adipiscing elit, sed diam nonummy nibh euismod tincidunt ut laoreet dolore magna aliquam erat volutpat.

Lorem ipsum dolor sit amet, consectetuer adipiscing elit, sed diam nonummy nibh euismod ut laoreet dolore magna aliquam erat

---

2 Unjustified, flush left
Auto hyphenation off
Word spacing
Minimum: 100%
Optimum: 85%
Maximum: 100%
Character spacing
Minimum: 0%
Optimum: −5%
Maximum: 0%

Lorem ipsum dolor sit amet, consectetuer adipiscing elit, sed diam nonummy nibh euismod tincidunt ut laoreet dolore magna aliquam erat volutpat.

Lorem ipsum dolor sit amet, consectetuer adipiscing elit, sed diam nonummy nibh euismod tincidunt ut laoreet dolore magna aliquam erat volutpat.

---

3 Unjustified, flush left
Auto hyphenation on
Word spacing
Minimum: 100%
Optimum: 110%
Maximum: 150%
Character spacing
Minimum: 0%
Optimum: 5%
Maximum: 15%

Lorem ipsum dolor sit amet, con-sectetuer adipiscing elit, sed diam non-ummy nibh euismod tincidunt ut laoreet dolore magna aliquam erat volutpat.

Lorem ipsum dolor sit amet, con-sectetuer adipiscing elit, sed diam nonummy nibh euismod tincidunt ut laoreet dolore magna aliquam erat

---

4 Justified
Auto hyphenation on
Word spacing
Minimum: 50%
Optimum: 100%
Maximum: 200%
Character spacing
Minimum: −5%
Optimum: 0%
Maximum: 25%

Lorem ipsum dolor sit amet, consectetuer adipiscing elit, sed diam nonummy nibh euis-mod tincidunt ut laoreet dolore magna ali-quam erat volutpat.

Lorem ipsum dolor sit amet, consectetuer adipiscing elit, sed diam nonummy nibh euismod tincidunt ut laoreet dolore magna aliquam erat volutpat.

Lorem ipsum dolor sit amet, consectetuer adipiscing elit, sed diam nonummy nibh euismod tincidunt ut laoreet dolore magna aliquam erat volutpat.

Lorem ipsum dolor sit amet, consectetuer adipiscing elit, sed diam nonummy nibh euismod tincidunt ut laoreet dolore magna aliquam erat

5 Justified

Auto hyphenation on

Word spacing

Minimum: 100%

Optimum: 100%

Maximum: 150%

Character spacing

Minimum:　 0%

Optimum:　 0%

Maximum:　15%

Lorem ipsum dolor sit amet, consectetuer adipiscing elit, sed diam nonummy nibh euismod tincidunt ut laoreet dolore magna aliquam erat volutpat.

Lorem ipsum dolor sit amet, consectetuer adipiscing elit, sed diam nonummy nibh euismod tincidunt ut laoreet dolore magna aliquam erat

6 Justified

Auto hyphenation on

Word spacing

Minimum:　75%

Optimum: 100%

Maximum: 125%

Character spacing

Minimum:　 0%

Optimum:　 0%

Maximum:　 0%

Lorem ipsum dolor sit amet, consectetuer adipiscing elit, sed diam nonummy nibh euismod tincidunt ut laoreet dolore magna aliquam erat volutpat.

Lorem ipsum dolor sit amet, consectetuer adipiscing elit, sed diam nonummy nibh euismod tincidunt ut laoreet dolore magna aliquam erat volutpat.

7 Justified

Auto hyphenation on

Word spacing

Minimum:　90%

Optimum:　90%

Maximum: 100%

Character spacing

Minimum: − 5%

Optimum: − 5%

Maximum:　 0%

Lorem ipsum dolor sit amet, consectetuer adipiscing elit, sed diam nonummy nibh euismod tincidunt ut laoreet dolore magna aliquam erat volutpat.

Lorem ipsum dolor sit amet, consectetuer adipiscing elit, sed diam nonummy nibh euismod tincidunt ut laoreet dolore magna aliquam erat volutpat.

8 Justified

Auto hyphenation on

Word spacing

Minimum:　80%

Optimum:　90%

Maximum: 100%

Character spacing

Minimum: −10%

Optimum: − 5%

Maximum:　 0%

Lorem ipsum dolor sit amet, consectetuer adipiscing elit, sed diam nonummy nibh euismod tincidunt ut laoreet dolore magna aliquam erat volutpat.

Lorem ipsum dolor sit amet, consectetuer adipiscing elit, sed diam nonummy nibh euismod tincidunt ut laoreet dolore magna aliquam erat volutpat.

9 Justified

Auto hyphenation on

Word spacing

Minimum: 100%

Optimum: 100%

Maximum: 110%

Character spacing

Minimum: − 5%

Optimum:　 0%

Maximum: − 5%

TRACKING VALUES

When text is output, by laser printer or imagesetter, it is scaled from a single outline printer font, and the character spacing values remain the same, regardless of output size. It may be necessary to adjust the spacing between characters ("tracking," as distinct from kerning which involves pairs of characters) on various sizes of text setting, depending on the characteristics of the typeface. Tracking values are normally expressed in fractions of em, the definition of which depends on the application you are using (QuarkXPress defines an em as the width of two zeros of the current type size, whereas DesignStudio defines an em as the square of the current type size). Values can be expressed as finely as 0.00005 em ($\frac{1}{20,000}$ em). In XPress a value of 1 equals 0.005 em ($\frac{1}{200}$ em).

Lorem ipsum dolor sit amet, adipiscing elit, sed diam nonummy nibh euismod tincidunt ut laoreet dolore magna aliquam erat volutpat. Ut wisi enim ad minim veniam, quis nostrud exerci tation ullamcorper suscipit lobortis nisl ut

7pt Gill Sans, 0 tracking

Lorem ipsum dolor sit amet, consectetuer adipiscing elit, sed diam nonummy nibh euismod tincidunt ut laoreet dolore magna aliquam erat volutpat. Ut wisi enim ad minim veniam, quis nostrud exerci tation

7pt Galliard, 0 tracking

Lorem ipsum dolor sit amet, adipiscing elit, sed diam nonummy nibh euismod tincidunt ut laoreet dolore magna aliquam erat volutpat. Ut wisi enim ad minim veniam, quis nostrud exerci tation ullamcorper suscipit lobortis nisl ut

7pt Gill Sans, 0.005 em tracking

Lorem ipsum dolor sit amet, consectetuer adipiscing elit, sed diam nonummy nibh euismod tincidunt ut laoreet dolore magna aliquam erat volutpat. Ut wisi enim ad minim veniam, quis nostrud exerci tation

7pt Galliard, 0.005 em tracking

Lorem ipsum dolor sit amet, adipiscing elit, sed diam nonummy nibh euismod tincidunt ut laoreet dolore magna aliquam erat volutpat. Ut wisi enim ad minim veniam, quis nostrud exerci tation ullamcorper suscipit lobortis nisl ut

7pt Gill Sans, 0.01 em tracking

Lorem ipsum dolor sit amet, consectetuer adipiscing elit, sed diam nonummy nibh euismod tincidunt ut laoreet dolore magna aliquam erat volutpat. Ut wisi enim ad minim veniam, quis nostrud exerci tation

7pt Galliard, 0.01 em tracking

Lorem ipsum dolor sit amet, adipiscing elit, sed diam nonummy nibh euismod tincidunt ut laoreet dolore magna aliquam erat volutpat. Ut wisi enim ad minim veniam, quis nostrud exerci tation ullamcorper suscipit lobortis nisl ut

7pt Gill Sans, 0.015 em tracking

Lorem ipsum dolor sit amet, consectetuer adipiscing elit, sed diam nonummy nibh euismod tincidunt ut laoreet dolore magna aliquam erat volutpat. Ut wisi enim ad minim veniam, quis nostrud exerci tation

7pt Galliard, 0.015 em tracking

Lorem ipsum dolor sit amet, adipiscing elit, sed diam nonummy nibh euismod tincidunt ut laoreet dolore magna aliquam erat volutpat. Ut wisi enim ad minim veniam, quis nostrud exerci tation ullamcorper suscipit lobortis nisl ut

7pt Gill Sans, 0.02 em tracking

Lorem ipsum dolor sit amet, consectetuer adipiscing elit, sed diam nonummy nibh euismod tincidunt ut laoreet dolore magna aliquam erat volutpat. Ut wisi enim ad minim veniam, quis nostrud exerci tation

7pt Galliard, 0.02 em tracking

Lorem ipsum dolor sit amet, adipiscing elit, sed diam nonummy nibh euismod tincidunt ut laoreet dolore magna aliquam erat volutpat. Ut wisi enim ad minim veniam, quis nostrud exerci tation ullamcorper suscipit lobortis nisl ut

7pt Gill Sans, 0.025 em tracking

Lorem ipsum dolor sit amet, consectetuer adipiscing elit, sed diam nonummy nibh euismod tincidunt ut laoreet dolore magna aliquam erat volutpat. Ut wisi enim ad minim veniam, quis nostrud exerci tation

7pt Galliard, 0.025 em tracking

Lorem ipsum dolor sit amet,
adipiscing elit, sed diam
nonummy nibh euismod
tincidunt ut laoreet dolore

10pt Gill Sans, -0.015 em tracking

Lorem ipsum dolor sit
amet, consectetuer
adipiscing elit, sed diam
nonummy nibh euismod

10pt Galliard, -0.015 em tracking

Lorem ipsum dolor sit amet,
adipiscing elit, sed diam
nonummy nibh euismod
tincidunt ut laoreet dolore

10pt Gill Sans, -0.01 em tracking

Lorem ipsum dolor sit
amet, consectetuer
adipiscing elit, sed diam
nonummy nibh euismod

10pt Galliard, -0.01 em tracking

Lorem ipsum dolor sit amet,
adipiscing elit, sed diam
nonummy nibh euismod
tincidunt ut laoreet dolore

10pt Gill Sans, -0.005 em tracking

Lorem ipsum dolor sit
amet, consectetuer
adipiscing elit, sed diam
nonummy nibh euismod

10pt Galliard, -0.005 em tracking

Lorem ipsum dolor sit amet,
adipiscing elit, sed diam
nonummy nibh euismod
tincidunt ut laoreet dolore

10pt Gill Sans, 0 tracking

Lorem ipsum dolor sit
amet, consectetuer
adipiscing elit, sed diam
nonummy nibh euismod

10pt Galliard, 0 tracking

Lorem ipsum dolor sit amet,
adipiscing elit, sed diam
nonummy nibh euismod
tincidunt ut laoreet dolore

10pt Gill Sans, 0.005 em tracking

Lorem ipsum dolor sit
amet, consectetuer
adipiscing elit, sed diam
nonummy nibh euismod

10pt Galliard, 0.005 em tracking

Lorem ipsum dolor sit amet,
adipiscing elit, sed diam
nonummy nibh euismod
tincidunt ut laoreet dolore

10pt Gill Sans, 0.01 em tracking

Lorem ipsum dolor sit
amet, consectetuer
adipiscing elit, sed diam
nonummy nibh euismod

10pt Galliard, 0.01 em tracking

Lorem ipsum dolor sit amet,
adipiscing elit, sed diam
nonummy nibh euismod
tincidunt ut laoreet dolore

10pt Gill Sans, 0.015 em tracking

Lorem ipsum dolor sit
amet, consectetuer
adipiscing elit, sed diam
nonummy nibh euismod

10pt Galliard, 0.015 em tracking

Lorem ipsum dolor sit amet,
adipiscing elit, sed diam
nonummy nibh euismod
tincidunt ut laoreet dolore

10pt Gill Sans, 0.02 em tracking

Lorem ipsum dolor sit
amet, consectetuer
adipiscing elit, sed diam
nonummy nibh euismod

10pt Galliard, 0.02 em tracking

A distinctive feature of computer-generated typography is that of horizontal scaling, whereby fonts are scaled along their horizontal axes only, as distinct from uniform scaling which is employed for varying the size of type. Although the technique is useful in many situations, it should not normally be used as a substitute for fonts which have a specially designed condensed or expanded version – the exaggerated distortions of horizontally scaled letterforms rarely surpass the esthetic properties of the real thing. However, rules are made to be broken …

thie

Univers 67 Bold Condensed, no horizontal scaling

thie

Univers 65 Bold, 83% horizontal scaling

Lorem ipsum dolor sit amet, consectetuer adipiscing elit, sed diam

12pt Gill Sans Light, no horizontal scaling

Lorem ipsum dolor sit amet, consectetuer adipiscing elit, sed

12pt Garamond, no horizontal scaling

Lorem ipsum dolor sit amet, consectetuer adipiscing elit, sed diam nonummy nibh euismod

12pt Gill Sans Light, 80% horizontal scaling

Lorem ipsum dolor sit amet, consectetuer adipiscing elit, sed diam nonummy nibh

12pt Garamond, 80% horizontal scaling

Lorem ipsum dolor sit amet, consectetuer adipiscing elit, sed diam nonummy nibh euismod tincidunt ut laoreet dolore magna

12pt Gill Sans Light, 60% horizontal scaling

Lorem ipsum dolor sit amet, consectetuer adipiscing elit, sed diam nonummy nibh euismod tincidunt ut

12pt Garamond, 60% horizontal scaling

Lorem ipsum dolor sit amet, consectetuer adipiscing elit, sed

12pt Franklin Gothic, no horizontal scaling

Lorem ipsum dolor sit amet, consectetuer adipiscing elit,

12pt Walbaum, no horizontal scaling

Lorem ipsum dolor sit amet, consectetuer adipiscing elit, sed diam nonummy nibh

12pt Franklin Gothic, 80% horizontal scaling

Lorem ipsum dolor sit amet, consectetuer adipiscing elit, sed diam

12pt Walbaum, 80% horizontal scaling

Lorem ipsum dolor sit amet, consectetuer adipiscing elit, sed diam nonummy nibh euismod tincidunt ut

12pt Franklin Gothic, 60% horizontal scaling

Lorem ipsum dolor sit amet, consectetuer adipiscing elit, sed diam nonummy nibh euismod

12pt Walbaum, 60% horizontal scaling

5
THE RIGHT SET-UP

WHO WILL USE IT?/WHICH DESIGN AREA?/
HOW FAR DO YOU WANT TO GO?/
HOW MUCH WILL IT COST?/CASE STUDIES

If you are new to computers, choosing one can be a pretty daunting task – as it can even if you are an old hand. The problem is further compounded by having to make decisions about everything else that you need to go with the computer (including software). Although some vendors offer complete systems, including a variety of peripheral hardware devices and applications, it will be very rare that one of those packages suits your precise requirements, even if you can identify those requirements in the first place – a difficult enough task in itself.

There are a few fundamental issues to consider before deciding on which configuration you require and these are discussed below, but the bulk of this chapter deals with the problems associated with selecting and evolving an appropriate setup by relating the experiences of a few professional graphic designers and design groups working in a diverse range of disciplines.

WHO WILL USE IT? At the most basic level, there is the freelance designer, working alone and theoretically requiring a relatively simple range of hardware, albeit with a professional level of performance capabilities. In such cases, the hardware configuration is fairly straightforward, and the choice of computer and peripherals is determined more by budget than anything else – as long as each model of equipment meets certain performance criteria.

If more than one person is to be equipped with a Mac, other considerations apply. For instance, while a single user will require one of everything – a printer, a scanner, a back-up device, etc. – this is not the case for multiple users, since a single printer and scanner can be accessed by several Macs. If you do need several Macs, you should consider whether you would benefit by linking them all together in a "network" – in fact, just sharing a printer is considered to be a network.

Although setting up a network requires another bout of learning, it has several practical as well as economic advan-

tages over "stand alone" Macs (Macs that are not net-worked). Just as you wouldn't expect two designers to use the same layout pad at the same time, so you wouldn't expect more than one person to work on the same file at the same time (even if it were possible), but the advantages of sharing manifest themselves in items such as a centralized, large-capacity hard disk which everyone uses – even if each individual Mac has a small internal hard disk for day-to-day work. A centralized hard disk can store the things everyone

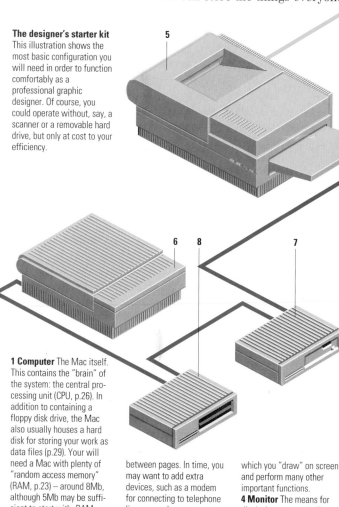

The designer's starter kit
This illustration shows the most basic configuration you will need in order to function comfortably as a professional graphic designer. Of course, you could operate without, say, a scanner or a removable hard drive, but only at cost to your efficiency.

1 Computer The Mac itself. This contains the "brain" of the system: the central processing unit (CPU, p.26). In addition to containing a floppy disk drive, the Mac also usually houses a hard disk for storing your work as data files (p.29). Your will need a Mac with plenty of "random access memory" (RAM, p.23) – around 8Mb, although 5Mb may be sufficient to start with. RAM chips (SIMMs) can be added as your need for RAM grows. The speed at which your computer is able to process data is important – complex page layouts may take a long time to "redraw" on screen, which can be very frustrating if you are often switching

between pages. In time, you may want to add extra devices, such as a modem for connecting to telephone lines, so make sure your Mac has enough space for extra expansion cards (p.47).
2 Keyboard Much of your interaction with the Mac will be by using the mouse, but the keyboard provides an opportunity for many short-cuts.
3 Mouse The means by

which you "draw" on screen and perform many other important functions.
4 Monitor The means for displaying your work. There are many permutations of choice, such as screen size, resolution, color, "bit-depth," and more. A 19in. screen is desirable for most work. Color is useful, but not absolutely necessary – you can still specify colors with a grayscale monitor even if you

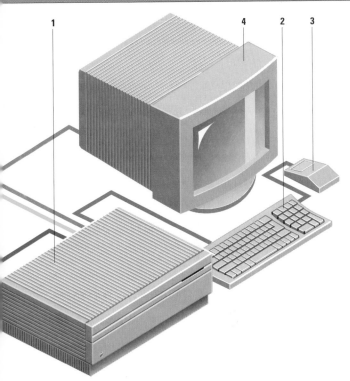

can't preview them. If you do opt for color, 8-bit will suffice unless you intend working extensively with scanned images, in which case you may find you need a 24-bit monitor (p.32).

5 Printer Some kind of laser printer is essential for proofing purposes. Most printers have a resolution of 300dpi, compared with up to 2450dpi on a high-resolution imagesetter, so you will still need to sample work on an imagesetter as laser-printed proofs will not display the subtleties you will need to make

esthetic decisions. A PostScript printer is essential even if you only use TrueType fonts (p.40).

6 Scanner You will find a scanner useful even if you intend using conventional methods of origination. You may, for instance, want to scan images for positional guides, or scan rough designs or, say, logos, for recreating on your Mac. A scanner resolution of 300dpi is sufficient for most purposes, but if you intend using scanned line art as high-resolution output, you

may require 600dpi or more.

7 Backup device Don't think, even for a moment, that nothing will go wrong – it will, so you will need some kind of device such as an external hard disk or a tape streamer (p.39).

8 Removable hard disk drive You will find removable media necessary for transporting large files, especially to service bureaus. A removable drive is also useful as a backup device and is often used as a primary means of storage.

SOFTWARE FOR STARTERS

Whichever field of graphic design you work in, you will need software which provides you with creative versatility and optimum professional standards. In addition to the system software bundled with the hardware, you will need applications for:
Page makeup for laying out pages (p.54).
Drawing to create artwork which you may wish to incorporate into your layouts (p.59).
Image-editing for creative work with scanned or "painted" images (p.64).
Type manipulation to enable you to design and manipulate fonts and other

graphic elements, such as logos, that you may wish to incorporate into a font (p.71).
Fonts As many as gives you the same creative freedom as hitherto (p.84).
System management utilities for enhancing the performance of both your computer and your applications. Among the most important are:
Font management for arranging menus and handling large numbers of fonts (p.78).
ATM (Adobe Type Manager) for making fonts look smooth on screen (p.78).
Backup for protecting your work (p.79).
Disk utilities for managing your disk (p.79).

needs to use, such as printer fonts, client databases and job files, so that everyone knows where they are and can examine them when necessary.

Networks can get quite complicated (especially the jargon surrounding them), so it is best to start at the simplest level (networking your Macs to a printer, say) and gradually expand the network. When you are embroiled in learning your way around the Mac and your applications, the last thing you need is the additional complication of networking.

WHICH DESIGN AREA? If your design activities are precisely focused, it may be an easier task for you to define which configuration to go for. For instance, a designer working mainly in information graphics (that is, the graphic representation of data – statistical or otherwise) will probably need to be concerned less, say, about a large selection of fonts, document length, text input and networking, and more about memory and application power. On the other hand, a designer whose main activity is book design (inside and out) will be concerned about text input, typographic power, document length, file size and the practicalities of moving files between several people working on the same job – such as authors and editors – and less about scanning and image manipulation.

A designer involved in more general graphics may need a full range of equipment, both hardware and software – including virtually every font available, to provide the same degree of flexibility that would have been possible without a Mac.

HOW FAR DO YOU WANT TO GO? This question really relates to how deeply into prepress activities you want to get. For instance, you may decide that the volume of your output justifies acquiring your own high-resolution image-setter, giving you even greater control over output, with the long-term benefit of reducing your costs to service bureaus. You can, of course, get much farther into prepress with a Mac – right up to color separation and page imposition (and, I dare say, one day even being on-line to a four-color printing press!) – but even though the technology permits you to venture into hitherto unfamiliar territory, you should be very aware of exactly where to draw the demarcation line between optimum graphic design activities and the traditional graphic arts and allied trades. As things stand, you should avoid the danger of usurping the skills of highly experienced prepress practitioners, even though you may have achieved this to a certain extent by bypassing the traditional typesetter.

HOW MUCH WILL IT COST? At the end of the day, your budget will determine what you *actually* buy. It is, of course, possible to set yourself up with the barest minimum of equipment, but doing so would be frustrating and, consequently counterproductive. Buying a complete Macintosh

etup that has a performance capable of allowing it to be used as a professional tool can be a very expensive business, so it is essential that you shop around. While the prices of Apple equipment appear to be fixed, most dealers offer substantial discounts, justifying them by persuading you to enter into a service agreement. A service agreement can be expensive, but it is no bad thing at first (for peace of mind, at least), although both your hardware and software will be under guarantee and, surprisingly, things rarely go wrong with the equipment – the problems occur more with system and application software when you can't solve a problem and need a patient, friendly and helpful voice on the other end of the telephone.

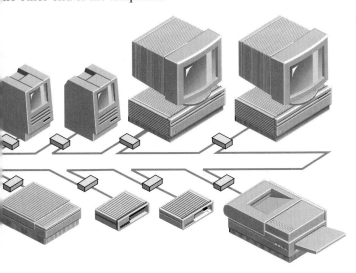

Networking If you work as part of a group and intend using several Macs, you will find many advantages in linking them together to create a "network." A network enables you to do such things as share hardware devices and programs with other computers, share your own files with people using other computers and *vice versa*, and automatically update files on other computers. A network can be, at its most basic level, simply two Macs sharing a single printer or, on a complex level, hundreds of computers using different operating systems and connected to each other across continents. As far as advantages to the average graphic designer are

concerned, probably the most relevant is the ability to minimize capital outlay by enabling many computers to share single hardware devices such as a printer, a scanner, a fax modem, a backup device and a removable media device. Automatic updating of files, using Apple's "publish and subscribe" feature, can also be useful to designers on a network where large jobs are concerned – say a corporate identity where logos and other graphic devices are constantly evolving. Central to a network is the "file server," a process by which information is shared between one device and another (individual devices on a network are called

"nodes"). The file server stores and manages the information that other users on the network can access (at the same time, if necessary). Sun Microsystems' TOPS (Transcendental Operating System) and Apple's own AppleShare are popular file servers. Networks using LocalTalk should always be arranged in a line (a so-called "bus" network) and not as a closed circle (although other networks may be configured as a "token-ring" whereby a continuously circulating file can be accessed by all nodes). A connector should be used for each device in a LocalTalk network.

RIGHT FOR THUMB Thumb Design Partnership, a group o nine designers, tackles a wide variety of general graphi design work, its clients ranging from multinational corpora tions to local arts exhibitions.

When Andrew Wakelin, Thumb's founding partner, firs bought a Mac in 1984, he had already been using an Apple I computer for accounts and spreadsheets. He used the Mac a "128K," mostly for word-processing since he was wary o using computers for design work – although he immediately took to the "friendliness" of the Macintosh. It was not unti he started using MacDraw that he realized the potential o the Mac as a design tool – especially when PostScript lase printers were introduced. By the end of 1988, Thumb wa producing page artwork from a Linotronic imagesetter via a service bureau. Eventually, they bought their own Linotron ic – and found that their typesetting costs amounted to a mere 3 percent of costs in the previous year.

Hardware Thumb now uses, as its main design work-hors es, one Mac II (with 4Mb RAM and a 40Mb hard disk), tw Mac IIx's (4/80) and three Mac IIcx's (4/80 – one has 8M RAM). One MacPlus (upgraded from an old 128K) is used a a dedicated print server. Three SEs (one with a 45Mb exter nal hard disk, the other with 140Mb), are used for account and copy preparation.

Monitors 13in. Apple RGB and 19in. mono monitors.

Printing For proofing, a LaserWriter IINTX with a 20M external hard disk for font storage. Film and bromide is out put on a Linotronic 300.

Scanning One Siemens 800dpi flat-bed scanner, althoug

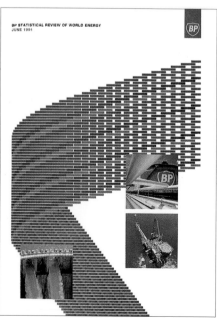

BP STATISTICAL REVIEW OF WORLD ENERGY
JUNE 1991

Left Thumb created the background pattern for the cover of this oil company report with FreeHand. To generate the pattern by conventional means (artwork) would have been difficult and time consuming, and would not have allowed any manipulation or modification. It is also likely that the number and complexity of tint patches would have ruled out this design solution on economic grounds, given the huge amount of hand work and the difficulty of tint fitting that would have been involved in its lithographic planning. The FreeHand file was imported into QuarkXPress, from which the final cover was output. The color photographs were conventionally scanned and stripped in.

most material is scanned at only 150dpi since scanned images are usually used only as positional guides. For scanning trannies (again, for position only), Thumb use a home video camera connected to a Neotech grayscale NuBus card.

Peripherals Two R45 drives (mainly for archiving), a 5¼in. (134mm) Apple PC drive for transferring PC-generated material, and a modem, which rarely gets used.

Software Thumb originally used PageMaker – whose pasteboard feature appealed to their designers – but only to produce layouts which were then used as a guide for conventional typesetting and paste-up. They eventually moved over to QuarkXPress as they preferred its greater power and accuracy even though, at the time, it did not feature a pasteboard. In 1989 they bought FreeHand to draw complicated maps for a ski brochure; from it, they went straight to four-color separated film. Thumb now uses several applications, including PhotoShop, Digital Darkroom and TypeAlign, but Wakelin estimates that around 80 percent of Thumb's design work is carried out with XPress and 15 percent with FreeHand. They still sometimes use PageMaker, but only on the rare occasions when a client has specifically requested them to do so.

Fonts To overcome the problem of which fonts to buy without spending a fortune (although, in the early years, choice was not what it is now), each of the designers was asked to come up with a list of the fonts they most commonly actually *used*. This produced a list of only about 12 fonts, to which they added about five new ones every couple of months. They now have approximately 60 typefaces.

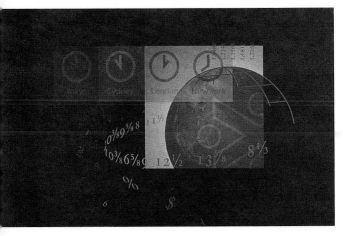

Above A detail from the cover of a brochure for a bank which was created with three separate applications; the background halftone images were scanned with Thumb's own desktop scanner and then manipulated with a variety of effects in Digital Darkroom. The hard-edged type was created, and colors were applied, in FreeHand. Both the Digital Darkroom and FreeHand files were imported into QuarkXPress (the picture boxes containing each image were laid one on top of the other), from which they were output.

Training Thumb has always trained its own designers, but never by forcing anyone into the environment. Wakelin used a technique of seduction by gradually introducing Macs into the studio, and then exploiting subsequent enthusiasm ("wow, let *me* try!"). Sharing knowledge and discovery was aggressively encouraged, right down to the format of an end-of-day session where everybody was asked to declare the best thing they had learned about the Mac that day.

Working methods Each desktop contains a "Today's work" folder from which, at the end of each day, work is copied into its appropriate "Job" folder. On some larger jobs, work is produced on an almost production-line basis: one designer may be working on copy preparation, another laying out the pages, with a third scanning images and then dropping them into their allotted positions on the layout – all having access to each other's files by way of TOPS networking utility. This way of working generates a form of backup where, by necessity, each file is copied onto the hard disk of the next person along in the process. Every desktop has a "Dump" folder into which finished jobs are, funnily enough, dumped. The contents of each Dump folder are disgorged on a regular basis. Wherever possible, Thumb asks that copy be provided by clients on disk, and most are happy to do this. In cases where that is not possible, copy is provided as clean typescript (handwriting and correction marks won't do), which is scanned using OmniPage OCR software.

Above For this invitation leaflet for a business convention, Thumb used FreeHand to create the logo and line work on the cover and QuarkXPress for the text and page layout. At the time, the halftone photographs were conventionally scanned and stripped in, although if they were creating the same job now, Thumb says that they would scan their own halftones and output them directly from within XPress.

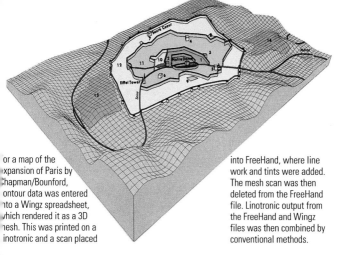

or a map of the expansion of Paris by Chapman/Bounford, contour data was entered into a Wingz spreadsheet, which rendered it as a 3D mesh. This was printed on a Linotronic and a scan placed into FreeHand, where line work and tints were added. The mesh scan was then deleted from the FreeHand file. Linotronic output from the FreeHand and Wingz files was then combined by conventional methods.

RIGHT FOR CHAPMAN/BOUNFORD Chapman/Bounford and Associates is a group of four designers who specialize in the graphic presentation of quantitative information.

Founding partner Trevor Bounford had always recognized the potential of computers for generating graphic imagery from data. He started dabbling with engineering graphics computers in the late 1970s, but found these to be both extremely expensive and very limited. Bounford first encountered the potential of Macintosh computers in 1985 while working with copywriters who used them, and where he learned what the Mac could do with page layout. However, it was not until 1988 that he bought the group's first Mac.

Originally, designers in the group took it in turns to use the Mac, but as their proficiency grew, so did their need for another machine. This need coincided with a commission to illustrate a large medical textbook, requiring over 600 illustrations, charts and diagrams, which provided a learning base for the group. Bounford is confident that without the Mac, they could not have fulfilled the contract.

Hardware The group now has four Macs – a Mac II (with 8Mb RAM and a 40Mb hard disk), a Mac IIx (8/80), and two Mac SE/30s (4/40). The Mac II runs with a 13in. color monitor, the IIx a 19in. color monitor, and both the SE/30s have 19in. monochrome monitors. For proofing they use a Laser-Writer II NTX and for scanning a Microtek MSF 300G. Work is backed up to a 105Mb external hard disk drive as well as to floppy disks.

Software Chapman/Bounford mainly use FreeHand, and occasionally, Illustrator. For page makeup they use Page-Maker as it's quick to set up pages, but for more complex work, they prefer the accuracy of QuarkXPress. Wingz is used to generate digital terrain modeling (3D maps – an important part of their work), even though the resulting file sizes tend to be massive.

6
THE DESIGN PROCESS

PRESENTING ROUGHS/FINE TUNING/STYLE
SHEETS/TEXT INPUT/CORRECTING TEXT/HANDLING
IMAGES/COLOR TRAPPING/ORGANIZING WORK
ON YOUR MAC/BACKING UP/USING SERVICE
BUREAUS

Installing a Mac into your working life will force you to make some fairly fundamental changes to your working methods. Nonetheless, you can always try to preserve your preferred procedures (at least, the creative aspects) by restricting the Mac to some of the more mechanical functions of your job – typesetting or camera-ready art, for instance; although, given the capabilities of the Mac, it is doubtful whether you would manage to sustain that restriction for long.

PRESENTING ROUGHS The Mac's ability to give a finished look to a design right from the word "go" has generated new expectations (sometimes unfavorable) from clients. You can easily take even the most rudimentary design to a finished-looking state by setting headings in an appropriate typeface, indicating text as dummy Latin copy and pictures as dummy scanned images, and then run it out on a laser printer in thumbnail form, at full-size, or even in color. However, because even preliminary designs at this level take a bit of time to set up on a Mac, and yet more time to produce alternatives to your original ideas, you should not think of aban-

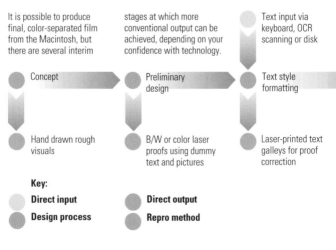

It is possible to produce final, color-separated film from the Macintosh, but there are several interim stages at which more conventional output can be achieved, depending on your confidence with technology.

Text input via keyboard, OCR scanning or disk

Concept → Preliminary design → Text style formatting

Hand drawn rough visuals

B/W or color laser proofs using dummy text and pictures

Laser-printed text galleries for proof correction

Key:

Direct input

Design process

Direct output

Repro method

doning your layout pad and markers just yet. In fact, the ability to produce such finesse at an early stage in the creative process can be bewildering to your client – because you now have fine control over tweaking an idea by infinitesimal degrees, the temptation exists to present your client with a rainforest of paper, with the client finding it difficult to distinguish one design from another. If your roughs are for a self-contained item such as a package design, it can be useful to use the Mac to run out typographic ideas which you can then trace using colored markers.

It is perhaps more usual for the Mac to be used in the secondary stage of rough presentations, after a broad concept has been agreed, when various typographic treatments and color permutations can be produced expediently. In such cases, you can use the Mac to output line art, either as laser proofs or as bromide prints from an imagesetter, onto which you paste color pictures, tints, etc. Alternatively, the designs can be output as color laser proofs complete with tints and scanned dummy pictures.

FINE TUNING One of the more immediate fears that you may have of using a Mac is losing control over the subtler aspects of design. This is perfectly justified, considering that you first see your design displayed by a very imprecise vehicle – the monitor screen. Your second view, on a laser-printed proof, is only marginally better, superb though laser printers are. The problem is that the success of a design can often rely on extremely subtle aspects, such as the typographic "color" of a piece of text, or the difference between, say, a hairline rule and a half-point rule. The difficulty of assessing these differences on a monitor or a laser proof is amplified when you consider that whereas in an application such as QuarkXPress you can specify a hairline rule, which is 0.25 points wide, it will print on a laser printer only at 0.5 points wide. The answer, then, is to run out your final ideas as bromide proofs on an imagesetter (this will show you

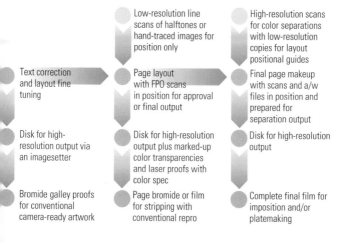

exactly what the end product will look like) before making a final decision.

STYLE SHEETS Having decided upon a design solution, you are now faced with the problem of setting up a grid and attributing styles to all the elements of your design. This is a particularly acute problem if you are working on a long document dripping with typographic styles and graphic devices. You can, of course, go through the laborious process of attributing styles to each item individually – by selecting a word, or whatever, and assigning it a typeface, size, weight, leading value, scaling value, tracking value, and so on. Fortunately, however, it is not necessary to go through this time-consuming process. Instead, you can set up a "style sheet" for every possible variation of text style and formatting in a document and assign it a keyboard command of its own; although this is not entirely necessary – you can simply select the style sheet from a menu. Thus you can format an entire block of text or an individual word with the desired styles in a single keystroke or menu selection.

Page grids can be set up using the "master page" feature that most page makeup applications offer. This enables you to set, as well as page margins, text columns, automatic page numbering and tints, repetitive items such as rules and running headings. Some applications allow you to set up a number of master pages – for accommodating design variations such as a different number of text columns – which you can assign to any page.

Style sheets and master pages are features that many designers I know have not yet come to grips with, even after using a Mac for some time. However, these features are very much worth learning since the benefits of doing so will soon prove indispensible.

TEXT INPUT The problems of entering text into a document once caused many designers perhaps more anguish than anything else attributable to the Mac. They found it difficult to see how they would avoid undertaking the tasks previously assigned to a typesetter – keying in text, formatting it, taking in corrections, getting their hands dirty with messy chemicals, etc – thus eroding the designer's creative time. Fortunately, technology has advanced to such an extent that those fears are rapidly becoming a thing of the past. It may still be necessary to do some work on copy, such as taking in corrections, but it is now possible to input text by one of a variety of means.

OCR scanning It is probable that a good deal of the copy you receive will come in the form of typewritten manuscript, or "hard" copy. In some circumstances, such as where the amount of copy is minimal, it's no big deal just to key it in yourself. Otherwise, hard text can be input to a Mac and converted to an editable form using one of the many

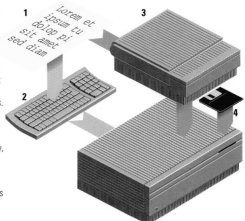

Text may be input to a Mac in several ways. Hard copy which may be type-written or printed **1**) can be entered by typing it in on the keyboard **2**) or directly by scanning it **3**), but you will need OCR software to accomplish this. Alternatively, text may be supplied in disk form (**4**), in which case it may need converting, as is quite likely, from another computer format. Apple's own Apple File Exchange will accomplish this if the disk is a 3½in. (90mm) floppy.

"optical character recognition" (OCR) applications that are available, such as **OmniPage** (Caere Corp.). These applications work in conjunction with most scanners. If you have no particular use for a scanner for any other purpose and the amount of text you need to scan is minimal, you may consider purchasing an inexpensive small hand-held scanner, which has been specially designed for scanning text but is not as efficient or as fast as a flat-bed scanner. By no means do OCR applications achieve a 100 percent success rate when scanning in text, but they have reached such a degree of sophistication that, provided the original copy is relatively clean, the error rate is generally low. Most OCR applications provide a means of automatically inserting special symbols to flag occurrences where a word may be suspect or where the scanner has not been able to "read" the copy, making it fairly easy to check scanned text for errors.

Text on disk The most efficient way of inputting text to a document is to have it supplied on disk and, if you can persuade your client to do so, this is the most desirable course to take. However, although it would be convenient if everyone used Macs, they don't, and it is quite likely that you will receive copy on a non-Macintosh format (it will probably be MS-DOS format) disk, even if it is a 3½in disk. Fortunately, if you have a SuperDrive, it is possible for your Mac to read a non-Mac disk and for you to convert its contents to a Macintosh file using a file conversion utility such as **Apple File Exchange**. If, as is also possible, you receive text on a 5¼in disk, you will need a peripheral device that reads MS-DOS disks, such as a **DaynaFile** (Dayna Communications, Inc.), which also reads high-density 3½in floppy disks (useful if you don't have a SuperDrive). In either case, the MS-DOS disks appear on your desktop in familiar style. If you have neither facility, most service bureaus offer disk conversion competitively.

Text by modem Another fairly efficient means of inputting text is to use a modem, by which you can take in text

instantly (called "uploading") – but, obviously, this is only possible so long as your client has a modem. A modem can also be useful for returning galleys for correction purposes, although if your client does not use Macs, you will need to transfer the galleys in an appropriate format such as a PostScript file. The most obvious format is ASCII (called "text only" format on the Mac), which any computer can read, but text in ASCII format does not retain any formatting instructions you may have given it, so may be inappropriate.

The old-fashioned way If no other means of inputting text is available to you, you may have to bite the bullet and do it the old-fashioned way – by keying it in. However, it is still not necessary for you to get directly involved, since most bureaus offer a typing service. Alternatively, you could use one of the ever-increasing Mac-based freelance typing services that are now available.

CORRECTING TEXT Taking in corrections to text is more problematical. If corrections are light (if you received text on disk in the first place, you would not expect many corrections), it is probably most expedient to take them in yourself. If, however, corrections are heavy, you would be well advised to put the work out to a Mac-based freelancer. If your client is a publisher, text corrections would most likely be supplied on disk.

HANDLING IMAGES Generally speaking, most designers do not scan in pictures or output them with reproduction in mind, although you would be forgiven for thinking otherwise when you read Macintosh magazines. Pictures are almost always scanned in as a guide for position only (FPO). Indeed, it is arguable that it is not necessary to scan in images at all, given the huge amount of disk space they occupy. However, a scanned image (even at low resolution) does allow you to indicate very precise crops to your printer or repro house and is worth doing for this purpose alone if you have the facility. Scanning images also allows you to make very precise text runarounds. As for the problem of disk space, a simple way around this is to keep the picture

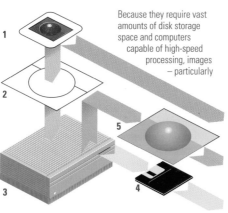

Because they require vast amounts of disk storage space and computers capable of high-speed processing, images – particularly color (**1**) – may be scanned at low resolution (**2**) and used for positional purposes only. Output from the Mac (**3**) is provided in the form of a disk (**4**) for imagesetting to film or bromide, with a laser proof (**5**) showing exact positions and crops. Increasingly, high-resolution scans are made first, a low-resolution copy being returned to the designer for positioning. The low-resolution version is substituted by the high during output (see p.133).

files on your hard disk only until you are ready to output your job to film – print out sets of laser proofs which include the images, for your reference as well as for the repro house, but delete them from the document prior to outputting it on an imagesetter.

If you intend using scanned images for reproduction, such as line art, halftones or color illustrations, you must not only leave them in the document file, but include the original picture files with the document file so that it can be output correctly by the imagesetter. For instance, if you are using a tone picture scanned as a TIFF file and a piece of artwork created in a drawing application and exported as an EPS file, both the TIFF file and the EPS file must accompany your document file to the bureau.

COLOR TRAPPING It is important to remember that when you are creating colored artwork, specifying tints or using colored typography, you may need to specify "trapping" values for each color. Trapping a color means that, to allow for imprecisions in printing, you increase the area of one color so that it overlaps an adjacent color. This overlapping only needs to be done to a infinitesimal degree – just enough to prevent white hairline gaps from appearing between colors. Fortunately, many applications support automatic trapping values, so you may not need to do much. Otherwise, you may need to add trapping values to tints manually. This can usually be done by adding a keyline with a thickness of about 0.25 point around a given tint area, making it the same color as the tint it surrounds and specifying that it should overprint the adjacent colors.

ORGANIZING WORK ON YOUR MAC There are no hard and fast rules as to how you should organize your work – everyone has their own way of doing it, depending as much on their hardware configuration as on the type of work that they do.

Naming files It is extremely easy to forget what is contained within a file, so it is important that you adopt a very logical and explicit method of naming them. This is particularly important if you share files on a network. Giving a file a number only is of no help to anyone; even if you work alone, it is likely to lead to confusion. Better to assign a code of, say, three letters, to each job that you are engaged in and then prefix every file belonging to that job with its code, followed by as explicit an explanation of the file contents as space permits (file names can be up to 31 characters long). Sometimes a date can be helpful as part of a file name, although you can ascertain the dates of both the creation and last modification of a file via the "Get Info" window ("File" menu).

If you are experimenting on different versions of the same design and are using the "Save As..." command to preserve previous versions, simply keep the same name as

Organizing work A clear and methodical approach to naming and organizing files and folders is essential – the speed at which you create new files that represent variations on a design makes it very easy to lose track of what's where. There are endless permutations of how work can be organized, and this example serves only as a guide. Try to categorize your work as much as possible so that you can create new folders in which to put items – it is much better to have folders within folders ("nested") than hundreds of files loose in a single folder for one job.

1 The hard disk window should contain as few items as possible, which, at this level, are easy to categorize.
2 Give each of your clients a separate folder.
3 Give each job for a client its own folder.
4 Break each constituent of a job into folders – including one for correspondence relating to that job.
5 If much text is involved, give each stage of proofs, prior to layout, a folder.
6 The files at this level should be those you are actually working on – put old ones into a folder or trash them. Give scans and a/w files other folders – don't mix them with layout files.
7 In naming images and a/w, be as explicit as possible and include the file type as part of the name (TIFF, EPS, etc.).

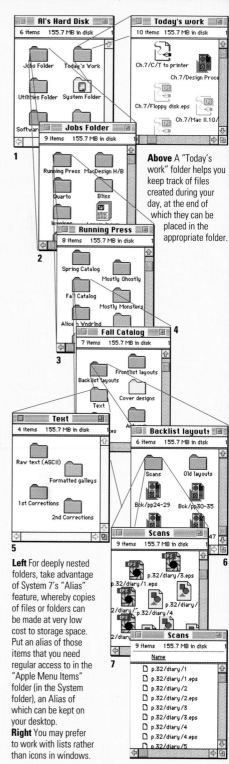

Above A "Today's work" folder helps you keep track of files created during your day, at the end of which they can be placed in the appropriate folder.

Left For deeply nested folders, take advantage of System 7's "Alias" feature, whereby copies of files or folders can be made at very low cost to storage space. Put an alias of those items that you need regular access to in the "Apple Menu Items" folder (in the System folder), an Alias of which can be kept on your desktop.

Right You may prefer to work with lists rather than icons in windows.

the original file, but number each new one consecutively. However, when you've finished experimenting and made a decision, be sure to delete all the other files to avoid confusing yourself.

Organizing folders The simplest way of keeping track of work is to create as many folders as necessary, giving each one a name that identifies the contents. If, for example, you create one folder per job and simply dump every file relating to that job loose in that folder, you may very soon lose track of where you are or, rather, where the files you want are. If you are generating a lot of scanned images, it makes sense to keep them in a folder with the document they relate to. If the scans relate to several different documents, you may decide to keep all of them together in their own folder. The important thing is to create a system that allows you easily to locate any file at any time.

One useful way of organizing your day-to-day work is to create a folder called "Today's Work" and position it on the desktop or put an Alias of it in the Apple menu. Every document you create during the day and every file relating to those documents gets put in this folder. At the end of the day, you decide how and where you want to keep those files and position them in appropriate folders relating to their job. If you are still working on a document, you put a copy of the document file back in the "Today's Work" folder and work on that version of the document, which replaces the previous version at the end of the day. This method gives you an instant view of your progress and of any current files.

If you share your Mac with other users, or if you are networked, it is a good idea to create folders with the names of the people sharing the computer and put everything relating to each person in the respective folder.

BACKING UP YOUR FILES If I were to stress the most important aspect of using a Mac, it would be that of backing up. No matter how long you go without anything untoward happening, one day it will – and you can be as sure of this as you are that the earth is round. If you don't back up, sooner or later you will be faced with a disaster – either your hard disk will irretrievably crash or your most important file will become irreversibly corrupted.

My backup policy verges on the paranoid, but I've lost too many important files and crashed too many disks for it to be otherwise. At the end of each day, I copy each job file in my "Today's Work" folder onto their respective floppy disks. I copy the same files into their respective folders on my hard disk, replacing previous versions of the files. I also make duplicate copies of the day's work into another folder on a separate part of my hard disk. To round off the day, I back up the files onto hard disks, using backup software which copies only those files that have changed since the

Backing up Much of the data stored on your hard disk will represent many hours of work and be irreplaceable. The most reliable disks are capable of failing, and the assumption must always be that one day they will. Even your disk fails but is repaired and your files are found to be intact, the disk may be out of service for some time. Thus it is of paramount importance that you copy, or "back up" everything that you do. There are many types of backup devices, from floppy disks to very high capacity tape streamers and hard disks, and there are many utility programs to make backup easier. The first backup you make is described as a "baseline," or "global," backup. Thereafter, using a suitable backup utility, you only back up work you have created or modified since your work was last backed up, and this is known as an "incremental" backup. Backing up onto floppies is impractical (40Mb uses around 60 disks). Although of limited capacity, removable hard disks give you greater flexibility over what you back up – by creating a folder or two for each backup disk that you have, you only need regularly back up the folders that you consistently work on. Use at least two sets of backup disks (preferably three, one of which you keep in another location) and rotate them alternately at each backup. Some backup utilities replace files that require updating (a good file may be replaced by a corrupt one), so you may like to keep an additional set of work in progress on floppy disks – before putting the current day's work away in the appropriate place in your "Jobs" folder, copy it to a floppy disk, putting it in a folder which you newly create each day. If a file corrupts, you can return to the last usable version (**5**).

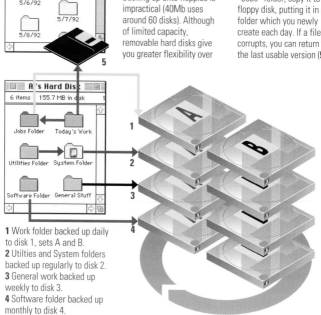

1 Work folder backed up daily to disk 1, sets A and B.
2 Utilties and System folders backed up regularly to disk 2.
3 General work backed up weekly to disk 3.
4 Software folder backed up monthly to disk 4.

last backup. This routine takes about ten minutes, and it's worth every one of them for the peace of mind it gives.

I keep four sets of backup disks in the form of removable media (plus further sets for each large job I am currently involved in), one for each of the folders at the root level of my hard disk – a "Jobs" folder for current work, a "General" folder for my own stuff, a "Software" folder for all my software except utility software, which goes on the fourth backup set, the System folder. Each of these backup disks has its own, second, backup disk (I've been advised not to trust removable media, although I've not yet had a problem with any of my removable hard disks). I keep one set of the disks

in a fireproof safe. Although I back up my jobs on a daily basis, I only back up my software and system folders every month since they do not change much during that time.

USING SERVICE BUREAUS Unless you intend owning your own imagesetter, you will need to have your files run out by a service bureau, which can provide either bromide for camera-ready art or final negative or positive film for printing. Most bureaus (though not all, so check first) are equipped to accept data on virtually any kind of media. What you actually choose to transfer your documents on depends on the file size of the documents themselves and of any other accompanying files, such as picture files (if your documents contain images, such as EPS files of Mac-generated art or TIFF files of scanned pictures, that you want included in the document you must send them to the bureau as well).

Depending on the application that you used to create your documents, you may also need to send some data files with the document – for instance, documents created with XPress must be accompanied by a copy of the XPress Data file. The bureau will want to know not only which fonts you used in the documents, but also who manufactured them – the character sets and kerning values of fonts from one foundry may be different from those from another.

Many bureaus also provide a variety of other services, such as color separation, color proofing (although check that by color proofing they mean as part of the four-color printing process and not just color laser proofing), disk conversion, slide production, image scanning, etc.

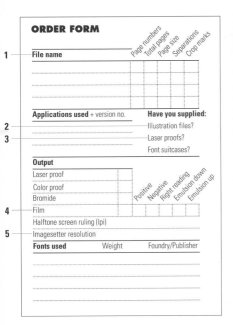

Left Provide your bureau with every detail about a job, or it may be output according to the information specified in the Page Setup dialog box the last time you printed the document. Supply the name of each file to be output (**1**) exactly as it appears on the file (if there are a lot, supply a print-out of the window of the disk you send the bureau). You must supply the illustration files used on the job if you want them to be part of the output (**2**) and also supply laser proofs so that they can check the output (**3**). If you are outputting to film, find out from your printer how it should be presented (**4**). Check with the bureau whether a very high resolution is necessary for your job as this could slow down output (**5**).

7
PREPRESS PRODUCTION
IMAGESETTERS/FILE FORMATS/SERVICE
BUREAUS/TINTS/COLOR REPRODUCTION/COLOR
CORRECTION/SCANNING RESOLUTION

Perhaps the paramount concern to graphic designers is the role that computers are increasingly playing in the transition of a design from final layouts (however they are prepared) to printing press. Traditionally, a designer's involvement in the prepress stages of print stops short either with a layout or type mark-up, or with camera-ready art prepared from bromide proofs supplied by a professional typesetter. However, each of the prepress crafts is rapidly being usurped by the capabilities of desktop computers.

The first of the traditional crafts to fall prey to computers was that of typesetting. Dedicated computer typesetting machines have been used by typesetters since 1963, but because of the sophisticated requirements of designers, typographers and typesetters alike, and the relative infancy of computer technology, these machines had to be operated by highly trained and skilled craftspeople – the same people, more often than not, who had previously been casting type in metal. The introduction of the desktop computer and, perhaps more important, the laser printer and PostScript, brought a quasi-professional level of print output to the fingertips of the masses. The potential of the desktop computer's graphic capabilities was quickly identified and exploited. While the original purpose of the technology may have been to enable anyone to produce documents of better quality than those hitherto generated on a typewriter or word processor, the rapid adoption of the technology by the graphics arts industries may have signaled the beginning of the end for the traditional typesetter.

At first, although it looked superb to the untrained eye, the quality of typography produced on desktop computers left a lot to be desired. For instance, one master was used to produce all sizes of a font, each size of type being an enlargement or reduction of the single master (as distinct from the traditional practice of "cutting" a different design for each size), and the kerning ability of fonts did not meet anything like the standards demanded by high-quality type-

setting. However, with the increasing typographic power of page makeup applications, and the fact that type foundries are now producing fonts for desktop computers which contain as much data as those used on high-end dedicated computer typesetting machines, it is now possible to originate typography on a Macintosh computer and output it at a quality that is indiscernible from high-quality typesetting.

There are designers who prefer to avoid involvement in the prepress processes and advocate the continuing necessity for trained and skilled operators, but the reality is that all those years of skill and experience are now increasingly contained within computer hardware and the software that runs it.

Nowhere in the graphics art industries is this more apparent than in the area of reproduction and color separation. At present, and for some time yet, graphic designers who use Macintosh computers leave the function of color separation to technicians using high-end scanning machines such as those manufactured by Crosfield, Scitex, Linotype-Hell and DaiNippon. But the huge gaps in hardware and software capability, output quality, capital expenditure and skill requirements between desktop color scanners and prepress scanners are rapidly being filled. Already, with such systems as Kodak's "Prophecy" and Scitex's "IPSO" systems, quality color separation has been brought a step nearer the capabilities and pockets (although still very expensive) of desktop computer users.

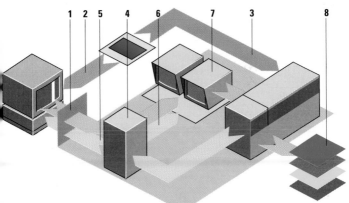

From Mac to film You can combine the power of high-end color scanning equipment and the skills of their operators with the work you do on your Mac by using a "gateway" link (**1**), a hardware/software setup designed to take advantage of appropriate technology at every stage of production, from Mac to final film. You use the originals as low-resolution scans for design purposes (**2**). When you have established image sizes, you send the originals for high-resolution scanning (**3**). Output is stored on high-capacity disks or tape (**4**). A low-resolution version is sent to you for positioning on your layouts (**5**). When you send your layout for output as film, the gateway setup automatically replaces the low-resolution scans with the stored high-resolution versions and converts your layout files to the maker's format of the high-end system (**6**). Cleaning up, if required, is made on an electronic page composition (EPC) system (**7**) before output to final film (**8**).

Output resolution and fonts Although printer fonts are outlines, printing devices recreate them by generating bitmaps of their shapes. Toner-based laser printers with a resolution of 300dpi are not able to match the quality of the light-generated shapes from imagesetters, which output at resolutions of up to 2540dpi.

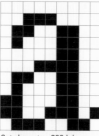

6pt character, 300dpi

6pt character, 1270dpi

Output resolution and halftones The quality of image output is determined by a combination of input resolution, bit-depth and output resolution. To achieve 256 grays (the optimum for quality reproduction), an 8-bit scanner must be used to scan originals (24-bit for color – 8 bits each for red, green and blue). For halftone output, input resolution should at least allow one pixel to be mapped to each halftone dot, but double the halftone screen is normal. Thus a halftone to be printed at 150 lpi should be scanned at 300dpi. Output resolution determines the quality of the dot itself and the number of grays each halftone dot is capable of reproducing. The number of grays is calculated by dividing the output resolution by the desired halftone screen ruling. This figure provides the axes for a matrix, the total number of pixels within that matrix being the number of possible gray levels. Thus a halftone to be printed with a screen of 75 lpi and output at 300dpi will achieve 16 grays (4 x 4 pixels).

Output resolution and lines A drawn, curved, object-oriented line ("path") is made up of straight segments. The number of segments in a path is described as the "flatness" value. Since PostScript limits the number of segments in any one path, and a high-resolution printer requires more segments to print a smooth curve than a laser printer, complex illustrations with low flatness values may cause printing problems.

Enlarged detail of 8-bit scan at 300dpi

The same detail printed with a 150 lpi halftone screen

Low-resolution halftone dot (5 x 5 pixels = 25 grays)

High-resolution halftone dot (16 x 16 pixels = 256 grays)

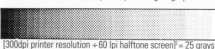

6.3% 12.5% 18.8% 25% 31.3% 37.5% 43.8% 50%

56.3% 62.5% 68.8% 75% 81.3% 87.5% 93.8% 100%

Halftone dot matrix of 4 x 4 pixels, producing 16 grays

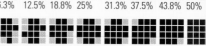

[300dpi printer resolution ÷ 60 lpi halftone screen]^2 = 25 grays

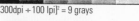

[300dpi ÷ 100 lpi]^2 = 9 grays

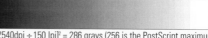

[2540dpi ÷ 150 lpi]^2 = 286 grays (256 is the PostScript maximum)

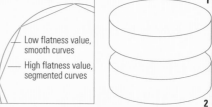

1

Low flatness value, smooth curves

High flatness value, segmented curves

2

Flatness values can be between 0 (**1**) and 100 (**2**)

Beyond color separation, things remain much as they have done for years, and unless – or rather, until – print technology changes dramatically, they will continue to do so. There are constant changes to print technology, but at a level that enhances the current processes – using computers to control ink ducts and impression, for instance – rather than at a radically new and different level. However, it's not entirely a fantasy to foresee the day when a printing press, using a more sophisticated development of the technology currently employed by, say, a laser or bubble-jet color printer, will be controlled directly from a desktop computer, eliminating such processes as film stripping and platemaking altogether.

In the meantime, the more immediate prepress issues that confront graphic designers are those of typesetting and reproduction.

IMAGESETTERS High quality output, whether it is bromide paper for camera-ready art or fully process-separated final film for imposition and platemaking, is produced on a machine called an imagesetter. Imagesetters work by means of a digitally controlled laser beam raking a photosensitive material such as bromide paper or film, thus exposing an image onto the material. Imagesetters are either flatbed – in which case the laser beam is projected via a series of mirrors and prisms onto the photosensitive material, which moves forward, one scan line at a time – or drum, whereby the film or paper, wrapped around a glass drum, is exposed by a rotating laser exposure assembly while the photosensitive material remains stationary. Drum imagesetters are thought to create fewer registration problems than flatbed types, because the material remains stationary and because the laser light source remains at a constant distance from the paper.

The process of a light beam raking the surface of a material is known as "rasterizing." In order that the imagesetter can understand the page description language (PDL) code, such as PostScript – which is used to "describe" the image to a printing device and thus translate it into machine code – it must contain, or have access to, a "raster" controller, or "raster image processor" (RIP). Desktop laser printers have RIPs built into them.

Imagesetter resolution Although both are laser printers, an imagesetter differs greatly from a desktop laser printer in that it is more precise, it produces a photographic, rather than toner-based, image, and it possesses greater RAM. Most important, it is able to reproduce an image at much higher resolutions than a laser printer, with the consequent advantage of extremely high-quality output. Normally, typographic matter will be output from an imagesetter at 1270dpi or 1800dpi (a typical laser printer outputs at 300dpi) – any higher resolution will be indiscernible and may slow

File formats When you save your work for storage on disk, the data that makes up the file is stored within a predetermined structure, or "file format." Many applications offer you a choice of format, your decision depending on what you ultimately intend using the file for. Sometimes the format is unique to an application and, although you may be able to use these files in other applications, it is possible that you cannot edit them outside the application that created them. However, there is a range of generic file formats which can be imported and exported by most graphics applications. Broadly speaking, there are two kinds of file formats, those that handle mainly text-based data (**above**), and those that are used for graphic images (**below**). The type of graphic image – whether it is object-oriented or bitmapped (see p.60) – often determines the file format that can be used, although some formats can contain either.

File formats for storing text and spreadsheet data

ASCII	256 standard character codes used by all computers. Often called "text-only" files. Text loses most formatting instructions.
DBS	Ashton Tate's proprietary database file format
DCA/RFT	IBM text format for word processing.
DIF	Format for exchanging data supported by some spreadsheet and database applications.
RTF	Microsoft's format for exchanging text documents while retaining text formatting information.
SYLK	Format for spreadsheets, used by Microsoft.
TEXT	Apple's extended version of ASCII for the Mac
WKS	Lotus's proprietary spreadsheet format.

File formats for storing images

DXF	AutoCAD's proprietary format for storing CAD files.
EPS, EPSF	Encapsulated PostScript Format. Primarily for storing object-oriented graphics files, but can also store bitmapped images (resulting files may be very large). EPS files are in either *ASCII* or *binary* subformats: **ASCII** Text-based description of an image, which contains two versions of it – one for printing on a PostScript device, regardless of resolution, and the other a low-resolution bitmap version for display. Often cannot be edited – even by the application that created it. **Binary** Similar to ASCII EPS format, but uses numbers rather than text to store data. Good format for converting TIFF files for color separation. Smaller file sizes than ASCII EPS format.
GIF	Graphic Interchange Format. CompuServe's format for sending compressed images over telephone lines.
Paint, PNTG	Original MacPaint low-resolution format used only for b/w bitmapped images of 72dpi. Limited to 8 x 10in.
PostScript	Uneditable text description of a file for printing with any PostScript device. Unlike some formats, PostScript files do not require the originating application.
PICS	Format for storing sequences of PICT and PICT2 images for animations in multimedia and 3D applications. File sizes can be very large.
PICT	Can store combination of bitmapped and object-oriented images. Limited to eight colors. Images copied to the Clipboard may be converted to PICT format.
PICT2	Development of PICT format for storing 8-bit and 24-bit color images. May not maintain resolution of an image when scaled. Not generally used for images requiring color separation, so more suitable where final output is either a computer display or photographic presentation.
RIB	Pixar's proprietary format for storing rendering and modeling files.
RIFF	Raster image file format. Letraset's own format as an alternative to TIFF. Originally only for 8-bit data, it now stores up to 32-bit information. Good for color separation files, but can mostly only be used with (some) Letraset applications, such as ColorStudio.
TIFF	Tagged image file format. The standard format for scanned bitmapped images and used extensively for color separations. There are several versions of the TIFF format, not all of them compatible with every TIFF-supported application. There are four subformats of TIFF 5.0: *TIFF B* for black and white; *TIFF G* for grayscale; *TIFF P* for images which store their color palette with the file; *TIFF R* for 32-bit color. May not maintain resolution when scaled.

down output to such an extent as to negate the quality versus cost ratio. Tint and halftone screens, however, will normally be output at resolutions of 2540dpi for screens of 150 lines per inch, or more if the halftone screen is finer. This is because imagesetter resolution only determines the quality of solid black since imagesetters cannot print grays. Imagesetter resolution, then, controls the quality of line and halftone dot – the higher the resolution, the better the quality of halftone dot and thus the opportunity to reproduce the original image with greater fidelity. However, final image quality depends on the relationship between input resolution, imagesetter resolution and halftone screen ruling.

Problems with high resolution concern the time it takes to output such files. The higher the resolution, the longer it takes to run out – a single, large image of around 30Mb may take as long as one hour to output four pieces of film. Documents of smaller sizes, but containing multiple images, may take even longer.

SERVICE BUREAUS If, as is typical, you will be using a bureau to output your work, there are many important criteria to bear in mind.

The first consideration is that of preparing your work for output on an imagesetter, which depends as much upon the application(s) you use as on what you need in terms of output. If, say, you require film separated into process colors from a document prepared using QuarkXPress, but which includes illustrations created in FreeHand, you probably won't encounter any problem. However, if that document also includes a color image which was "imported" into the layout as a TIFF file, you will find that QuarkXPress cannot separate that image. In such cases, the image must first be imported into an application with color separation capabilities, such as PhotoShop, that can convert the file using CMYK color information, "saved" as an appropriate EPS file and then re-imported into XPress. Some page makeup applications, such as DesignStudio, have built-in color separation capabilities.

Other separation problems may occur when PANTONE colors are specified in an illustration, say, in one application and then exported as a file to be used in another application. In such cases it may be necessary to recreate the same PANTONE color in the application finally used to produce the document.

However, the majority of problems encountered when outputting documents through an imagesetter in a bureau concern fonts and typography. Type foundries are constantly "tweaking" their products – just as software houses do – and a font may go through as many as five upgrades, during which it will have been reconstructed or the data within it changed. The problems occur when the latest version bears no identifying features from the previous versions (although

Gradated tints Many applications offer features for specifying gradated tints which can be made up from any mix and any percentage of process colors. However, you should be aware of the limitations imposed by the combination of halftone screen ruling and output resolution (p.126). This determines the maximum number of shades of a single color that it is possible to reproduce and thus the rate at which one shade changes into the next (called "stepping," or "banding") in a gradated tint. To achieve a visually smooth blend of shades, there must be as many steps as possible up to the maximum of 256 levels allowed by PostScript. Stepping may become more visible when the percentage values of a single color are very close (e.g. 30%–40%) over a large area, or when the same percentage values are specified at the beginning and end of a gradation comprising two or more colors. To achieve a smooth blend in gradated tints of more than one color, each color should have a different percentage value at one end of the gradation.

Calculating steps To calculate the number of steps in a gradated tint, subtract the end percentage value of the tint from its start value (*note: the start and end values are based on 0–1, where 100% = 1, thus 60% = 0.6 and 30% = 0.3*) and then multiply that figure by the number of grays (p.126). For example, if you specify a gradation starting with 60% and ending with 30%, you subtract 0.3 from 0.6. Multiply the answer, 0.3, by the number of gray levels, say 256, giving 76.8 steps which, over an area 1in. (25mm) wide would produce a smooth blend with slightly more than one step every point (one inch = 72pts).

100% Black — 0%

60% Black — 30% Black

50% Black — 40% Black | 50% Black — 40% Black

60% Cyan + 60% Magenta — 30% Cyan + 30% Magenta

40% Cyan + 60% Magenta — 30% Cyan + 20% Magenta

50% Magenta — 50% Cyan

30% Cyan + 50% Magenta + 40% Yellow — 30% Cyan + 30% Black

20% Magenta + 50% Yellow — 40% Cyan + 30% Yellow + 30% Black

100% Magenta + 100% Yellow — 100% Cyan + 100% Magenta

some fonts, such as those produced by Bitstream and Com-pugraphic, bear version numbers in the "Get Info" dialog boxes of their printer fonts), and even though the bureau may possess the same font manufactured by the same foundry, it may be a different version – the possible conse-quence being that the differences, however tiny, may cause the text to run out at a different length.

Sometimes, a font used in a document is replaced by an altogether different font when the job is run out. This hap-pens because of the difference in system software configurations between your computer and the bureau's. They may, for instance, have used a utility program to reas-sign font identification (ID) numbers to avoid conflicts, whereas you did not – the result being that although both your computer and theirs identified fonts with the same ID numbers, they were different fonts.

Fortunately, there is an easy way of avoiding these prob-lems simply by providing a suitcase containing all the screen fonts you used for a job, and, if you use PostScript fonts, copies of the outline printer fonts. *Un*fortunately, however, doing this means that you will almost certainly be breaching the terms of the license agreement between you and the font license holder, but to get the job done by your deadline, and in the most problem-free and cost effective way, you may have little choice. If it makes you sleep better at night, bear in mind that the likelihood is that your bureau, particularly if it is a large one, in all probability pos-sesses the identical font already – and in any case will entirely delete the folder created for your job, containing your fonts, from their hard disk after a few days.

Another way of solving the font problem may be to sup-ply your document as a PostScript file (usually an option in the "Print" dialog box), in which case you elect to "print" your document to disk as a PostScript file rather than to your laser printer. The problem here may be that the result-ing file size may be too large to transport if it contains many images or graphic devices (page 68 of this book occupies 4.4Mb of disk space when saved as a PostScript file).

Some page makeup applications may require you to include certain data files – such as hyphenation and justifi-cation files – with your document in order that the bureau version of the application uses your data rather than their own. If you change such things as kerning values, for instance, this information may be stored in the application's data file rather than in the document itself.

If you import image files, such as EPS files, into page makeup documents, you will need to include them with your document when you send it to a bureau, since the information the imagesetter needs in order to output it is contained within the image file rather than in the document into which you imported it.

Input resolution and halftone image quality The quality of a printed color halftone depends on the combined relationship between scanner resolution, imagesetter resolution and halftone screen ruling. Theoretically, the higher the input resolution, the better the printed result. However, since normal high-quality color printing rarely uses screen rulings beyond 150lpi, there is little to be gained from scanning images at resolutions of more than double the screen ruling – which is regarded as the rule of thumb for optimum quality. Another factor is the size of file generated – an image scanned at 300dpi will be more than twice the size as at 200dpi, and yet the difference in printed quality between the two will be very subtle. These illustrations compare different scanning resolutions with halftone screen rulings. They were imageset at 2450dpi.

300dpi scan; 150 lpi screen

300dpi scan; 128 lpi screen

200dpi scan; 150 lpi screen

200dpi scan; 128 lpi screen

150dpi scan; 150 lpi screen

100dpi scan; 128 lpi screen

Sometimes, the density of printing film produced by bureaus can be a problem, particularly that output by small bureaus that cater more for the desktop publishing user. Before using a bureau for the first time, establish that they have experience in preparing film for quality printing. This is more likely if, for instance, they make regular use of a densitometer in calibrating their equipment.

Although other problems may occur, these are more or less unique to particular jobs, and your bureau will be able to advise you on what to do to solve them or avoid them altogether. It can often save you untold grief if you explain to them the nature of a job *before* you send it, so that they can instruct you as to the best way of presenting it.

There are several ways of transporting documents to bureaus. Larger bureaus will possess equipment compatible with virtually any form of media. Floppy disks are probably the most common medium for presenting documents, but larger files require the greater capacity of removable cartridges such as those made by Bernoulli, Ricoh and Syquest. Alternatively, file compression utilities such as Disk Doubler can be used to compress files and even split up single files so that they fit onto floppies. If you have *really* large files, most will be quite happy to accommodate your external disk drive unit. Alternatively, you may prefer to transmit files via a modem, but because it is likely that you will be

Controlling image quality

When you make modifications to an image, such as rotating and scaling, using an appropriate image-manipulation application, pixel values are constantly being recalculated by the program in a process called "interpolation." Sometimes interpolation causes an image to lose its sharpness – as does "resampling up" (increasing the resolution of an image from its original scanned resolution). In such circumstances, it may become necessary to use a so-called "filter" which sharpens the image and may restore it to somewhere near its original state. This technique is often referred to as "unsharp masking." Care should be taken not to oversharpen an image since this may cause graininess. A wide range of other filters for image enhancement, and special effects are also available in image manipulation packages.

Original scanned at 100dpi

Noise filter

Resampled to 200dpi

Diffuse filter

Unsharp masking applied

Emboss filter

generating large files and because modems use telephone lines, cost may rule out this method.

COLOR REPRODUCTION Generally speaking, most designers who use Macs deal with the problem of halftone reproduction, particularly color, traditionally – by leaving it up to the operators of high-end color scanners. A desktop scanner may be used to scan images – or even hand-drawn line tracings of images – at low resolution which are then used as guides for position only, the final origination being undertaken by conventional methods.

Color reproduction generated by desktop scanners – sometimes referred to as "commercial color" – is improving steadily. In some situations it may be deemed acceptable, but it still comes nowhere near the quality demanded by most graphic designers. Even using desktop scanners, if you consistently work with large numbers of images, you will require powerful data storage facilities, a powerful computer – and eons of time.

However, although truly high-quality desktop color reprographics may still be some way away, facilities are already in place that enable you to take advantage of the fact that a Macintosh can be linked to a repro scanner to produce final page film.

This is done via a "gateway link," whereby your completed document is passed to the repro house who, having

previously scanned your color originals, electronically strip the images into your page. The gateway itself is usually a hardware/software combination which converts your Macintosh PostScript document into a form that enables the high-resolution repro scanned images to be placed into your page layout – just as the RIP does in an imagesetter. A typical gateway system is Crosfield's Lightspeed StudioLink. This

Color correction curves

Many applications allow you to make color modifications to a scanned image by manipulating a line which represents the tonal values of the scanned image relative to the screen image. Modifications can be made to the image as a whole, or separately to each of the process colors or RGB colors. Being able to make judgments on subtle color adjustments is only possible with a 24-bit color monitor. The monitor must be calibrated to the specifications of the application in which the corrections are being made in order to establish a direct relationship between displayed and output color. Many applications will calibrate your monitor automatically, but also offer controls for manual calibration. For consistency you should keep your monitor brightness and the ambient light temperature of your workspace constant.

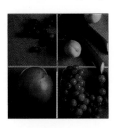

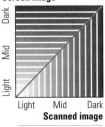

Screen image

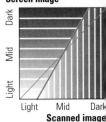

Screen image

Original image In its unchanged state, the color values of shadows, middle tones and highlights of the displayed image exactly match those which were scanned. In this case the color curve is represented as a straight, 45° line.

Increased contrast Increasing the angle of the line squeezes out the extreme shadows and highlights, spreading the middle tones over lighter and darker values. A vertical line would increase contrast to maximum – black and white.

Color proof corrections

Final adjustments to a color image should only be made after it has been proofed on a four-color printing press. Even if the original transparency was perfect, other factors can affect the outcome. Among these is "dot gain" – where the size of halftone dots increases either during the transfer of the image from film to printing plate, or because of the effect of inking. Proofing may also reveal other aberrations which are impossible to detect on your monitor or on a laser proof. One of the most common of these is "moiré" (see p.136).

Correct image

Too much contrast

Detail too soft

Detail too sharp

provides the link to the Crosfield Studio System (Crosfield also have their own page make-up application, called Lightspeed CLS – Color Layout System – to complement StudioLink, although any page make-up application can be used with it). Another gateway is Scitex's Visionary, which is based on QuarkXPress and is designed to interface with the Scitex Response System.

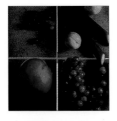
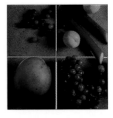

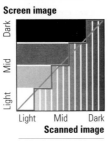
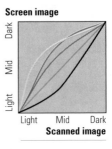

Reduced contrast
Reducing the angle of the line compresses all the tones of the image into the middle tone range of the monitor.

Posterization This technique confines the continuous range of colors to "flattened out" bands.

Color correction To make accurate corrections, it is usually necessary to make adjustments to individual process colors in an image rather than identical adjustments to all the colors. Results must be proofed for final assessment.

Too much yellow

Too much cyan

Too much magenta

Too little yellow

Too little cyan

Too little magenta

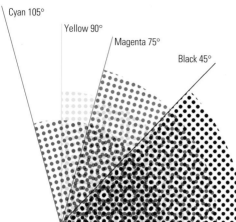

Halftone screen angles
Halftone screens must be set at the correct angles to avoid a picture printing with an undesirable screen clash ("moiré," **below**). The screen angles shown (**left**) are common for 4-color printing and are the default angles for most applications.

SCANNING RESOLUTION When you use a gateway link, an original is scanned at a suitably high resolution and a low resolution (72dpi) file can be automatically generated, which is returned to you so that you can show the exact crop and final position. The low-resolution scan is replaced by the high-resolution version prior to final output. Using this method still means that you need to know the final size that you want the image to be, since the scan resolution is set at the time of scanning, and any subsequent enlargement may reveal pixelation (10 percent enlargement may just about be acceptable). Repro scanner input resolution is typically 300dpi; while this may seem very low compared to imagesetter output, it must be remembered that the typical halftone screen ruling for color images is only 150lpi, and higher input resolution is really only required for very fine halftone screen rulings, such as those over 200lpi. Another confusion may arise when repro scanner operators refer to scanned images as "contones" (continuous tone images) – a relic of the days when mechanical color separations produced continuous tone negatives prior to halftone screening – whereas, in fact, the images will already have been digitized.

Color trapping When two solid areas of color print side by side, imperfections in register sometimes create white hairline gaps. To avoid this, a technique called "trapping" is employed, whereby the edges of an image printing in one color are increased to slightly overlap those of the adjacent color. Conventionally, this would take place during film makeup or platemaking by varying exposures or by the use of "fatties" – interleaved film which causes light to spread, fractionally increasing an image size. Some Mac applications feature automatic trapping controls, but it may be necessary for you to create your own trapping by adding a rule (**1**) of, say, 0.25pt around a shape (**2**). The rule should be specified in the same color as the area it surrounds and set to overprint.

8

TROUBLESHOOTING

PRECAUTIONS/SYSTEM ERRORS/STARTUP ERRORS/
MEMORY PROBLEMS/PROBLEMS WITH FILES/
PRINTING PROBLEMS/FURTHER READING

No matter how well a computer is built – or how well the parts, devices and programs that serve it are built (or written) – things go wrong. Problems can occur almost anywhere: a hardware fault, a software bug, a corrupted program or data file, incompatibilities of software, viruses – and so on. Fortunately, however, major problems are rare, and you should regard this chapter more as a safety net than as a cause for concern.

You *will* encounter problems, but these can be kept to a minimum if you observe the few simple preventative guidelines listed here. Also listed are remedies for – or at least explanations of – some of the more alarming problems that you may suddenly be presented with. The list is by no means comprehensive, and if you are confronted with a problem that isn't addressed here or in your manuals, contact your dealer or a User Group. Problems with individual applications are not included here, since many of these occur in new upgraded versions of the software and are usually identified fairly quickly – "bug-fixes" are issued. Sometimes, a problem may occur simply because the person who wrote the application you are using didn't anticipate that particular string of commands or the action you just made. Of course, *you* won't know if that's the case, but if it seems that it is a recurrent problem – let the publisher know (every other possibility having been eliminated). At least then the problem can be fixed for future releases of the software.

PRECAUTIONS

Check that everything is plugged in
This may seem obvious, but even one unplugged item may cause problems.

Never plug in or unplug any item while it is switched on or while the

Mac is switched on
While there are exceptions to this rule (modem, printer and audio ports), it is safest never to plug in or unplug anything while the computer is live – even the ADB port (mouse and keyboard).

Don't obstruct the cooling vents of your Mac or any piece of hardware

Electrical components, and power supplies in particular, give off a lot of heat.

Don't move or jar your Mac or any device containing a hard disk while it is switched on
Doing so may cause a disk to crash, with subsequent loss of data.

Always turn off your Mac by selecting the Shutdown command from the Special menu
Using the power switch to quit the Finder may damage system files.

Don't keep more than one System folder on your startup disk
Doing so will confuse your Mac and cause system errors.

Turn on peripheral SCSI devices *before* you switch on your Mac
Some (not all) SCSI devices need to be switched on all the time the Mac is on. If you switch on a device *after* you switch on your Mac, it may not be recognized. The Mac may even ask for a startup disk. Turning off a SCSI device while your Mac is in use may cause a system error.

Ensure that no two SCSI devices have the same SCSI address number
There are eight SCSI numbers (0 – 7) although number seven is allocated to your Mac's CPU and zero is usually your internal hard disk, if you have one. Make sure that each device connected to your Mac has a different number before you switch the Mac on or it will crash. The SCSI address number, or ID, is usually located on the back panel of the device, but it may occasionally be allocated by means of software.

Save your work regularly
Get into the habit of saving your work to disk as often as you can (type Command-S). Always Save when you turn away from the Mac – to answer the telephone, for instance. Save at least every 15 minutes – and more frequently unless your document is so large that it takes several minutes to save. Save before you print a document, and save before you hide the application you are working in or switch to another application.

Print out documents before closing them
This may seem overly paranoid, but by doing this at least you have a hard copy of a design or illustration you may have been working on all day if the unthinkable happens – the file corrupts.

Back up your work regularly
Always back up your current work files every day (if not more) and your complete system every week or so. Keep backup copies of all your original application and font floppy disks. While saving and backing up work will not actually prevent problems from happening, you'll be thankful you did when your hard disk crashes.

Periodically reinstall system and application software
System software and application files may corrupt over a period of time and should be replaced if problems begin to occur with increased frequency (frequent system errors may speed up the corruption of system files).

Rebuild your desktop file regularly
The desktop file is an invisible file that keeps track of all the files on your disk. Because it also retains information about files you delete, it just gets bigger and bigger, eventually causing Finder operations to slow down or even prevent you from opening a file altogether. To flush out the desktop file, you "rebuild" it by holding down the Option and Command keys while you start up or restart your Mac.

Defragment your hard disk regularly
When data gets written to your hard disk, it is placed in the next available – and largest – space, each file side by side to begin with. If you continue working on a file, it outgrows the space

it's in, and the new data has to be placed elsewhere on the disk. Eventually, all the large spaces get used up, and even new files must be split up and the pieces positioned wherever there is space. When this happens, your disk is said to be "fragmented." The result of a badly fragmented disk is a slow Mac, because it takes longer to find the pieces of file and thus retrieve the data. Fortunately there are many utility programs available which will defragment ("optimize") disks, which they do by picking up all the bits of files and rearranging them contiguously on your disk. Alternatively, you can back up your entire hard disk, reformat it and then restore all your backed-up files to the disk. The files will be written to the disk contiguously

Keep a spare startup disk
Your Mac may one day fail to recognize your startup disk (which could be due to a variety of reasons, such as corrupt system files), so a spare floppy startup disk will at least enable you to gain access to your hard disk, identify the problem and, if possible, rectify it – always supposing that the disk has not completely gone feet up, for which you will need a disk recovery utility.

Keep a virus detection program on your hard disk
Computer viruses are deliberately mischievous programs written to create havoc with any computer that they come into contact with. Viruses spread by copying themselves to and from hard disks via floppy disks and also over networks. Use a virus detection utility to check every disk you insert into your Mac and run a regular check on your hard disk. Make sure you keep your virus detection program up to date to combat new viruses.

SYSTEM ERRORS

The most alarming problem you are likely to encounter (a hard disk crash notwithstanding) is a system error – a crash, or "bomb" – or an application error. If this happens the first rule is: **keep calm** and don't panic – you *may* be able to do something about it. Before you try any of the remedies below, sit back and look at the screen – try to remember the last time you saved your work to disk. If it was very recently, you may not lose much. If you can't remember, write down or draw everything that you can see on the screen (there's no hurry), such as a layout, or newly-defined colors or type specifications, the details of which may be visible on palettes. Next, go through each of the following procedures in turn, always remembering that each of them is a long shot and that the likely outcome is that you will have to restart your Mac:

The Mac will not respond to keyboard commands and nothing happens when Menu Bar titles are clicked – even though the pointer moves.
Establish that the Mac isn't just taking a long time to execute a command – particularly if you are working on a very complex illustration or using an application for 3D rendering. If the pointer has changed its shape to a wristwatch, you may have to wait – but even that isn't necessarily an indication that the Mac hasn't crashed. Try typing Command-period – this may cancel any task that the computer is currently carrying out. If still nothing happens, try the next remedy.

The pointer has "frozen" on the screen and the Mac will not respond to keyboard commands
Check that the mouse and keyboard ADB connections are secure. The error may

have occurred within the application rather than the system. Try pressing the Option-Command-Esc keys together. This may present you with a dialog box asking if you want to quit the application you are in and return to the Finder, and advising you that if you do so all changes you made since you last saved will be lost. Click OK and with a bit of luck you should return to the Finder. When you do, your Mac may be in an unstable state, so save any open documents in other applications and restart your Mac.

A dialog box appears, saying "Sorry, a System Error occurred"
This is characterized by the icon, pictured above, of a bomb. Your Mac has crashed, and there's not a lot you can do about it. There are usually two buttons in the dialog box, a Restart button and a Resume button, the latter rarely enabled and unlikely to work even if it is. However, you might try this extreme long shot: press the Interrupt button which is paired with the Reset button on the Programer's Switch, found on the case of your Mac. Hopefully, you will be presented with a dialog box containing the greater-than symbol (>) in its top left corner. Type the following:
SMFA700A9F4 (carriage return) – the box should fill with numbers. Then type:
PCFA700 (carriage return)
G (carriage return). This may take you back to the Finder (it worked for me – but only twice) where you should save any open documents and restart your computer. If all fails, press the Reset button to restart your Mac.

A system error may occur for a number of reasons. Among the most common are:

Application error Many crashes will be for a one-off reason and may never re-occur under the same circumstance. To check, restart your Mac, open the document you were working on, and try to repeat the actions you made before the crash. If you Mac crashes again, there is something wrong with the application – either it has corrupted (reinstall it) or it is a bug (notify the publisher). Either way, avoid the sequence of actions which caused the crash.

External hard disk or other SCSI device switched off or disconnected Switching on your Mac before you switch on a hard disk – or switching off a hard disk before your Mac – may cause it to crash. Either way, switch on the disk before restarting the Mac.

Incompatible init files or system extensions Init files are startup documents and may cause system errors during the startup sequence or when called upon while you work in an application. If the problem occurs shortly after installing a new init, remove it and restart. If that solves the problem, your new init is probably to blame. Otherwise, you may have to remove all your inits and reload them one by one, restarting each time you do so until you find the guilty one. Renaming the offending init may eliminate conflicts, but it's more likely that you will have to use that init selectively – find out what it conflicts with (trial and error) and don't use those two together.

System software corrupted Reinstall the System and Finder files.
Damaged disk The boot blocks (startup information) on your hard disk may be damaged, in which case you can restore them by reinstalling the drivers on your hard disk (by using the setup program for your hard disk – if it's an Apple disk, use HD SC Setup).

STARTUP ERRORS

No hard disk icon on the desktop

If your hard disk fails to mount after an otherwise successful startup, try rebuilding your desktop file. Alternatively, it may be possible to mount your disk using a shareware utility called SCSI Probe (Robert Pilic). If the disk still doesn't mount, there may be a problem with the hard disk itself; try using a disk repair and recovery utility. If that fails, have your hard disk serviced – it may still be possible to retrieve the data stored on it.

Flashing question mark appears at startup

This indicates that the Mac is asking you to insert a startup disk – either there isn't one, or the Mac can't find it. If you use an external drive as your startup disk, make sure it's turned on. Make sure all your SCSI devices are switched on. You may have switched on your Mac too soon after turning on your SCSI devices – try starting up again. Check that all cables are securely connected. Reinstall the system software from the installer disks (the first one of these, "Installer 1," is a startup disk). If none of these remedies work, you will have to start up from another disk and run a disk maintenance utility to check and repair your startup disk.

MEMORY PROBLEMS

"Memory low" warnings

You are most likely to get these while working in an application – either the application will warn you, or it will unexpectedly quit, returning you to the Finder.

An application may run out of memory if you are working on a very complex document. If you encounter such problems, reset the application memory size: quit the application (if it hasn't done so itself), select the application icon and then Get Info (File menu). At the bottom of the window are two boxes, one with a suggested memory size, the other with the current size. For many applications, the suggested size is enough (memory size must not be lower than that suggested), but it is quite likely that many design tasks you undertake will require more than the suggested size. Increase the current size (make sure you have enough RAM to accommodate it) and relaunch the application.

Not enough memory to open an application

If you are presented with a dialog box advising you that there is not enough memory to open the application you just launched, and asking you if you want to try opening it using what memory is left – click "Cancel." This generally happens when you have other applications open – they are all using up memory. Close one of those applications and then relaunch the one that failed. If the warning pops up again, you may have to close another or *all* open applications. This is because RAM is allocated in contiguous blocks and can't be split up as can a file on a hard disk. Closing one application may still not free up a large enough block, even though the total memory allocated to open applications mathematically leaves enough memory for the newcomer. Find out the size of your largest unused block of memory in About This Macintosh … item in the Apple menu. If you have no other applications open, you can free up some memory by removing a few fonts or inits from your system folder or

by reducing the current size of the application memory (not below its suggested size). Best advice: get more RAM.

PROBLEMS WITH FILES

Document won't open

If a document will not open by double-clicking on its icon in the Finder, you may need to open it from within the application in which it was created. If that doesn't work, there may be a problem with the disk – make a copy of the disk and try to open the file from the copy. If the file has corrupted, there's not much you can do, and you will probably have to revert to an earlier version of the document (thus the reason for frequent backups). Try using a disk maintenance utility to recover the file. If the file contains text, you may be able to recover it by using Microsoft Word's ability to open any file (press Shift while pulling down the File menu); much of what you see will be gobbledegook, but the text may appear somewhere among it.

Can't save a document

Try using the Save As… command and giving the file a different name. If the disk is full, save to another disk.

PRINTING PROBLEMS

Problems are most likely to occur if the documents you create are graphics-intensive – you may see the words "Limitcheck," or "PostScript Error" appear in dialog boxes. If your document contains EPS files created in a drawing application, try applying a higher "flatness" value to its paths and then exporting it as a new EPS file. If you keep getting errors while trying to print a long or complex document, try printing it one page at a time.

FURTHER READING

BOOKS

GENERAL

Most of the general books published about the Macintosh tend to be very large and go into considerable detail. They are usually aimed at the general Macintosh user and much of what is contained within them is of little relevance to graphic designers. However, the following books are well-written and offer a wealth of technical information and tips, and you are advised to arm yourself with at least one of them. Because they contain a great deal of technical detail, it is likely that these books will be out of date rapidly, so check that you have a recent edition (that it refers to System 7, for instance) and go for ones that are constantly revised or offer regular updates.

The Big Book of Amazing Mac Facts
Lon Poole, 514 pages
(Microsoft Press)
A book full of general tips.

The Big Mac Book
Neil J. Salkind, 1020 pages
(Que)
Detailed general reference.

The Macintosh Bible
Sharon Zardetto Aker et al. edited by Arthur Naiman, 1118 pages
(Goldstein & Blair)
Wittily and well written, and regularly updated.

The Macworld Complete Mac Handbook
Jim Heid, 548 pages

(IDG Books Worldwide, Inc.)
Expanded compilation of the Macworld *Getting Started* column.

SYSTEM 7

The Macintosh Bible Guide to System 7
Charles Rubin, 254 pages
(Goldstein & Blair)

Macworld Guide to System 7
Lon Poole, 356 pages
(IDG Books Worldwide, Inc.)

The System 7 Book
Craig Danuloff, 388 pages
(Ventana Press)

PROBLEM-SOLVING

The Macintosh Bible "What Do I Do Now" Book
Charles Rubin, 191 pages
(Goldstein & Blair)
Tells you what to do instead of panicking.

TYPOGRAPHY

The Macintosh Font Book
Erfert Fenton, 260 pages
(Peachpit Press)

Typefaces for desktop publishing
Alison Black, 106 pages
(Architecture Design and Technology Press)

SCANNING

The Scanner Handbook
Stephen Beale and James Cavuoto, 253 pages
(Computer Weekly)
An introduction to desktop scanning.

REPRODUCTION

The Linotype Color Book
Dominique Legrand, 80 pages
(Linotype-Hell)
A guide to digital color reproduction.

MAC-graphics
Lim Ching San and Gim Lee, 288 pages
(Octogram Publishing/ COMPUTERbooks)
Macintosh type and tint effects, to show what they look like in print, plus very comprehensive process color tint charts.

JOURNALS

GENERAL

MacUser (U.S.)
(Ziff-Davis Publishing Co.)

MacUser (U.K.)
(Dennis Publishing Ltd.)

Macworld (U.S.)
(Macworld Communications, Inc.)

Macworld (U.K.)
(IDG Communications)

GRAPHICS

XYZ
(Haymarket Publishing)

PrePress
(Newsfield Ltd.)

QuarkXPress In-Depth Ready,Set,Go!/Design- Studio In-Depth PageMaker In-Depth
(MindCraft Publishing Corp.)

9

GLOSSARY AND INDEX

Here you will find brief definitions both of Macintosh terms and of design terms in the context of the Mac. Italic figures at the end of entries refer to the page number(s) where that topic is discussed in the main body of the book.

Key:
abb: abbreviation
adv: advertising
app: application
fin: finishing and binding
pap: paper/papermaking

pho: photography
pri: printing
rep: reproduction/prepress
Sys.6: Versions of the operating system prior to System 7

typ: typography/ typesetting
util: utility program
→ see
● Apple Menu

A

abort → cancel.

About MultiFinder
(● menu, *Sys.6*) Shows the version number of the Finder and System files on your startup disk, gives total RAM in the Mac and shows the amount of memory set aside for operating the system, Finder and open applications.

About the Finder (● menu, *Sys.6*) Shows the version number of the Finder and System files on your startup disk, gives total RAM in the Mac and shows the amount of memory set aside for operating the system and Finder.

absolute leading
→ leading.

absolute page number
The actual position of a page in a document, relative to other pages, regardless of any other page number.

accelerator card/board
An add-on board with a faster central processing unit and/or coprocessor to speed up computer operation. *28, 47–8*

accent Mark added to a character to denote pronunciation in a given language.

accent characters Type characters that print with accent marks, usually accessed via the Option (or

Shift-Option) key on Apple keyboards.

accessory → desk accessory.

access time Of disk drives, the average combined seek time (the time taken for the drive head to reach data being accessed) and latency time (the time taken for the data sector to rotate beneath the head).

activate To select an item, or make it "live" on screen, usually by clicking on it or within it.

active icon The currently selected icon, or icons, on the desktop. An active icon is highlighted, usually as a negative of its inactive, or unselected, image.

active window The currently selected window on the desktop, an active window has its title bar highlighted by horizontal lines and is always in front of (or on top of) all other windows.

ADB *abb:* → Apple Desktop Bus.

additive colors The primary colors of light – red, green, and blue (RGB) – that may be mixed to form all other colors in computer monitors and in photographic reproduction.

add-on board → expansion card.

address A number identify-

ing a location in a computer's memory.

address lines Paths on a central processing unit chip used to carry data addresses. The more address lines, the larger the amount of memory that can be used simultaneously.

Adobe Font Metrics A brandname specification for storing font information (metrics) in a file. *91*

Adobe Multiple Master format *97*

Adobe Type Manager (ATM) *(util.)* A brandname font utility which improves the screen display of PostScript Type 1 fonts by scaling the outlines contained within their printer files, rather than by using bitmapped screen fonts. *41, 78, 88–9, 91, 94*

Adobe Type Reunion *(util.)* *78*

advertising, *software for 70–1*

AFE *abb:* → Apple File Exchange.

AFM *abb:* → Adobe Font Metrics.

After Dark *(util.)* *79*

AI *abb:* → artificial intelligence.

airbrush A mechanical painting tool producing a fine spray of paint or ink, used in illustration, design, and retouching.

airbrush tool A tool used in some computer drawing and painting applications, the function of which is to simulate, on screen, the effects provided by an airbrush. 61, 54

Alarm Clock Standard Apple desk accessory, supplied with all Macs, which displays date and time and allows you to set an alarm.

alert (box) A message box which appears unsolicited, usually accompanied by a sound, to pass on information or give a warning.

algorithm A set of precise predetermined procedural steps for solving a specific problem.

algorithmically defined Description of a font which draws each character according to calculations made by a program, the program being unique for each character.

alias A copy of a file's icon – but not a copy of the file itself. The alias icon works in the same way as its original but occupies very little disk space, no matter how many copies are made.

aliasing → jaggie.

aligned left/right → ranged/left, right.

aligning numerals → lining figures.

alphabet (length) A measure derived from the length, in points, of the 26 lowercase alphabet letters. Thus 39 characters have a measure of 1½ alphabets.

alphanumeric set *(typ.)* A full set of letters and numbers, sometimes also including punctuation marks and certain commonly used symbols.

alpha test Early testing of a product, to debug it, by the company developing it.

alpha version First version, for testing, of a program. It is followed by beta and then release versions.

analog computer A computer using a physical variable, i.e. voltage, to represent numbers in arithmetical calculations.

anchor In some applications, the facility to lock, or anchor, one item to another; a picture or rule can be anchored to text so that it flows with it.

annotation (1) A type label added to an illustration. (2) Explanatory notes or names printed in the margin of a text.

antialiasing A technique which reduces the jagged effect of bitmapped screen images by averaging the density of pixels at the edges of images with their background, thus softening the stepped appearance of the image.

antiqua (1) Early typeface based on 11th- and 12th-century Italian scripts. (2) A German term for roman type.

API *abb:* application programming interface, a term describing applications with built-in features for simple modification.

append In some applications, the facility to copy a set of user-defined specifications from one document or library to another.

Apple Desktop Bus (ADB) The standard connection path provided on most Macs (early Macs and the Mac Plus use a different connection) to allow peripheral devices such as keyboards, mice, trackballs, and digitizing tablets to connect to your Mac. 30

Apple equipment, *purchase* 109

Apple File Exchange (AFE) A Macintosh application which comes with your Mac and allows you to translate data to or from MS-DOS-compatible and most Apple II computers. 117

Apple HD SC Setup The standard Apple utility that comes with your Mac which you use for initializing, partitioning, or testing your hard disk.

Apple key → command key.

Apple menu A standard menu, identified by the Apple logo on the left of the menu bar, from which you can access items placed in the Apple Menu Items folder and get information about memory and open applications.

AppleShare The Apple file server on a computer for users of an AppleTalk network, enabling them to share files on that computer.

AppleTalk Apple's local area network (LAN) system,

built into every Mac, which you can use to connect your Mac to other Macs or to share printers and other devices. Physical links are made with Apple's LocalTalk connectors and cabling.

application files 22

application heap The portion of RAM set aside for use by software applications.

Application Memory Size The portion of RAM reserved by each application.

Application Menu A standard menu, located at the extreme right of the menu bar, which lists open applications and is where you can choose to hide or show open windows.

application (program) A program written to create or manipulate data for a specific purpose, such as word processing or page layout, but which is distinct from nonapplication programs such as system software. 19

application programming interface → API.

application support file An auxiliary file used by applications for special purposes, such as a spelling dictionary or help file.

arabic numerals The numerical symbols 1234567890.

archival backup → backup, archival.

arrow keys The four keys on the keyboard which move the text insertion point, or pointer, left, right, up or down, or move you through list boxes.

arrow pointer The basic arrow cursor, a left-leaning arrow (▶), used in the Finder and most applications, which is controlled by the mouse.

art(work) (a/w, A/W) Any illustrative matter prepared for reproduction, such as illustrations, diagrams, and photographs, as distinct (usually) from text.

artificial intelligence (AI) A term describing programs that deduce, to a specific set of rules, a solution from original and subsequent criteria provided by you – in other words, the program learns by its own experience.

ascender The portion of a lower-case letter rising

above its body, or x-height; i.e. the upper part of the characters b, d, f, h, k, l, t.

ascent The height of text above its baseline, as specified by font designers.

ASCII Acronym (pronounced askee) for the American Standard Code for Information Interchange, a standard by which most computers assign code numbers to letters, numbers, and common symbols. *128*

assembled negative *(rep.)* A film negative of combined line and halftone copy used in the conventional preparation of a film positive or printing plate for photolithography.

asynchronous communication A communication protocol by which a start-and-stop signal denotes the beginning and end of each character transmitted, thus enabling two devices to communicate without rigid timing signals. As distinct from synchronous communication.

ATF Type Designer *(app.)* 98

ATM *abb:* → Adobe Type Manager.

audio port The sound output port on a Mac which enables you to replace or enhance its internal speaker by adding one externally. *30*

authoring programs, multimedia *75*

author's proofs Galley or laser proofs, checked and marked by a proofreader, to be read by the author, who may then mark any necessary correction.

Authorware Animator *(app.)* 75

Authorware Professional *(app.)* 75

autoflow The facility, in some applications, to flow text automatically from one page to another or from one box to another.

auto leading → leading.

automated publication Published work of which a copy is kept on disk, tape, or film for future publication with revised matter or format.

automatic curvature The default curve of a path which some applications, with drawing tools, draw between two points.

automatic font downloading → font downloading.

automatic hyphenation A facility, in some applications, to break a word in a suitable place with a hyphen at the end of a line of text.

automatic text box In some frame-based page layout applications, a text box on an automatically inserted page into which text will automatically flow.

automatic text chain → autoflow.

auto page insertion A facility, in some applications, to add pages automatically when an amount of text greater than the space available to accommodate it is imported into a document.

autotrace A facility, in some applications, to create a freeform path by automatically tracing solid elements of an image. *59*

auxiliary dictionary A user-defined dictionary for checking spelling, which may be based upon the built-in dictionary of the application in which it is created.

A/UX *abb:* Apple/UNIX, Apple's version of the AT&T UNIX operating system.

auxiliary file An application support file.

axis (pl. axes) Imaginary line defining the center of an object around which the object rotates or is symmetrical to on a flat plane.

a/w (A/W) *abb:* → artwork.

B

b/f (**1** *typ.*) *abb:* bold face. Instruction to set copy in a bold face. (**2**) *abb:* brought forward. Copy or matter which has been brought forward from the previous page.

back *(fin.)* The part of a book nearest the fold or the edge at which the pages are bound.

backbone → spine.

backed → back up (**2**).

background Description of a program which runs at the same time as another is running in the foreground, as when two or more programs are open.

background color/tint A color or tint which has been applied to the background of any item, whether it be an illustration, page, or boxed feature.

backgrounder Apple's pri[nt] spooler software for its LaserWriters. Backgrounder will only work if its file is in your system folder along with the PrintMonitor file.

background printing The facility to print documents and use your Mac at the same time for something else.

background processing The facility of a program run ning in the background, to process data without interfering with the program operating in the foreground.

back matter → end matter

back panel The rear surface of a computer or peripheral device which houses the power switch, power connector, and communications ports.

back-to-back *(pri.)* Refers to the process of printing on both sides of a sheet.

back up (**1**) To make a duplicate of a disk, application, or document as a precaution against losing the original. *106–7, 121–3, 138* (**2** *pri.*) To print the second side of a sheet of paper. Backed refers to the sheet when it has been backed up.

backup A duplicate of a file, folder, or disk. → back up (**1**).

backup utilities *79*

backup, archival A backup which specifically saves the previous versions of your backups, thus avoiding the possibility of your losing files which may be deleted and rewritten by a mirror-image backup.

backup, global/baseline An exact duplicate of everything on your disk. A global backup is usually the first one you make from a source disk. Thereafter, backups are either incremental or archival.

backup, incremental A backup of only those files which you have worked on or changed since your last backup.

backup, mirror-image A backup achieved by copying the exact contents from one disk to another, thus replacing older versions of files with updated ones.

backup, same disk A backup copy of a document,

...aved onto the same disk as the original.

backup set A set of backup disks or files containing duplicate, or backed-up, files from a source disk.

Balloon Help A cartoon-like device for giving on-line help about icons and menu commands. The Balloon Help menu is represented in the menu bar by a question mark in a balloon.

bar code A pattern of vertical lines identifying details of a product, such as country of origin, manufacturer, and type of product, conforming to the Universal Product Code (UPC) — there are several different formats for product coding.

base alignment In computer typesetting, the automatic alignment of type of different sizes on a common baseline.

base artwork/black art Artwork requiring the addition of other elements such as halftone positives before reproduction.

base film *(rep.)* The basic material for contact film in platemaking for photomechanical reproduction, to which film positives are stripped.

base line The last line of space on a page containing type matter.

baseline An imaginary line on which the bases of upper-case letters, and the bases of the x-heights of lower-case letters, rest.

baseline backup → backup, global/baseline.

baseline grid In some applications, an invisible grid to which lines of text can be locked so that their baselines align from column to column.

basic-shape tools In most graphics applications, the tools for drawing basic shapes, i.e. lines, squares, rectangles, circles and ellipses.

batch mode The facility of an application to process data processed in batches as distinct from data which is processed as you input it interactive mode, or real-time); e.g., when you run a spelling checker through a whole document.

battery The lithium battery

in your Mac, which supplies power to an area of RAM called parameter RAM (PRAM).

baud The unit of measure equating to one unit per second describing the speed of data transfer, e.g. by a modem, sometimes inaccurately referred to as bit rate (two or more bits can be contained in a single event). The greater the baud rate, the faster the transmission of data.

BBS *abb:* bulletin board system/service. → bulletin board.

begin even *(typ.)* Instruction to the typesetter to set the first line of a piece of text without a paragraph indent; i.e., full out.

beta test Testing of a software product by a person designated, although not employed, by the company developing it.

beta version Second version of a program used for testing. It follows the alpha version.

Bézier control handle → Bézier curve.

Bézier curve In object-oriented drawing applications, a mathematically defined curve between two points (Bézier points). The curve is manipulated by dragging, from an anchored point, control handles which act on the curve like magnets. → object-oriented.

binary code The code by which sets of data are represented by binary digits. → bit.

binary digit → bit.

binary system Numbering system using only two digits, 0 and 1 (binary = of, or involving, pairs), rather than the decimal system of 0-9. *15–16*

binding edge → spine.

binding methods *(fin.)* Methods of securing multiple leaves of a printed item, such as a book. Mechanical binding methods include plastic comb binding, ring binding, and metal clasp attachments. Bookbinding methods include Smyth-sewn, side-sewn, section-sewn, and perfect binding.

bit *abb:* binary digit. The smallest unit of information your computer uses. It is

expressed as 1 or 0, meaning on or off, yes or no, positive or negative, something or nothing. Eight bits are required to store one alphabet character.

bit density The number of bits in a given area or length; e.g., per inch of magnetic tape.

bit-depth The number of bits used to define a device's capability to reproduce grays or colors — the greater the bit-depth (e.g., 32-bit), the more colors you will have available.

bit map At its simplest, a text character or graphic image comprised of dots. In fact, a bit map is the set of bits that represents the position and binary state (on or off) of a corresponding set of items to form a bit image such as your display screen.

bitmapped font A font comprised of bitmapped letters, characterized by their jagged edges, as distinct from the smooth edges of an outline font used by printers. *88–9, 91*

bitmapped graphic An image comprised of dots, as distinct from an object-oriented graphic. *59, 60* → object-oriented.

bit rate The number of bits per second (data and non-data) carried by a communications channel. Sometimes, inaccurately, referred to as baud rate.

Bitstream *131*

black letter Heavy style of typeface based on broad-nib script, also called Old English (U.S.) and Gothic (U.K.).

black patch/out *(rep.)* A piece of black (or red) material used to mask the image area on base artwork or positive film, leaving a window in the negative for stripping in a halftone image.

black printer *(rep.)* Term for the film which provides the image to print in black ink in the four-color printing process.

blanker → screen saver.

blanking interval The term describing the brief moment of time in which the beam of electrons in a video monitor switches off. This happens when the beam moves from

one horizontal line to another (called the "horizontal blanking interval"), and when it moves from the bottom of the screen to the top at the end of each frame (called the "vertical blanking interval").

blank screen *(Sys.6)* The screen state of virtually all applications after closing, rather than quitting a document (which takes you back to the Finder) – that is, the screen is completely blank except for the menu bar.

bleed The part of an image that extends beyond the edge of a page. Images which spread to the edge of the paper allowing no margins are described as "bled off".

blending 59, 61
blessed folder → system folder

blind folio Page number counted for reference or identification, but not printed on the page itself.

blind P The character ¶, used to indicate new paragraphs. Also called a "paragraph mark" or "reverse P."

block A group regarded as a unit, usually referring to data or memory in which data is stored.

block letter A term used to describe large display sansserif characters, deriving from letters cut in wooden blocks, which were used for embossing or printing.

blues, blueprint *(pri.)* Low quality proofs, usually produced by the printer rather than origination house, for a final check before printing. → diazo; Ozalid.

board, circuit board The name given to the support upon which chips and other components are mounted. A printed circuit board (PC board) is one that has been stamped with metallic ink to connect the components. A motherboard, or logic board, is the main board in your computer that bears the CPU, ROM, RAM and expansion slots. A board that plugs into an expansion slot is often called a card.

body copy/matter Printed matter forming the main part, usually text, of a work.

body type The type used in setting the main part of a text.

bold (face) Type with a conspicuously heavy, black appearance. It is based on the same design as mediumweight type in the same type family.

bomb The name given to an error in your system software of which the net result is that you will almost certainly be forced to restart your Mac. It is often identified by an icon of a bomb in a message box. The term has been extended to mean any condition where your Mac fails to respond to input from the mouse or keyboard, thus requiring you to restart. This is also described by the terms "System error," "crash," "freeze," and "hang." 139

book face Old term for a particular typeface, but now used to mean any type suitable for the text of a book.

book make-up The collation and identification of copy prepared for printing.

book paper *(pap.)* A general classification of papers suitable for book printing.

book proof *(pri.)* Imposed proofs or page proofs put together in book form for checking before binding.

boot blocks Specifically designated areas on a disk set aside to give your Mac the information it needs to start up, such as the allocation of RAM for different purposes (the number of files that can be opened, for example).

boot disk → startup disk
boot(ing) (up) The process of starting up a computer or any application by loading the necessary program – in the Macintosh's case, the System and Finder – into memory. In Mac parlance, more commonly called "starting up." → cold boot; warm boot.

bottom out To arrange text so there are no unsuitable breaks at the bottom of a page, or so that the page does not end with a widow.

bounding box In some applications, a box enclosing an item.

bowl The curved part of a type character that encloses the counter.

box In some applications, a frame into which text or pictures can be inserted.

box feature/story Information in a book or publication presented separately from the running text and illustrations and either surrounded by a box rule or underlaid with a tint patch. Also called a "sidebar."

boxhead In a table arranged in columns, the heading to each column appearing under the main heading.

box rule A rule or border surrounding an item of type or other graphic matter.

bpi *abb:* bits per inch → bit density.

bracketed type Type in which the serif is joined to the main stem in an unbroken curve.

breve A mark indicating pronunciation of a short vowel (˘).

bridge The most basic hardware and software connection between similar computer networks, from one AppleTalk network to another. → gateway; network.

brightness → HSB.
brightness control A control wheel (and in some cases, a control panel device) on most monitors that enables you to adjust its screen brightness.

bromide (1) A photographic print on paper coated with light-sensitive silver bromide emulsion. (2) General term for high-quality output from an imagesetter, made on photographic paper rather than film.

buffer Refers to an area of memory – either in RAM, on a separate cache, or on a hard disk – set aside to undertake a task when required. Buffers are commonly used in output devices to speed up that activity and to free the computer for use → print spooler.

bug A software program error, made at the time of its creation, which causes the program to behave erratically or incorrectly. Buggy software is not so much a mistake as the result of the complexities of programs being so great that it is virtually impossible to test every possible sequence of

commands likely to occur.

bullet A large dot used to precede listed items, separate items of text, or add emphasis to particular parts of a text. It is available in most fonts by keying Option-8.

bulletin board (BBS) A facility for sharing information by using a telephone link from your computer, via a modem, to another computer dedicated to serving that purpose.

bull's eye → hickie.

bundle (**1** *pap.*) Two reams of paper (1,000 sheets). (**2**) A resource used to associate file references and icon lists for the Finder.

bureau → service bureau.

burnout *(rep.)* The masking of copy being exposed in a reproduction process, to make space for new insertions.

bus A series of wires or paths along which information is shared within a computer or between one device and another. → Apple Desktop Bus, NuBus, SE Bus.

button (**1**) In dialog boxes, any control you can click which allows you to designate, confirm, or cancel an action. A default button is one which is activated by the "return" or "enter" key on your keyboard and is generally identified in dialog boxes by a heavy border. (**2**) The mouse button on top of your mouse which you use for clicking.

by Color (View menu, *Sys.6*) The command which, on color monitors, lets you view the contents of a directory window according to the color you have given it using the "Color" menu (the order of colors is the same).

by Date (View menu) The command which lets you view the contents of a directory window according to the date on which it was created, with the most recent heading the list.

by Icon (View menu) The command which lets you view the contents of a directory window with full-size icons.

by Kind (View menu) The command which lets you view the contents of a directory window according to

whether it is a document, folder, or application.

by Label (View menu) The command which lets you view the contents of a directory window according to an assigned name and/or color which can be changed in the Labels control panel.

by Name (View menu) The command which lets you view the contents of a directory window according to document names, alphabetically. If you want a specific document to head the list, just add a space before its name.

by Small Icon (View menu) The command which lets you view the contents of a directory window with icons of smaller sizes than normal.

by Version (View menu) The command which lets you view the contents of a directory window according to the version number of any applications contained within it.

byte A unit of information made up of eight bits (0s and 1s), which can represent any value between 0 and 255 (256 is the total number of possible configurations of eight 0s and 1s). One byte is required to make up a single text character. *14–16*

C

© The mark agreed by the Universal Copyright Convention to signify, when accompanied by the date of publication and copyright owner's name, that an item is protected by international copyright laws. → copyright; Universal Copyright Convention.

c *abb:* → cyan.

C/C++ Programming language commonly used, like Pascal, for compiling Mac applications.

CAD *abb:* computer-aided design. A term describing any design that is carried out with the aid of a computer.

CAD/CAM *abb:* computer-aided design and manufacturing, where computers are used to control, in many cases, the entire production process from design to manufacture. *65, 78*

CADD *abb:* computer-aided drafting and design. → CAD.

CAG *abb:* computer-aided graphics, as in graphic design.

Calculator A desk accessory (● menu) that looks and works like a pocket calculator, operated by using your mouse or the keypad. Calculations can be pasted into a document via the Edit menu.

callout A piece of explanatory text, separated from the main body and linked, usually by a leader line, to an illustration.

CAM *abb:* computer-aided manufacture. Usually used in the context of CAD/CAM and rarely seen as an abbreviation on its own. → CAD/CAM.

cameo A term for typefaces in which the characters are reversed to show white on a dark ground.

camera-ready art(work) Copy or any material that is ready for photographic reproduction. Also called "mechanicals." → paste-up.

camera-ready paste-up → paste-up.

cancel/abort A button, present in most dialog boxes, giving you the option to cancel the command which generated the box.

Canvas *(app.)* 61

cap, capital The term for an upper-case letter, deriving from the style of inscription at the head, or capital, of a Roman column.

cap height The height of a capital letter measured from its baseline.

cap line An imaginary horizontal line running across the tops of capital letters.

caps and smalls *(typ.)* Type consisting of capitals for initials and small caps in place of lower-case letters.

caps lock A modifier key that allows all letters (and only letters — numbers, punctuation marks, and symbols are not affected) to be typed to appear as capitals.

caption Strictly speaking, the descriptive matter printed as a headline above an illustration, also called a "cutline," but more generally used to refer to information printed underneath or beside a picture.

card → board.

caret, caret mark Symbol

used in preparing copy and proof correction to indicate an insertion.

carry forward/over → jump; take over.

cartridge, removable hard disk Hard disks that come in cartridge form to make them ejectable from their media, thus making it easier to transport large amounts of data than a floppy disk will permit.

case (**1** *fin.*) The stiff cover of a book, consisting of two boards, a hollow and a binding material. (**2** *typ.*) A box with separate compartments in which pieces of type are kept. This is the origin of the terms "upper-case" and "lower-case," referring to the areas of each case reserved for capital and small letters.

casting off → copyfitting (**1**).

catchline The temporary heading for identification at the top of a galley proof.

cathode ray tube (CRT) Vacuum tube producing information display electrostatically, the standard video display device.

CCD *abb:* charge-coupled device, a means of translating light into data in a scanner or non-tube video system. *43*

CCITT *abb:* Consultative Committee on International Telephony and Telegraphy, a data compression standard.

CD *abb:* compact disk → optical disk.

CD-I (*abb:* compact disk - interactive) A multimedia standard allowing you to store sound and video on the same CD.

CD-ROM *abb:* compact disk read-only memory. Non-erasable storage systems of huge capacity – around 650MB, which is enough space for a type foundry's entire font library. CD-ROMs are similar to audio CDs, but come in cartridges. *39, 98*

CD-ROM-XA (extended architecture) A CD-ROM which runs the CD at high speed, thus enabling the use of real-time video sequences. A CD-ROM-XA drive will read both CD-ROM and CD-I disks.

cdev *abb:* → control panel device.

central processing unit (CPU) Generally used to mean the central computer, built around a CPU chip (itself sometimes referred to as the CPU), that performs the computer's calculating functions and to which other devices are connected. *29*

center-aligned → centered.

centered Description of type which is placed in the center of a sheet or type measure, with both the left and right edges of text being ragged.

CGI *abb:* computer-generated image.

chalking (*pri.*) A printing fault caused by ink soaking into the paper and leaving pigment deposited on the surface.

chancery italic A 13th-century style of handwriting on which italic type designs were based.

Chapman/Bounford & Associates, *case study 113*

character An individual letter, figure, punctuation mark, or sign, including, on your Mac, such invisible characters as "space," "return," and "tab."

character assembly (*typ.*) An alternative term for typesetting, especially in reproduction methods not using metal type.

character attribute The complete specification of a character, including font, size, color, style, scale, kern, etc.

character generator A system of hardware or software that provides code for a computer font.

character set The complete repertoire of letters, figures, and other symbols in a font.

character space The distance between characters, based on the values allocated by the font designer. → kerning; letterspace/fit; tracking.

character width → data bits.

charge-coupled device → CCD.

checkbox A square box in dialog boxes that, when clicked on, shows an x, indicating that an option is enabled. When the box is empty, the option is disabled.

Chicago The bitmapped font specially designed for the Mac which appears in dialog boxes and menus. Like Geneva, it is built into your Mac's ROM, so you can't delete it.

chip A small piece of silicon impregnated with miniaturized computer circuits. Chips comprise the basis of computer functions in the form of CPUs or memory chips.

chip family An evolving series of related chips, usually produced by the same manufacturer.

choke A method of altering the thickness of a letter or solid shape by overexposure in processing or by means of a built-in option in some Mac applications.

choose To select a menu entry by clicking on its menu title and dragging the pointer to the desired entry before releasing the mouse button.

Chooser A desk accessory (● menu) supplied by Apple that enables you to choose between printers or other network devices by displaying icons of their drivers. The Chooser also allows you to turn background printing on or off.

Chooser documents Files in your system folder that represent devices found as icons in the Chooser. These are known as device resource files.

chroma The intensity or purity of a color.

Cibachrome (*pho.*) An Agfa process for obtaining photographic color prints direct from transparencies.

cicero A unit of the European Didot system of measurement for measuring the width, or measure, of a line of type and the depth of the page. One cicero = 4.511mm (³⁄₁₆in.) or 12 didot points. → pica. *86*

circuit board → board.

circular screen (rep.) A photomechanical screen that can be adjusted to prevent moiré patterns in color reproduction.

circumflex → accent.

clean proof (*typ./pri.*) A typesetter's or printer's proof which is free from correction marks.

Clean Up (Special menu)

Available only if you have selected view By Small Icon or By Icon (View menu), this command tidies up icons to the nearest available space on your (invisible) desktop grid.

Clear (Edit menu) A command that removes selected items without copying them to the clipboard, thus leaving the contents of the clipboard intact.

Clear key A key on Apple keyboards that duplicates the function of the Delete key, although, in certain applications, such as some spreadsheets, it may have a specific purpose. → Delete key.

CLI *abb:* → command line interface.

click, clicking (on/off) To press and immediately release the mouse button when the pointer is appropriately positioned, for instance, to select an icon. To "click and drag" is to position the pointer as desired and then click and hold down the mouse button while moving the pointer; for instance, to move an item.

client-server A network system in which data is accessed by "clients" from a central computer, or "server," rather than peer-to-peer in which there is no central server.

clip art Libraries of copyright-free illustrative or design material, of widely varying quality, available either in book form or in various file formats on computer disk.

Clipboard The file used by the Scrap Manager and applications for holding the last item that you cut or copied. Such items can subsequently be pasted into an appropriate place or document. Each process of cutting or copying deletes the previous item from the Clipboard. → Show Clipboard.

clipping Limiting a drawing to within the boundary of a particular area.

clipping path In some drawing applications, a closed path into which an element can be pasted as a fill.

clock speed/rate The num-ber of instructions per second, regulated by the pulses of a quartz crystal, that can be processed by your Mac's central processing unit. The pulse frequency is measured in megahertz (millions of cycles per second) – the more megahertz, the faster the clock speed. Clock speed determines such things as the speed of screen redraw and RAM or disk access.

clone A machine made by one manufacturer that imitates the operation of, and is sometimes compatible with, another made by a different manufacturer.

Close (File menu) A command that closes the active window. If it is a document window, you may be asked whether you want to save any changes. The Close command performs the identical function to the close box.

close box The small box at the top left, in the title bar, of a directory or document window which, when clicked, closes the active window. Also called go-away box. Holding down the Option key while clicking the box closes all windows on the desktop.

close up An instruction to delete a space to bring characters closer together.

closed file A file to which you cannot gain access and which thus cannot be read from or written to.

cloverleaf/pretzel/propeller symbol The symbol used to identify the command key.

club line A short line ending a paragraph, which should not appear at the top of a page or column. → orphan; widow.

CMC7 A character set used in magnetic ink character recognition.

CMY *abb:* cyan, magenta, and yellow. Color model based on the subtractive color theory that is used, in some applications, to produce spot colors which have been mixed from these colors.

CMYK Acronym for the process colors of cyan, magenta, yellow, and black inks used in four-color printing.

Coated paper *(pap.)* A gen-eral term for art, chromo, and enamel papers or similar groups, in which the surface has a mineral coating applied after the body paper is made. It is also known as surface paper.

cocked-up initial → raised cap(ital).

cock-up figure/letter → superior figure/letter.

code The instructions in a program, written by a programmer, that make the program work. The efficacy of a program depends upon how well written its code is.

codet → color control bar.

cold boot Turning on or restarting your Mac with the power switch. A warm boot is preferable. → warm boot.

collate *(fin.)* To put the sections or pages of a book or loose-leaf publication in their correct order.

ColorStudio *(app.) 65, 68–9*

Color (menu) *(Sys 6)* A pull-down menu of colors (only available on color monitors) that enables you to attribute colors to icons in the Finder by selecting an icon and then choosing a color from the menu. This enables you to organize items on your desktop by choosing By Color from the View menu – this sorts colored icons in the same order as the colors in the color menu.

color *(typ.)* The apparent light or heavy appearance of a particular typeface.

color bar → color control bar.

color black → black.

color break *(pri.)* The edge between two areas of color in an image.

color control bar/codet *(rep./pri.)* The standard set of marginal strips placed on each of the four pieces of film used in making the plates for color printing. When printed, they superimpose to form a colored bar in various densities which enables the platemaker and printer to check by eye or instrument the nature of each ink film, the strength and evenness of ink, and the registration of colors.

color correction The adjustment of the color values of an illustration either (**1** *pho.*) by the original photographer using color

balancing filters, or (**2** *rep.*) by adjusting the color scanner to produce the correct result. Subsequently, corrections can be made on the color separated films or on a computer by means of an image-manipulation application. *134–5*

color filters Thin sheets of colored glass, plastic, or gelatin (**1** *pho.*) placed over a camera lens to modify the light entering the camera, or (**2** *rep.*) used in color separation, color correction, or for special effects.

color library A text-only document containing predefined colors that can be imported into some graphics applications.

color model In graphics applications, the manner in which colors can be defined or modified. The most common color models are RGB (red, green, and blue); HSB (hue, saturation, and brightness); or HLS (hue, lightness, and saturation); CMY; CMYK (process colors); and PANTONE (spot colors).

color monitors *33–5*

color palette In graphics applications, the menu (usually tear-off) that contains the colors available for use within that application.

color picker (1) The Control Panel device that allows you, if you have a color monitor, to select colors for your display from a color "wheel." (**2**) A sample book of carefully defined and graded colors from which you can select spot colors and which a printer can use to achieve fidelity.

color positives (*rep.*) A set of positive color separations.

color printers *42*

color rotation/sequence (*pri.*) The order in which the four-color process inks are printed.

color scanner → scanner

color separation (*rep.*) In color reproduction, the process of separating the colors of an image, by means of a scanner or process camera, into a form suitable for printing. *125*

color seps/separations (*rep.*) A collection of images (subjects) that have been, or will be, separated in the color separation process.

color sequence → color rotation.

color swatch A sample of color, usually selected from a color picker, and used as a guide for the reproduction of spot colors.

color temperature (*pho.*) The term describing the color composition of a light source in photography – measured in degrees Kelvin, a system based on a supposed absolute darkness rising to incandescence.

color transparency/ tranny (*pho.*) A photographic image produced on transparent film as a color positive.

color trapping → trapping.

color value The tonal value of a color, as distinct from a light-to-dark scale of pure grays.

color wheel → color picker.

column (1) A section of a vertically divided page, containing text or other matter. (**2**) A vertical section in tabulated work.

column grid → grid.

column inch/centimeter A measure of space used to define text areas or advertising matter in a newspaper or periodical.

column rule A light-faced rule used to separate columns in a newspaper.

combination line and halftone (*rep.*) Halftone and line work combined onto one set of films, plates, or artwork.

command An item, usually in a menu or dialog box, that describes an action for your computer to perform next. A command which is inactive, and thus cannot be selected, appears dimmed, or gray.

command key A keyboard modifier key which, when used in conjunction with another key, provides a shortcut to menu commands or, in some applications, a method of canceling an operation in progress, such as printing. The command key is identified by a "propeller" symbol or, on Apple keyboards, the Apple logo, or both. → command.

command line interface A user interface in which instructions are given by

means of a line of (usually) keyboard commands. The opposite of GUI.

commercial color The term describing color separations produced by desktop scanners as distinct from high-resolution repro scanners.

comp (1) *abb:* → compositor (**2**) *abb:* comprehensive, a mock-up showing how a finished design or publication will look.

compact disk → optical disk

compact Mac A Macintosh computer with the monitor built into the casing, such as the Macintosh Classic and SE/30.

compatibility, *in modems 47*

compiler Software used in programming that converts high-level program code into machine language. A compiler converts a program in its entirety, as distinct from an interpreter which converts a program a piece at a time.

compose (*typ.*) To set type by any method.

composite artwork Artwork that combines a number of different elements.

composition size (*typ.*) Term used to describe any type up to a size of 14 points, these being the sizes that, traditionally (in hot metal), could be set on a compositing machine.

compositor (*typ.*) The person who sets type, originally by hand, but now by any method.

comprehensive → comp.

compression, *of files 79, 132*

Compugraphic *131*

computer A device or machine capable of processing information, expressed in logical terms, according to a predetermined set of instructions.

computer, *choice 105, 106–7*

computer aided design → CAD.

computer aided design and manufacture → CAD/CAM.

computer input device → input device.

computer languages Coding systems developed

to deal with specific types of communication with computers.

computer output device → output device.

condensed type A typeface with an elongated, narrow appearance.; a condensed font that will have been specifically designed so that the anomalies of optical condensing (→ horizontal scaling) are eliminated.

configuration, → set-up

connectivity *30, 32*

constrain In some applications, the facility to contain one or more items within another item; e.g., a text or picture box within another text or picture box.

constrained item An item that is contained within another.

constraining box An item that has others constrained within it.

contact screen *(rep.)* A halftone screen made on a film base which has a graded dot pattern. In conventional reproduction, it is used in direct contact with a film or plate to obtain a halftone negative from a continuous tone original. → halftone screen.

contiguous Adjoining, next in order. Thus, of memory and storage, contiguous space is that which is not broken up into chunks of data such as programs and files. → fragmented.

continuous tone, contone *(rep.)* An original illustration which contains continuous shades between the lightest and darkest tones without being broken up by the dots of a halftone screen or reduced to a single shade as in a line illustration.

control character A character produced by use of the control key and another character to issue a command. → keyboard equivalent.

control key The key on Apple ADB keyboards that is used by some applications as a modifier key to provide keyboard equivalents.

controlling dimension The width or height of an image taken as the basis for its enlargement or reduction.

Control Panels A folder located in the system folder

(and represented in the Apple menu) where you can access programs that allow you to set up your Mac in the way that you want it (speaker volume, mouse tracking, etc.) and to access other, third-party control panel devices.

control panel device (cdev) A utility program which, when dragged to your system folder, is repositioned in the Control Panels folder, which can be accessed via the Apple menu.

control point In some drawing and graphics applications, a point in a line or path by which you can control its shape or characteristics. → Bézier curves; handles.

controls The term describing buttons, checkboxes, scroll bars, etc., that appear in windows, dialog boxes, and palettes.

coprocessor A microprocessor chip that assists the central processing unit with data-intensive or specific activities, such as large databases or graphics tasks. Also called a floating-point unit (FPU). *27*

copy (**1**) Manuscript, typescript, transparency, artwork, or computer disk from which a printed image is to be prepared. (**2**) To make an exact duplicate of a file or document or of anything within it. Your Mac automatically places the copied item in the Clipboard, from where it can be pasted in the same or any other place. Copy is accessed via the Edit menu or Command-C. → cut and paste.

copyfitting (**1**) Calculating the amount of space typeset copy will fill when set in a specific font, size, and measure. (**2**) Forcing typeset copy to fit within a given area by modifying it; i.e., cutting or adding words, increasing or decreasing character space, horizontal scaling, etc.

copy-protected Description of software that has been produced in such a way as to prevent its unauthorized duplication or use.

copyright The right of the creator of an original work to control the use of that work.

While broadly controlled by international agreement (→ Universal Copyright Convention), there are substantial differences between countries, particularly regarding the period for which a work is protected by copyright. In the U.S. copyright of an intellectual property is generally established by registration, whereas in the U.K. it exists automatically by virtue of the creation of an original work. Ownership of copyright does not necessarily mean ownership of the actual work (or vice versa), nor does it necessarily cover rights to that work throughout the world (the rights to a work can be held territory by territory). *54, 75*

copywriting A term applied to the writing of copy specifically for use in advertising and promotional material.

corner marks Marks on original artwork, film, or a printed sheet acting as cut/trim/crop marks during finishing or register marks during printing.

corner radius The roundness of the corners of a round-cornered rectangle expressed in the currently defined unit of measurement.

corporate identity/house-style The elements of design by which any organization establishes an appropriate, consistent, and recognizable identity through communication, promotion, and distribution material. → letterhead; logotype.

correcting text *118*

cosmetics A term occasionally used to describe the general appearance of a computer-generated image; e.g., sharpness, tonal contrast, etc.

counter The enclosed or partially enclosed area of a type character; e.g., the center of an "o" or the space between the vertical strokes of an "n."

cover *(fin.)* The outer layer of paper, board, cloth, or leather to which the body of a book is secured by any binding method.

cpi *abb:* characters per inch. In copyfitting, the number of type characters per inch.

cpl *abb:* characters per line. In copyfitting, the number of type characters per line.

CPS *abb:* characters per second, referring to the output speed of a computer printer or imagesetter.

CPU *abb:* → central processing unit.

CPU chip A silicon microprocessor that is the brain of your computer. It determines the speed of your computer and what software can be run, as well as performing the main information processing tasks.

crash (1) → bomb. **(2)** A more-or-less serious breakdown of an electronic system caused by the failure of a component or by a reading head damaging the surface of a disk.

Creator A field in a file containing a four-letter code (signature) that identifies the application that created the file. Creator signatures are registered with Apple Computer so that each is unique.

credit/courtesy line A line of text accompanying an illustration giving the name of an individual or organization which supplied it.

crop To trim or mask an illustration so that it fits a given area or to discard unwanted portions.

crop marks → corner marks.

Crosfield Studio System *135*

crossbar/crosshair pointer In some applications, a cross-shaped cursor (+) that, when you click on an appropriate tool, indicates that a certain drawing or selection function is activated. → pointer.

cross-head(ing) Subsection, paragraph heading, or numeral printed in the body of text, usually marking the first subdivision of a chapter.

crossline screen → halftone screen.

cross-section View of an object showing it "cut through" to expose its internal characteristics.

CRT → cathode ray tube.

c/t *abb:* → color transparency.

current startup disk The disk containing the system folder that your Mac is currently using. The icon for the startup disk always appears in the top right-hand corner of the Finder.

cursor → pointer.

Cut *(Edit menu, Command-X)* The command that removes a selected item from a document and places it on the Clipboard. → Clipboard.

cut and paste The action of removing an item from a document and then, via the Clipboard, pasting it elsewhere in the same, or another, document.

cut dummy *(rep.)* Cut proofs of illustrations used in sequence as a guide to the make up of pages.

cut-line → caption.

cut-marks → corner marks.

cutout (1 *rep.)* An illustration from which the background has been removed to provide a silhouetted image. **(2** *fin.)* A display card or book cover from which a pattern has been cut by means of a steel die.

cyan *(C)* The special shade of blue that is one of the four process colors used in four-color printing, sometimes called process blue.

cylinder The total number of disk tracks that can be accessed from a single position of the drive's read/write heads. A cylinder is two tracks of a double-sided floppy disk, and four or more tracks of a hard disk. → platter.

D

DA *abb:* → desk accessory.

DA Handler *(Sys.6)* A System file which enables desk accessories to run normally under MultiFinder.

DA suitcase → suitcase.

daisy-chain (network)/daisy-chaining The linking, in sequence, of several peripheral devices to your Mac. Depending on the type of device, daisy-chains may be made to your Mac's ADB or SCSI ports.

dash A punctuation mark usually known as an em dash/rule (—) or en dash/rule (–), as distinct from a hyphen (-). → em; en; hyphen.

data Any information, but in computing usually used to mean information processed by a program.

data bank Any place or computer where large amounts of data are stored for ready access.

database Virtually any information stored on a computer in a systematic fashion and thus retrievable.

data bits Communications bits that contain data, as distinct from the bits that contain instructions. Sometimes called character width. → bit.

data bus The path along which data is transmitted. The wider the bus, measured in bits, the more data that can be transmitted simultaneously.

data compression → file compression.

data file → document.

data fork The part of a Macintosh file that comprises data; that is, the digitized code for the text and graphics generated by you, as distinct from the resource fork, which contains information relating to an application.

data interchange format → DIF.

data processing The processing of information by means of a computer or other mechanical or electrical device.

data transfer rate The speed at which data is transferred from a disk drive into RAM after it has been read.

Date setting → Alarm Clock.

datum The singular of data, although data is now commonly accepted as a singular noun in computer usage.

daughter board Sometimes used to describe a circuit board that connects to a motherboard. → board.

DaynaFile *117*

DCA *abb:* document content architecture, a file format for transferring partially-formatted text documents.

DCS *abb:* desktop color separation. → color separation; commercial color.

deadline The final date set for the completion of a job.

dead matter Any leftover matter that is not used in camera-ready art or page makeup.

debug To hunt out and correct errors in software pro-

grams. → bug.

decimal tab In word-processing and page make-up applications, the facility to align decimal numbers along their decimal points.

decryption The process of removing the protection afforded to a document by encryption. The same software must be used to decrypt a document as was used to encrypt it.
→ encryption.

dedicated A system or equipment with a unique function that can be used only for that purpose and is not otherwise adaptable, such as a dedicated word processor.

deep-etch halftone *(rep.)* A halftone image from which unwanted screen dots have been removed, so that areas of plain paper will be left on the printed sheet.

deep-etching *(pri.)* The etching of long-run lithographic printing plates to reduce the printing areas of the plate to slightly below the surface.

default The settings of a program in the absence of user-specified settings; in other words, the settings it came with until you change them, e.g., the settings in the Control Panel. → preferences; preset defaults.

default button → button.

default settings → default.

defragment The process of eliminating small blocks of space on a hard disk by rearranging files that have become fragmented, so that they are stored contiguously.
→ fragmented.

Delete key The key that, in text, moves the insertion pointer back one character, deleting it in the process, or removes a current selection. Items deleted by the Delete key are not placed on the Clipboard. On some Mac keyboards the Delete key is called the Backspace key.

delimit To indicate the end (limit) of a line or to separate one field or record from another by using a specially defined character. The standard characters for some Mac databases are the Tab key to delimit fields and the Return key to delimit records.

densitometer An electronic precision instrument used to measure density and other properties of color and light in transparencies, film, reflection copy, or computer monitors.

density (1) The amount and compactness of type set within a given area or page. (**2** *pho./rep./pri.*) The weight of tone or color in any image. A printed highlight can be no lighter in color than the surface it is printed on, while the shadow can be no darker than the quality and volume of ink the printing process will permit.

descender The part of a lower-case letter that falls below the baseline of the x-height as in g, q, and p.

deselect To deactivate highlighted text or an active item, usually by clicking your mouse. → activate.

designers, *as typesetters* 124–5

design process 108, 114–23

DesignStudio *(app.)* 55, 58

desk accessory (DA) A utility program for system enhancement generally found under the Apple menu, i.e. Alarm Clock, Scrapbook, etc. In System 6 or earlier versions of the System software, DAs are installed either by using the Apple-supplied Font/DA Mover application (this permits only 15 DAs to be installed), or by using applications such as Suitcase II and MasterJuggler. DA files are identified by their icon of a suitcase with a grid pattern on the side (as distinct from screen font file icons which have a letter A on the side of the suitcase). For use with System 7, the desk accessory application must be removed from its suitcase and dragged to the Apple Menu Items folder in the System Folder (if you want it to appear under the Apple menu). → suitcase.

desktop The name given to the environment in which you work on screen. *16, 20*

Desktop file The invisible file created by the Finder to record information about the files and folders on your disk. Each disk you use has its own Desktop file.

desktop publishing (DTP) A term coined at the advent of the Macintosh, before the potential of the machine in the professional design and reproduction industries was fully realized. Used to describe the activity of generating text, page layout, and graphics on a computer and then printing, or publishing, the result.

device Short form referring to any peripheral device.

device resource file
→ Chooser documents.

diacritical mark A mark indicating the particular value or pronunciation of a character. → accent.

dialog box A box that appears on your screen, usually in response to a command from you, requesting information or approval in order to execute an action. Unprompted dialog boxes (often requiring no more from you than to click "OK") are more often called "message" or "alert" boxes. Boxes in which you open or save documents are called Standard File dialog boxes.

diapositive *(pho.)* A photographic transparency in which the image is positive.

diazo(type) *(rep.)* abb: diazonium. A method of printing from a transparent or translucent original onto paper, cloth or film. The print may be blue (called blues/blueprints), brown (browns/Vandykes), or black. Also known as Ozalids and dyelines, diazos are widely used in preprint stages for checking imposed film as well as by architectural and engineering draftsmen.

dictionary The file, in word-processing applications, that enables you to check words and documents for spelling.

didot point The European unit for type measurement, being 0.38mm (0.0148in) compared to 0.35mm (0.013837in) of the Anglo-American point.

DIF abb: data interchange format, a file format for transferring (without text formating) database and spreadsheet data. *128*

differential spacing The spacing of each character of type according to its individual width.

digit Any numeral (0 to 9).

Digital Darkroom (app.) 65, 68

digital typesetting 90

digitize To convert anything, such as an image or a sound, into a form that can be electronically processed, stored, and reconstructed.

digitizer A peripheral device such as a tablet or camera that digitizes signals so that your computer can understand them.

digitizing fonts 98

digitizing/graphics pad/ tablet An input device that allows you to draw or write using a pen-like instrument as if you are working on paper. 49, 64

dimmed command In menus and dialog boxes, if a command is gray, rather than black, it is said to be dimmed and unavailable for use, or disabled.

dimmed icon A dimmed icon indicates that a file or folder is open or that a disk has been ejected.

DIN abb: Deutsche Industrie-Norm. The code of standards established in Germany and widely used throughout the world to standardize such things as the size, weight, or speed-rating of certain materials and manufactured items that depend on universal compatibility.

DIN-8 The 8-pin modem and printer port connection on your Mac.

dingbat A decorative font, the modern form of decorations traditionally called printer's flowers, ornaments, and arabesques.

DIP abb: dual in-line package. The way in which some chips, such as memory chips, are mounted so that they can be plugged into your Mac.

DIP SIMM A high-profile SIMM.

Direct Slot The expansion slot of the Mac SE/30, incompatible with any other Mac slot. → expansion slot. 32

directional The term used to describe a word such as "left," "right," "above," and "below," used in a caption to direct the reader to a relevant picture or item.

directory An invisible catalog of information about all the files on a disk. The volume directory contains general information, whereas the file directory logs specific information such as where the files are stored on the disk.

directory dialog box → Standard File dialog box.

directory window The window that displays the contents of a disk or folder.

disabled The condition of an item in a menu or dialog box that is not available for selection, thus it appears dimmed. → dimmed command; dimmed icon.

discretionary hyphen character In some applications, a manually inserted character that indicates a word break.

Disinfectant (util.) 79

disk A circular platter coated with a magnetic medium (unless it is an optical disk) on which computer data is stored. Disks may be rigid (hard) or flexible (floppy) and may be permanently installed in your computer, in a peripheral device, or in removable cases. Floppy disks for the Mac are typically 3½in. diameter and may be single-sided (400K capacity, and you probably will not come across any), double-sided (800K), or high density (1.4MB). Single- and double-sided floppy disks can be used in any Mac floppy drive, whereas high-density floppies can only be used in high-density drives (called SuperDrives). Floppy disks are also called diskettes. The capacity of hard disks ranges from around 10MB to 300MB (and rising – capacity is now being discussed in terms of gigabytes). Hard disks also come in a variety of removable cartridges with around 40-80MB capacity. 37–9

disk buffer An area in RAM, similar to a RAM cache, where frequently used information from a disk can be stored temporarily. → RAM cache.

disk controller Hardware that converts signals from a bus into instructions usable by a disk drive.

disk directory → directory.

DiskDoubler (util.) 79, 132

disk drive The hardware that reads data to and from disks. → disk; floppy disk drive; hard disk drive.

disk drive head → read/ write head.

disk drive port A port, on some Macs, used to attach external floppy disk drives.

Disk Driver The disk controller for 3½in. (90mm) floppy disks.

diskette → disk.

disk fragmentation 138

disk icon An icon that indicates the presence of a disk on your Mac. The startup disk icon is always positioned in the top right-hand corner of your screen and subsequent disk icons appear vertically beneath that, in the order in which they mount. → icon.

disk optimizers 79

disk recovery 79

disk window → root directory.

display → monitor.

display matter/type Larger typefaces used for headings, etc., as distinct from the smaller types used for text and captions.

dithering A technique used by some input and output devices to simulate grays by varying the pattern and proximity of black pixels to each other.

ditto mark A symbol (″) indicating repetition of the text matter directly above.

dock To connect one stand-alone computer to another, such as connecting a laptop to your Mac.

document Any file that you create or modify with an application on your Mac, such as a page layout or simply a letter. The document file is created on your disk when you enter text or draw a line and then save it (when you save a document for the first time, a dialog box will appear, asking you to name the document and indicate where you want to put it). 22

document content architecture → DCA.

document window The window that an application opens to display a document created, or about to be created, with that application.

DOS abb: disk operating systems. → MS-DOS.

dot (**1** *rep.*) The smallest basic element of a halftone. (**2**) Alternative term for a pixel.

dot area (*rep.*) The pattern of a halftone; that is, both the dots and the spaces in between.

dot etching (*rep.*) The process of reducing the size of halftone dots on negative or positive film, using chemicals, in order to modify the tonal values of a halftone image.

dot for dot (**1** *pri.*) Printing color work in perfect register. (**2** *rep.*) A method of producing printing film by photographing a previously screened halftone image. Generally, on fine-screened images, a maximum limit of 10 percent enlargement or reduction is desirable.

dot gain (*rep./pri.*) An aberration occuring during the reproduction chain from original to printed image, caused by the tendency of halftone dots to grow in size. This often leads to inaccurate results, but if the dot-gain characteristics of a particular printing press are known, compensation can be made during reproduction.

dot loss (*rep./pri.*) The devaluation or disappearance of a halftone dot on a printing plate, the opposite of dot gain.

dot-matrix printer A crude, but usually cheap, printer that uses a grid of pins to create characters, with hammers hitting the correct combination of pins for each letter.

dots per inch (dpi) The unit of measurement that represents the resolution of a device such as a printer, imagesetter, or monitor. The closer the dots are together (the more dots per inch) the better the quality. Typical resolutions are 72dpi for a monitor, 300dpi for a LaserWriter, and 2450dpi (or much more) for an imagesetter.

dot pitch The distance between the dots, or pixels, in your monitor, measured in dots per inch (dpi).

double burn/print down (*rep.*) To use two or more negatives to expose an image onto a sensitized

plate – often one for line work and a second for halftones.

double-click Clicking of the mouse button twice in rapid succession while the pointer is positioned in an appropriate place. Double-clicking is a short-cut to performing functions such as opening documents or highlighting words in text.

double print down → double burn.

double-sided floppy disk → disk.

double spread/page spread → spread.

double truck → spread.

download To transfer data from a remote computer to your own. Opposite of upload.

downloadable font A font that must be loaded into the RAM of your printer, as distinct from a font that is resident in its ROM.

dpi *abb:* → dots per inch.

dpsi/dpi² *abb:* dots per square inch.

drag To carry out an action by holding down the mouse button while you move the pointer, then release the mouse button to complete the action. You use dragging to perform such tasks as selecting and moving items, selecting pull-down menu commands, selecting text, and, in some applications, creating items with an appropriate tool selected,.

DRAM *abb:* dynamic random access memory (pron. dee-ram) → dynamic RAM.

draw(ing) application/ program Drawing applications can be defined as those which are object-oriented (they mathematically define lines and shapes), as distinct from painting applications which use bitmaps. → object-oriented; bitmapped. *59–64*

Drive In appropriate dialog boxes, a button which allows you to select a different volume to the one identified in the dialog box. Sometimes, clicking on the disk on volume name will achieve the same result.

drive → disk drive.

driver An item of software that tells your Mac how to handle or operate a piece of hardware, such as a printer.

Drivers are located in your system folder.

drive head → read/write head.

driving out Arranging the spaces in a line of type to fill the measure.

drop (**1**) A gap, usually at the top of a page or column, before the printed image starts. (**2**) Of text, the number of lines in a column permitted by the page grid.

drop cap *abb:* drop capital. A large, sometimes decorative, initial at the beginning of a text or paragraph that drops into the lines of type beneath.

drop folios Numbers printed at the bottom of each page, generally referred to simply as folios.

drop letter → drop cap.

dropout (**1** *rep.*) During reproduction, to use filters or other means to prevent an item from appearing on final negative or positive film. (**2**) → reverse onto.

dropout blue/color Pencil or other marker, used to write instructions on artwork, which makes a mark that does not reproduce.

dropped initial → drop cap.

dropped-out halftone (*rep.*) Areas removed from a halftone negative, positive or plate by masking.

dropped-out type Type that is reversed out of its background. → reverse out.

dropping-out The repro house term for the replacement of a low-resolution scan by a high-resolution scan, prior to final output.

drop-shadow An area of tone forming a shadow behind an image or character, designed to bring the image or character forward.

drop tone → line conversion.

DTP *abb:* → desktop publishing.

dummy (**1**) The prototype of a proposed book or publication in the correct format, binding, paper, and bulk, but with blank pages. (**2**) A mock-up of a design showing the position of headings, text, captions, illustrations, and other details.

duotone (*rep.*) Technically, two halftones made from the same original to two differ-

ent tonal ranges, so that when printed – in different tones of the same color – a greater tonal range is produced than is possible with a single color. However, the term is generally used, wrongly, to describe a duplex halftone.

dupe abb: duplicate.

duplex Simultaneous, two-way communication over telecommunication lines. → half duplex.

duplex halftone (rep.) Two halftones made from the same original, but printed in two different colors. Generally called a duotone, although this is technically incorrect. → duotone.

Dvorak keyboard An alternative keyboard layout to the familiar and widely-used QWERTY arrangement found on typewriters and Mac keyboards. Essentially, a Dvorak layout is one where the more frequently typed keys are positioned most comfortably in relationship to your dominant typing fingers

dyeline → diazo.

dynamic RAM (DRAM) Memory that is only active while supplied by an electric current, and is therefore lost when power is turned off. The more expensive static RAM does not lose its memory in the absence of power. DRAM chips for the Mac come largely in the form of SIMMs. → RAM; SIMMs.

Dynodex (app.) 78

E

Easy Access A system feature to help people who have difficulty typing with both hands, or manipulating the mouse. "Sticky Keys" allows modifier keys to be used without having to press the keys simultaneously, while "Mouse Keys" enables you to manipulate the pointer by using the numeric keyboard instead of the mouse.

edition (pri.) The whole number of copies of a work printed and published at one time, either as the first edition, or after some change has been made (revised edition, second edition, etc).

Edit menu One of the three standard Mac menus, this

one contains commands for such actions as Cut, Copy, and Paste.

egyptian A collective term for a group of display typefaces with heavy slab serifs and little contrast in the thickness of strokes.

eight-bit The allocation of eight bits of memory to each pixel, giving a screen display of 256 grays or colors (a row of eight bits can be written in 256 different combinations: 0000000, 00000001, 10000001, 00111100, etc). → four-bit color; twenty-four-bit color.

Eject The command found under the File menu when you are in the Finder, or in dialog boxes, that enables you to eject floppy disks or removable hard disk cartridges.

electronic design (ED) Any design activity that takes place with the aid of electronic devices, including computers.

electronic mail → E-mail.

electronic publishing (EP) A term sometimes used as an alternative to desktop publishing.

element In some drawing applications, any object such as a shape, text, or image.

ELF abb: extremely low frequency, referring to the electromagnetic field generated by certain types of electrical current which research has shown to be potentially carcinogenic (cancer-causing), particularly in the event of sustained exposure. Computer monitors emit ELF radiation in greater or lesser quantities, depending on various factors such as the size of the monitor and whether it is mono or color. The sides and back of your monitor emit greater amounts of radiation than the screen. VLF (very low frequency) radiation is also emitted by monitors, but it is easier to filter and considered to be less harmful than ELF. In any event, you should not sit closer than 28in (800mm) from the front of your monitor. → radiation shield.

eligible The term given to a file that can be translated by Apple File Exchange.

ellipse/oval tool In many

graphics applications, a tool for drawing ellipses and circles.

ellipsis (**1**) A sequence of three dots (…) indicating that part of a phrase or sentence has been left out. (**2**) The three dots following a menu command indicating that a dialog box will need to be given additional information before the command can be carried out.

elliptical dot screen (rep.) A halftone screen with an elliptical dot, producing more even changes in the mid-tones of a halftone illustration.

em Traditionally, the area (usually a square) taken up by a capital M, but giving rise to a linear measurement equal to the point size of the type being set, so a 6 point em is 6 points wide. A 12 point em is generally called a pica, or pica em, and measures 4.22mm (0.166ins). Half an em is called an en. → pica.

em dash/rule A dash one em wide, the actual width depending on the size of type being set. → em; dash.

em quad (typ.) Alternative term for an em space, being a square of the type size.

em space A space one em wide, the actual width depending on the size of type being set.

E-mail abb: electronic mail. Communication between computers, either locally through a network, or using modems to transmit over telephone lines, usually via a central computer which stores messages until their recipients are ready to receive them.

Empty folder The name the Finder gives a folder when you select New Folder (File menu). Give it a name as soon as you put something in it.

Empty Trash (Special menu) The command that flushes out the Trash if it has something inside (indicated by a bulging garbage can icon).

emulation The simulation of otherwise incompatible software or hardware in order to make them compatible.

emulsion side (rep.) The matte side of photographic

m which holds the emul-on and which is placed in rect contact with the emul-on of another film or a ate when printing down to uarantee a sharp image.

n A measurement equiva-nt to half the width of an m. → em.

n dash/rule A dash half e width of an em dash.

n quad (typ.) A space half e width of an em quad.

n space A space half an m wide, the actual width epending on the size of ype being set.

ncapsulated PostScript → EPS.

ncryption The scrambling f data to protect a file from nauthorized access.

nd even (typ.) Instruction o end a paragraph or sec-on of copy with a full line.

nd/back matter The final ages of a book, following he main body, such as the ndex. Also called postlims."

nd-of-line decisions The erm used to describe a pro-ram's ability to hyphenate words and justify lines of ext.

nter key On the Mac key-oard, the key that dupli-ates much of the function f the Return key. It confirms n entry or command or may orce a carriage return. In ome applications, it may ave a specific function.

O abb: erasable optical. An ptical disk that can be written to as well as read rom. → optical disk. 39

EP abb: → electronic pub-ishing.

EPS(F) abb: encapsulated PostScript (file), a standard graphics file format based on vectors (information giv-ng both magnitude and direction). → object-oriented; PostScript. 128

erase An option in some dialog boxes to erase the selected volume.

Erase Disk (Special menu) The command to reinitialize or reformat the selected disk on the desktop.

error message A message box that automatically appears when, at its mildest, you have attempted a task that an application won't permit or cannot do, or, at worst, your computer bombs.

→ bomb.

error/result code The num-ber that often accompanies alert and bomb dialog boxes and sad Mac icons to indi-cate the nature of the prob-lem.

Esc key abb: Escape key. Like the Control key, the function of Esc depends on the application you are using, or you can use it as a modifier key.

Ethernet A local area net-work hardware standard that offers fast data transfer.

E13B A type font of numer-als and symbols used in magnetic character recognition.

even smalls Small capitals used without an initial full capital at the beginning of a word.

even working (pri.) A printed work divided into a number of sections of equal size, such as 16, 32, 48 pages.

event The term used to describe any occurrence that the system or an application may need to respond to, such as a mouse click or a disk insertion.

event-driven Description of a program in which actions are based on events gener-ated interactively by the user.

event manager The part of the System (Operating System Event Manager) or Toolbox (Toolbox System Event Manager) that handles hardware-related events such as mouse clicks.

exception dictionary A list of user-defined word breaks that are exceptions to the standard breaks contained within an application's hyphenation dictionary.

exotic A traditional term for a typeface with characters of a language not based on Roman letterforms, e.g., Hebrew.

expanded/extended type A typeface with a flattened, stretched out appearance. An expanded font will have been specifically designed so that the anomalies of optical expansion (→ hori-zontal scaling) are elimi-nated.

expansion card/board A circuit board, attached via your computer's expansion

slot, which allows you to expand the capabilities of your computer (e.g. an accel-erator).

expansion slot The place in your computer where you can add an expansion card. 31, 32

expenditure 26, 108–9

expert system → artificial intelligence.

export The facility provided by some applications to save a file in an appropriate for-mat for use by another application: a text file may be saved as an ASCII file or an illustration as an EPS file.

extension → system extension.

external command/exter-nal function (XCMD/XFCN) Extensions to the scripting language of authoring appli-cations, enabling the pro-gram to perform specialized commands or functions. 75

external device → periph-eral device.

external disk drive Any disk drive that is not internal – inside your Mac – is said to be external.

extremely low frequency → ELF.

F

face Traditionally, the print-ing surface of any type char-acter. It now means a group or family to which any par-ticular type design belongs, as in typeface.

face/fade out blue → drop-out blue.

facsimile → fax.

fadeback → ghosting (1).

false double → spread.

family A group of type fonts with a common design, dis-tinguished from each other only by weight – light, roman, bold, etc. – and their corresponding italic styles.

FatBits A magnification of the screen image that enables you to edit bitmapped graphics pixel by pixel.

fat face A typeface with extreme contrast in the widths of thin and thick strokes.

fat matter A term for copy with a large proportion of spacing. Dense copy is known as lean matter.

fatty (rep.) In conventional reproduction, the name given to the piece of film

placed between the negative (or positive) film and a plate in order to create traps – the slight spread of two adjacent colors to achieve perfect registration. → choke; lap; trapping.

fax *abb:* facsimile transmission. The electronic transmission of copy and artwork from one location to another, using telephone lines. Fax cards (→ board) are available to fit into an expansion slot in your Mac to enable you to send and receive faxes direct, without the need for a separate fax machine.

FDHD *abb:* floppy drive high density → floppy disk drive.

feet/foot margin The white area at the bottom of a page between the image and trimmed area.

field In some applications (mainly databases), a self-contained area into which data is entered and which is generally interactive with another field in the same (or another) record, or the same field in another record.

figure (1) A number, as opposed to a letter. **(2)** An illustration.

figure number The reference number given to an illustration.

file A collection of data to which a name has been given and which is stored on a disk. *19, 22*

file compression The condensing of data within a file so that it is smaller, thus occupying less space on a disk and being quicker to transmit over telecommunication lines. *79, 132*

file creator → Creator.

file directory → directory.

file format The way in which a program saves data. In order to help you work on one job that requires the use of several applications, or to work with other people who may be using different applications to yours, file formats tend to be standardized. *128*

file fragmentation → fragmented.

File menu One of the three standard Mac menus (it appears in the menu bar of virtually every application). The File menu is where you give commands to, among other things, create, open,

save, print and close files, quit applications and eject disks.

filename The name given – or that you give – to a file. Macintosh filenames can be up to 31 characters long, although most dialog boxes show fewer than that. *119, 121*

file partition → partition.

file, *problems 140*

file recovery The act of resurrecting a file after you have deleted it. A deleted file remains on a disk (only its name is erased from the directory) and, until the space it occupies is used by your computer for something else, it can sometimes be recovered. Many utilities are available for recovering deleted files.

file server A computer on a network, with special software so that all the network users can access the applications and documents stored on it.

file sizes *44, 45*

file tag Information relating to data stored within each sector of a disk, designed to enable you to recover deleted files.

file transfer To send a file from one computer to another over telecommunication lines, using a modem.

file type The four-letter code assigned to every Mac file when it is created, to identify its format, i.e., APPL for an application, TEXT for text files, MPNT for MacPaint, and so on.

fill In most graphics applications, the color, tone or pattern applied to the inside of a closed path or shape.

fill character In some applications, the user-defined character that is inserted between specified tab stops.

film assembly/stripping *(rep.)* The process of assembling film negatives or positives in correct positions for the preparation of printing plates.

filmsetting → phototypesetting.

film speed *(pho.)* The rating given to photographic film so that an exposure can be calculated.

filter (1) → import/export filter. **(2)** A feature in many

paint and image-editing applications that enables you to apply predefined (but sometimes editable) visual effects to an image.

final draft Copy ready for typesetting.

final film *(rep.)* The positive or negative used for platemaking, incorporating all corrections and in which the halftones are made with a hard dot.

Finder The program that provides the desktop, file and disk management and the ability to launch applications. The Finder is one of the three basic components of the Mac's operating system (the others are the System file and the ROM chips). → desktop; System; system folder. *16, 18, 52*

Finder desktop → desktop

Finder flags Attributes, such as locked, invisible, busy, etc., for every file on your disk.

Find File (● menu, *Sys.6*) An Apple-supplied desk accessory to enable you to find any file or folder on the selected disk.

fine rule → hairline rule.

fine tuning, *of designs 115–16*

finished artwork → artwork.

finished page area The area on your monitor that will form the page after it is printed and trimmed, or the area on a printed sheet that will form the page after the sheet is trimmed. → trimmed page size.

finished rough → mock-up

finishing *(fin.)* All operations after printing.

firmware The term given to the permanent software contained within your Mac's ROM, which forms an integral part of your computer's hardware.

first generation copy A copy of a photograph or other item made directly from the original, as distinct from a copy made from another copy of the original.

fit (1) → letterspace/letter-fit. **(2** *rep.*) The alignment and register of individual areas of color or images within a printed page, as distinct from the register of the colors on an entire printed sheet. Errors of fit

ccur in film stripping, whereas errors of register occur in printing.

it in window The facility of some applications to enlarge or reduce a page to the size of the window within which you are working on your monitor.

ixed-size font → bitmapped font.

ixed word spacing A standard space between characters and words, used for unjustified typesetting, as distinct from the variable spacing required for justified setting.

key A term (derived from "function keys") used to describe the keyboard equivalents for basic functions like ejecting disks (shift-command-1).

ash (*rep.*) A second exposure in conventional halftone processing that reinforces the dots in dark areas. These would otherwise run together and print solid.

at (**1** *pri.*) An assembly of composite imposed film, used in preparing plates for printing. (**2** *rep.*) A halftone of insufficient contrast.

latbed scanner → scanner.

at-file database A database program in which each file is self-contained and cannot exchange data with another file, as distinct from a relational database in which files can exchange data.

latness In object-oriented drawing applications, a term that refers to the number of straight lines, or segments, that make up a curve (which is how PostScript treats curved lines) to be printed on a PostScript printer – the lower the number, the smoother the curve.

latplan A diagrammatic plan of the pages of a book used to establish the distribution of color, chapter lengths, etc. Also called a flowchart.

lat-tint halftone A halftone printed over a background of flat color.

licker Image vibration on your monitor, caused by a low refresh rate. Also called a "strobe" effect.

ip → flop.

loating palette A palette

which you can position anywhere on your screen by dragging its title bar. → palette.

floating point unit (FPU) → coprocessor.

flop To reverse an image from left to right (horizontal flop) or top to bottom (vertical flop). Sometimes called flip. → lateral reverse.

floppy disk → disk.

floppy disk drive A hardware device for reading and writing data from and to a 3½in. (90mm) floppy disk. An internal floppy disk drive is standard on every Mac (some Macs have a slot for an optional second drive). Floppy disk drives are also available as external devices.

flowchart → flatplan.

flowers → dingbat.

flush → Clear.

flush left, right → ranged left, right.

flush paragraphs Paragraphs in which the first word is not indented, but which aligns with the left edge of the text. → full out.

foil Clear, stable film used as a backing during film assembly.

folder A place on your Mac, represented by an icon of a folder (which it emulates), where you keep your documents and applications. Folders form the basis for the organization of all your data on your Mac. 20–2, 121

folder bar In Standard File dialog boxes (such as Open and Save), the bar above the scrolling list that, when clicked on, reveals a list of the folder hierarchy. → HFS.

folio (**1**) Technically, the number of a leaf of a book when it is not numbered as two separate pages. However, a folio number is generally said to mean a page number. (**2**) The size of a book that is formed when the sheet containing its pages is folded only once, thus making the pages half the size of the sheet. A folio-size book is generally said to mean a large-format book.

follow copy (*typ.*) Instruction to a typesetter to follow the spelling and punctuation of a manuscript, even if unorthodox, in preference to the house style.

follow on → run on.

FOND *abb:* font family descriptor. The log of a font family (all the sizes and styles of a typeface) kept in a suitcase or in your System file.

FONT → font ID conflict.

font/fount Traditionally, of metal type, a set of type of the same design, style and size. On the Mac, a font is a set of characters, including letters, numbers and other typographic symbols, of the same design and style – although some definitions of the term include, wrongly, all styles: light, roman, bold, etc. → outline font; printer font; screen font; TrueType. 71–4, 88–9, 91, 98, 99, 129, 131

font downloading The process by which a printer font file is downloaded, or sent, to your printer. A font may be available in your printer's built-in ROM chips, on its hard disk, manually downloaded into its RAM, or automatically downloaded, when it is needed, by the printer driver. To download PostScript fonts automatically, the printer font files must be in your system folder or, if you are using a font management utility such as Suitcase II, the printer font files may be kept in the same folder as any open suitcase file. → suitcase.

font effects, *diagram 73*

font family The set of all the characters of a typeface design in all sizes and styles.

font file The file of a screen font, called a suitcase.

Font Harmony (*util.*) 97

font ID conflict An aberration that may occur as the result of an Apple-imposed limit (in the early days of the Mac) of 128 identity numbers (actually 256, but the first 128 were reserved), called (confusingly) FONTs, for all PostScript fonts you may have installed on your Mac. This results in such anomalies as a screen font that you specified in a document being different from the one that prints. The problem was partially solved with the introduction of NFNTs (new font numbering table) which allows for some

16,000 ID numbers. Version 3.8 of Font/DA Mover *(Sys.6)* also improved matters (by being able to convert FONTS to NFNTs) as have utilities such as Suitcase II and MasterJuggler, both of which include programs to resolve ID conflicts. Adobe Systems Inc. maintains a registry of unique font ID numbers and names for PostScript Type 1 fonts. *97*

font ID number → font ID conflict.

Font/DA Mover An Apple-supplied application for moving fonts and desk accessories in and out of your System and suitcase files. *89*

FontMonger *(app.)* 74, 96

font names, *table 99*

Fontographer *(app.)* 71, 72, 74, 91, 98

font organization 97–8

FontStudio *(app.)* 71, 72, 74, 98, 99

font/type series The identification of a typeface by a series number, i.e. Univers 55.

font substitution A facility of LaserWriters to substitute outline fonts for the basic system bitmapped fonts: Geneva (for which Helvetica is substituted) and Monaco (Courier).

font usage In some applications, a facility that lists all the fonts used in a document.

foolscap Standard size of printing paper 13½ x 17in. (343 x 432mm).

foot The margin at the bottom of a page or the bottom edge of a book.

footer (1) In some applications, particularly word processing programs, the facility to place text and numbers automatically at the bottom of printed pages. **(2)** A running headline that appears at the bottom of a page.

footnotes Short explanatory notes, printed at the foot of a page or at the end of a book.

footprint The exact space on a surface occupied by a piece of hardware.

foreground application The application that is currently active and whose menu bar occupies the top of your screen.

foreign file A document created in a different application to the one you are using, and one which you may wish to import.

format (1) The size of a book or page or, in photography, the size of film. **(2** *typ.)* To attribute type characteristics such as font, size, weight, tracking, leading, etc., to a text. **(3)** The arrangement of sectors and empty directories on a disk in preparation for its initialization. **(4)** In some applications, to specify paragraph, and other, attributes such as indents, hyphenation and justification, tabs, etc.

formatting The process of preparing a new disk for use on your Mac. When a disk is formatted, sectors, tracks and empty directories are created, and the disk may be verified (a test of the integrity of the data blocks).

forme *87*

for position only (FPO) An instruction on layouts and artwork that an item is displayed only as a guide for positioning.

forward delete key A key found on extended keyboards which deletes characters to the right of the text insertion point rather than to its left, as with the delete key of standard keyboards.

fount → font.

four-bit color The allocation of four bits of memory to each pixel, giving a screen display of 16 colors (a row of four bits can be written in 16 different combinations: 0000, 0001, 1001, 0110, etc.). → eight-bit color; twenty-four-bit color.

four-color process *(rep./pri.)* The printing process that reproduces full-color images by using three basic colors – cyan, magenta and yellow plus black for added density.

FPD *abb:* → full-page display.

FPO *abb:* → for position only.

FPU *abb:* floating-point unit → coprocessor.

fractions, *table 96*

fragmented The condition of disk storage space when, in time, tracks get broken into non-contiguous chunks, leaving only small blocks of

free space into which new files can be written, thus making it necessary for the new files to be split apart so that they will fit onto the disk. This means that both the disk and the files on it become fragmented. The result can be a dramatic increase of access time. *138*

frame A decorative border. → box rule.

frame-based A term sometimes used to describe applications which require you to create text or picture boxes in a document before text or pictures can be added.

FrameMaker *(app.)* 58

frame rate → refresh rate.

freeform tool In graphics applications, any tool which allows you to draw free shapes.

FreeHand *(app.)* 60–1, 62–3, 74, 94, 111, 113

freehand tool In graphics applications, the tool that allows you to draw a line as you click and drag the mouse.

free line fall → unjustified.

free space A memory block that is available for allocation.

freeware Any software that is declared to be in the public domain and free of copyright restrictions, as distinct from shareware. *78*

freeze → bomb

front matter The pages of a book preceding the main text, usually consisting of the half title, title, preface and contents. Also called "prelims."

fugitive color *(pri.)* A colored ink that is not stable and may change or fade when exposed to certain conditions of light or atmosphere.

full color Term usually used synonymously with "four color." → four-color process.

full out Description of type set to the full measure, without indents.

full-page display (FPD) Name given to a 12in. (300mm) monitor (measured diagonally). → monitor.

full word wrap The transfer of a whole word to the following line to avoid a word break.

function key A key on an extended keyboard that can be assigned to a specific

junction. Not to be confused with Fkey.

G

galley proof *(typ.)* A proof of typeset text before it is laid out into a page design. The term derives from the days when metal type was proofed from a long, shallow, metal tray called a galley.

gang up (1 *pri.*) To print two or more jobs on the same sheet, which would then be divided appropriately. (**2** *rep.*) To place a group of originals of the same proportions together for reproduction.

garbage The term given to meaningless characters which may appear on your monitor, signifying that something is wrong.

gateway (link), router A hardware/software connection between dissimilar computer networks. → bridge; network. *125, 133–5*

Gb *abb:* → gigabyte.

General Controls The basic Apple control panel device that allows you to modify the desktop settings, such as the time and date, that are stored in your Mac's parameter RAM (PRAM).

generic disk drive A disk drive with a mechanism that is common to many brands.

Geneva A system font that is a bitmapped version of the typeface Helvetica. Like Chicago, it is built into your Mac's ROM, so you can't delete it.

Get Info (File menu) Invoking this command, having first selected a folder or file, produces a window that gives you information about that folder or file, such as its size, when it was created and to which disk it belongs. You can also lock or unlock a file (but not a folder), and you can make a file into a template (→ stationery). You can make comments in the box provided, although those comments will be lost if you rebuild the desktop. If the selected file is an application, you will also be able to see which version it is unless the application is open) and adjust its memory heap.

host icon The term for the

grayed icon of a disk (or its contents, if it was open) left on the desktop after it has been ejected, as distinct from the grayed icon indicating that a file or folder is open.

ghosting (1 *rep.*) To decrease the tonal values of the surrounding parts of an image in order to make the main object stand out more clearly. (**2**) In illustration, particularly technical illustration, to depict parts of an image that would not normally be visible, such as parts of an engine covered by its casing.

GIF *abb:* graphic interchange format. A file format used for transferring graphics files between different computer systems via the CompuServe information service. *128*

gigabyte (Gb/gig) A unit of measure to describe 1,024 megabytes. → byte; kilobyte; megabyte.

gigo *abb:* garbage in – garbage out. A principle, particularly in computer programming, that poor quality input produces equally poor quality output.

global backup → backup, global/baseline.

glossary (1) An alphabetical list giving the definition of terms, usually related to a particular subject. (**2**) In some word processing applications, the facility to insert frequently used text by means of a keyboard shortcut.

g/m²/gsm/grams per square metre *(pap.)* A unit of measurement indicating the substance of paper on the basis of its weight, regardless of the sheet size.

go away box/region → close box.

golden section A formula for division of a line or area supposed to give harmonious proportions. If a line is divided unequally, the relationship of the smaller section to the larger section should be the same as that of the larger section to the whole. It is in practice a ratio of about 8:13.

gothic → black letter.

grabber (hand) tool In some graphics applications, the tool which allows you either to move a picture

around inside a box, or to move the page around in its window.

gradated fills *59, 61*

gradated tints *130*

gradation/graduation (1) The smooth transition from one tone or color to another. (**2**) The range of values between black and white.

graphic (1) A typeface originating from drawn rather than scripted letter forms. (**2**) A general term describing any illustration or design.

graphical user interface → GUI.

graphic interchange format → GIF.

graphics tablet → digitizing pad.

grayed command → dimmed command.

grayed icon → dimmed icon.

grayscale (1) A tonal scale printed in steps of no-color through to black and used for quality control in both color and black-and-white photographic processing. (**2**) Of monitors, the ability to display a pixel in a range of grays from white to black. (Monochrome monitors can only display black pixels, in which case grays can only be achieved by the varying density of black pixels to white pixels. → dithering)

greek(ing) To indicate type by substituting rules or a gray tint for the actual letters. This is common practice when preparing rough visuals, or scamps. On a Mac, this is a feature of some applications (some even allow pictures to be greeked by substituting a flat gray tint) and using it speeds up the process of screen redraw.

grid (1) A measuring guide used in book and magazine design to guarantee consistency. The grid usually shows such things as column widths, picture areas, trim sizes, etc. (**2**) In some applications, a background pattern, usually invisible, of equidistant vertical and horizontal lines to which elements such as guides, rules, type, boxes, etc., can be locked, or "snapped," thus providing greater positional accuracy.

group In some applications,

the facility to combine several items so that a single command can be applied to all the items in the group, or so that all the items can be moved around together.

GUI *abb:* graphical user interface. The feature of a computer system, such as a Mac, that allows you to interact with it by means of pointing at graphic symbols (icons) rather than by typing coded commands. Also called WIMPs or pointing interface. *17, 19, 52–3*

guides In some applications, visible but non-printing horizontal and vertical lines that help you to position items with greater accuracy.

gutter Strictly speaking, the space on a sheet, imposed for printing, comprising the foredges of the pages, plus trim. Commonly, however, the term is given to the margin down the center of a double-page spread, or to the vertical space between adjacent columns on a page.

gutter bleed An image allowed to extend into the fold, or to extend unbroken across the central margins, of a double page spread.

H

H&J, H/J *abb:* → hyphenation and justification.

hairline rule Traditionally, the thinnest line that it is possible to print. In applications that list it as a size option for rules, it is about 0.25 point thick.

hairlines The very thin strokes of a typeface.

hairspace Traditionally used for letterspacing, the term generally refers to a very narrow space between type characters.

half duplex Communication, over telecommunication lines, between two devices but in one direction at a time. → duplex.

half up A term that describes artwork prepared at one-and-a-half times the size at which it will be reproduced. Artwork that is drawn half up will need to be reduced by one third, to 66 percent, to print at its intended size.

half-title (1) The title of a book as printed on the recto of the leaf preceding the title page. **(2)** The page on which the half-title appears.

halftone (1 *rep.)* The process by which a continuous tone image is simulated by a pattern of dots of varying sizes. **(2** *rep.)* An image reproduced by the halftone process. *126, 129, 132*

halftone screen Conventionally, a sheet of glass or film cross-hatched with opaque lines. Also called a crossline screen or contact screen, it is used to translate a continuous tone image into halftone dots so that it can be printed. → contact screen; elliptical dot screen; moiré. *136*

handles (1) In applications which feature drawn lines and boxes, text boxes or picture boxes, the small black squares positioned at each corner (and sometimes also at other places) that enable you to resize those items. → control point. **(2)** → Bézier curve.

handshake The term given to the procedure that two networked computers or other devices go through when initial contact is made, so that they can establish data transmission protocols.

hang → bomb.

hanging cap/capital An initial character that is larger than the text to which it belongs and which is positioned outside and to the left of the paragraph.

hanging indent An arrangement in typeset text where the first line of each paragraph is set full out to the column measure and the remaining lines are indented to the right of the first line.

hanging punctuation Punctuation marks allowed to fall outside the measure of a piece of text.

hard copy (1) A copy of matter prepared for printing, used for revision or checking. **(2)** A printout of a computer document.

hard disk → disk; hard disk drive.

hard disk drive A hardware device for reading and writing data from and to a hard disk. The term "hard disk drive" – or even just "drive" – is often used to mean an external device, as distinct

from "hard disk" which usually refers to the disk inside your Mac, even though both are drives. Most connect to Macs via a SCSI port. The disk itself may be non-removable and may be made up of several platters, depending on its storage capacity, or it may be removable, in which case it will consist of a single platter housed in a rigid plastic case, or cartridge. Also *38, 106–*

hard dot *(rep.)* A halftone film produced either directly from a scanner or as final film and which, being dense has a dot that can only be minimally retouched or etched.

hard hyphen The term sometimes given to a hyphen that will not permit the hyphenated word in which it appears to break at the end of a line.

hard space The term sometimes given to a space that will not permit two words between which it is placed to separate at the end of a line. A hard space can sometimes be generated by pressing Option-Spacebar.

hardware A term for equipment. It generally applies to the physical apparatus of a computer environment, as distinct from firmware (built-in programs) and software (programs). *26–49*

hardware, *case studies 110–11, 113*

hardware, *choice 105*

Hayes-compatibility *47*

HD SC Setup → Apple HD SC Setup.

HDTV *abb:* high-definition television.

head → read/write head.

head crash The breakdown of a disk drive caused by a read/write head coming into contact with, and damaging the surface of a platter.

header In some applications, particularly word processing programs, the facility to place text and numbers automatically at the top of printed pages.

heading The title introducing a chapter or subdivision of text. A crossheading, or crosshead, appears in the body of the text.

headless paragraph A paragraph set apart from other text, but without a

head to head/foot/tail *(pri.)* In page imposition, the placement of the heads and tails of pages on each side of a sheet to suit the requirements of binding.

heap The portion of memory set aside for use on demand by the System or by applications. → application heap; system heap.

heavy Of type, an alternative term for bold or, sometimes, type heavier than bold.

help A feature of most applications to provide on-line explanations and advice.

help balloon → Balloon Help

hertz (Hz) The measurement of a unit of frequency. One hertz is one cycle, or occurrence, per second.

hex *abb:* hexadecimal, meaning the use of the number 16 as the basis of a counting system.

HFS *abb:* hierarchical file system. The name given to the way you and your Mac organize and store files and folders so that they can be accessed by any program: you organize your files inside folders which may, in turn, be inside other folders, thus creating a hierarchy. This is the hierarchy in which you move up or down within Standard File dialog boxes. Files or folders bearing the same name may exist on the same disk, but only if they are not at the same level in the same folder.

hickie/hickey/bull's-eye *(pri.)* A common printing defect, visible as a spot surrounded by a blank halo, caused by a speck of dirt pushing the paper away from the printing plate.

hierarchical file system → HFS.

hierarchical menu A menu that contains items which, when highlighted, generate their own menus, called submenus. The presence of a submenu is indicated by a ▶) symbol to the right of the menu item. → menu.

high density → disk.

high key *(pho.)* A photographic image exposed or processed to produce overall light tones.

high-level language Any programming language that is based as closely as possible on English rather than machine code.

highlight (**1** *pho./rep.*) The lightest tone of a photograph or illustration. (**2**) To mark an item, usually text or a menu command, to indicate that it is selected or active. The form in which an item is highlighted depends upon what type of monitor you have (color, grayscale or monochrome) and what application you are using.

high-profile SIMM → SIMM.

high-resolution printer → imagesetter.

hinting, hints The set of instructions contained within Type 1 fonts which modifies character shapes so that they appear better when displayed or printed at low resolutions

HLS *abb:* hue, lightness and saturation → HSB.

holding line → keyline (1).

hologram An image created by lasers to give an illusion of three dimensions.

horizontal blanking interval → blanking interval.

horizontal scaling In some applications, the facility to condense or expand type. By retaining the exact attributes of the source font, horizontal scaling distorts its appearance and, while the facility can be a bonus, you may prefer to use a specially designed condensed or expanded version of the font. → condensed type; expanded type. *104*

hot spot The specific place on the pointer that activates the item on which it is placed.

house organ A publication produced to give information about a company to its own employees or customers.

house style (**1**) The style of spelling, punctuation and spacing used by a publishing house to maintain a consistent standard and treatment of text throughout its publications. (**2**) → corporate identity.

HSB *abb:* hue saturation and brightness. A color model based upon the light transmitted in your monitor, hue being the spectral color, saturation the intensity of the color pigment (without black or white being added) and brightness representing the amount of black present. Called HLS (hue, lightness and saturation) in some applications.

H/T *abb:* → halftone.

human interface → interface.

HyperCard An Apple-supplied application with which you can design your own programs or modify the models provided. *75*

HyperTalk The "scripting" language used in HyperCard to create programs.

hypertext A programming concept that links any single word of text to an unlimited number of others.

hyphen A mark (-) used to divide broken words or to link two words.

hyphenate To divide a word between syllables at the end of a line of text or to create a compound form from two or more words, using a hyphen.

hyphenation and justification (H&J; H/J) The routines of an application that distributes spaces correctly in a line of type to achieve the desired measure in justified text. When this cannot reasonably be done without breaking words at the end of a line, hyphens will be introduced at a position determined by the application's built-in dictionary or H&J rules. *100–1*

hyphenation exceptions The facility, in some applications, for you to modify, add or delete words that can be hyphenated.

hyphenation zone In some applications, a (sometimes) user-definable area, at the right of the column in which type is being set, in which words can be hyphenated.

Hz *abb:* → hertz.

I

IAC *abb:* interapplication communication architecture. A protocol used by applications developers to allow their programs to share and exchange data.

I-beam pointer The shape the pointer usually adopts (I) when it is used to edit text, as distinct from the insertion point. Sometimes

called the text tool.

IBM PC → PC.

icon A graphic representation of an object, such as a disk, file, folder or tool, or of a concept or message. *18, 20–1*

ideal format *(pho.)* A size of photographic film measuring 2.3 x 2.7in (60 x 70mm).

ID number (1) A number sometimes given in bomb alert boxes, indicating the likely cause of the system error. → bomb; error code. **(2)** → SCSI ID number. **(3)** → font ID conflict.

Illustrator *(app.) 60–1, 74, 94*

image The subject to be reproduced as an illustration on a printing press. *132–3*

image area (1) In design, the space within which a particular image is to fit. **(2** *pri.)* The printing or ink-carrying area of a litho plate.

image, *editing 65, 68–9*

image, *handling 118–19*

image master *(typ.)* A film-based font.

image, *storage, file formats 128*

imagesetter *(typ.)* A high-resolution output device that is used to produce reproduction-quality copy for printing, either as camera-ready artwork on photographic paper or as film negatives or positives. *108, 127–33*

imagesetters, *and bureau 129, 131–3*

ImageStudio *(app.) 65, 68*

ImageWriter A low-quality dot matrix printer for use with Macs.

import To bring text, pictures or other data into a document. Some applications allow you to import material in a variety of file formats such as ASCII or EPS.

import/export filter In some applications, a file that enables the translation of a file format to or from another application.

impose/imposition *(pri.)* To arrange pages – in the correct sequence and with the appropriate margins for folding and trimming – before printing.

imposed proof *(pri.)* A proof of imposed pages prior to the final print run.

imprint The printer's imprint is the name of the printer

and the place of printing (a legal requirement in many countries if the work is to be published). The publisher's imprint is the name of the publisher, usually printed on the title page of a book.

imprint page The page of a book carrying details of the edition, such as the printer's imprint, copyright owner, ISBN, catalog number, etc.

incremental backup → backup, incremental.

incremental leading → leading.

indent Of type set to a narrower measure than the column measure, the term given to the distance that the beginning or end of the line is from the left or right edges of the column.

index The section of a publication giving an alphabetical listing of subjects, proper names, etc., mentioned in a book, with page number references.

index letter/number A character or number used to key a reference between an illustration and the caption or text.

inferior character Letters or numbers set smaller than the text and set on or below the baseline, as H_2O. In most Macintosh applications, inferior characters are called "subscript."

information bar/palette/window In some applications, an area or window containing information, such as measurements, about the document you are working on.

information service A commercial service that provides a facility, via telephone lines, for information, messages, and sharing software. → bulletin board.

init *abb:* initialization program. A small utility program that runs automatically when you start up and which modifies the way in which your Mac operates. An init is activated by placing it in your system folder and restarting your computer. → system extension.

init conflict A problem caused by some inits being incompatible with other inits, system files, or applications, which may cause your Mac to crash. An init

conflict may be resolved by renaming the offending init, thus changing the startup loading order (inits load alphabetically), although be warned that some inits must not be renamed.

init manager An init that enables you to manage other inits, such as turn one off if you don't need it (inits use up memory) without having to remove it from your system folder, or rename one if it conflicts with others.

initial cap/capital (1) Instruction to set the first letter of a word or phrase as a capital. **(2)** The initial letter of a paragraph that may be enlarged and set as a drop, hanging or raised cap.

initialization file/resource → init.

initialize To create or clear the directory of a disk so that new data can be stored. When a hard disk is initialized or reinitialized (which you can do again and again) its directory is emptied of file information, but the data itself remains (although it is invisible) until written over by the new files. When a floppy disk is initialized, the disk is formatted as well as initialized, thus the files stored on it, if any, as well as the directory, are deleted. → formatting.

inline lettering Any typeface with a white line inside the shape, that follows the outline of the character.

in pro *abb:* in proportion. **(1)** Individual subjects for reproduction that are to be enlarged or reduced in proportion to each other, either all together or separately. **(2)** An instruction that one dimension of an item is to be enlarged or reduced in proportion to the other.

input Any data entered into a computer, by whatever means.

input device Any hardware device capable of entering data into a computer; i.e., keyboard, scanner, digitizer, etc. *48–9*

input resolution *132*

insertion point The point, indicated by a blinking vertical line, where the next action you type on the keyboard will appear. The insertion point can be positioned

in an appropriate place by using the I-beam pointer and clicking.

install To add new system files or resources to the system folder of a startup disk.

Installer The Apple-supplied program for installing system software onto your hard disk. The Installer should also be used for installing system upgrades rather than simply drag-copying the files to your system folder.

Installer programs The programs that come with many applications, particularly those that occupy several floppy disks, to enable you to install the application onto your hard disk. Installer programs will also put the application files in their appropriate places, creating folders for them and putting files, if necessary, into your system folder.

integrated circuit The electronic circuit embedded in a microchip.

interactive Term describing the immediate and reciprocal action between person and machine.

interactive mode The facility of an application to process data as you input it, as distinct from processing data which is processed in batches (batch mode), say when you are interrupted by a spelling checker as soon as you make a spelling mistake. Also called "real-time" processing.

interface The physical relationship, or point of interaction, between systems and/or machines, or between person and machine (which is called "user" or "human" interface). → GUI. *19*

Interleaf Publisher *(app.) 58*

interleave ratio The numbering order of track sectors on a disk. A ratio of 1:1 means that the sectors are numbered consecutively, whereas 3:1 means that the numbers run consecutively only in every third sector. This ratio is an indication of how many times a disk must rotate in order for all data in a single track to be read – a computer with a slow data transfer rate requires a disk

to spin more times so that it has time to absorb all of the data in a track (so a 3:1 interleave ratio requires a disk to rotate three times because it only reads every third sector). A ratio of 1:1 is the fastest, since all the data in a track will be read in a single revolution of the disk. If your disk has the wrong interleave ratio, reading and writing data may become very slow – even if your computer has a fast data transfer rate.

interleaving (1 *pri.)* Sheets of paper placed between newly printed sheets in order to prevent ink transfer. Also called slip-sheeting. **(2)** Blank pages between the printed pages of a book, provided for handwritten notes. **(3)** → interleave ratio.

interlinear spacing → leading.

interlock To run type characters into each other by reducing character space.

internal disk drive → floppy disk drive; hard disk drive.

internal modem A modem that is manufactured as an expansion card to fit inside your Mac.

international paper sizes *(pap.)* The standard range of metric paper sizes laid down by the International Standards Organisation. The papers are designated A, B and C series and are available in proportionate sizes, divided in ratio to the largest sheet, A0 (trimmed – untrimmed sizes are prefixed with R, or SR for bled work), which is one square meter in area (841 x 1189mm): the shortest dimension of a sheet is equivalent to the longest dimension of the next size down.

interpolation The term describing the technique of recreating the color values of pixels in bitmapped images which have been modified (i.e. by rotating or skewing).

interpreter Software used in programming that converts program code into machine language. An interpreter converts a program one piece at a time as distinct from a compiler which converts a program in its

entirety.

interrupt button One of two buttons on the programmer's switch, the interrupt button is the rear one and is used by programmers for debugging software. → programmer's switch; reset button.

invisible character/invisibles The term used to describe characters that may be displayed on screen, but do not print, such as spaces (·), paragraphs (¶), etc.

invisible file A file that exists, but is not visible on your desktop; i.e. desktop file.

I/O *abb:* input/output.

ISBN *abb:* International Standard Book Number. A unique ten-figure serial number that appears on every book published and which identifies the language in which it is published, its publisher, its title and a check control number. An ISBN is often included in the bar code on a book.

ISO *abb:* International Standards Organization. A Swiss-based organization that has been responsible for standardizing many elements common to design, photography and publishing.

ISSN *abb:* International Standard Serial Number. A unique eight-figure number that appears on magazines and journals and which identifies the country of publication and the title.

italic The specially designed sloping version of a roman typeface deriving from handwriting and calligraphic scripts, intended to be distinctive from, but complementary to, that face. A version of italic, often called oblique or sloped roman, can be generated electronically on your Mac by slanting the roman style to the right.

ITC *abb:* International Typeface Corporation, a type foundry.

item General term describing objects such as text boxes, picture boxes and rules created in some graphics applications.

item tool In some applications, the tool that selects, modifies or moves items.

J

jaggie/staircasing The

term, technically called aliasing, given to the stepped appearance on monitors of bitmapped images and fonts, particularly when they are enlarged, caused by pixels consisting only of straight, square sides. → antialiasing.

jobbing *(pri.)* Description of general printing, not specializing in any field (such as book work) and usually comprising short runs.

JPEG *abb:* Joint Photographic Experts Group, a data compression standard.

jump In a publication, printed matter carried over to continue on a succeeding page.

jump line The reference on a page indicating that matter is continued elsewhere; i.e., "continued on page X."

justification The spacing of words and letters so that the beginning and end of each line of text share the same vertical left and right edges. → H&J. 87, 100–1

K

K *abb:* key, used to describe the process color black, deriving from the key, or black, printing plate in four-color process printing. Using the letter K rather than the initial B avoids confusion with blue, even though the abbreviation for process blue is C (cyan).

K(b) *abb:* → kilobyte.

Kbit *abb:* → kilobit

kern The part of a type character that overhangs the next.

kerning Adjusting the space (usually reducing it) between a pair of type characters to optimize their appearance. Traditionally, in metal type, kerned letters were those that physically overhung the metal body of the next character and were particularly important in italic typefaces – the roman versions of most metal fonts being designed so that they did not require kerning. As distinct from tracking, which is the adjustment of space over several characters.

kerning pair Any two characters that normally require kerning or to which a kerning value has been applied.

kerning table In some applications, the table describing the automatic kerning values of a font, which you can modify.

kerning value The space between kerning pairs.

key **(1** *rep./pri.)* Any printing plate (traditionally the black, called the key plate) or piece of artwork that provides a guide for the position and register of other colors. **(2)** To input matter via a keyboard.

keyboard 48, 106–7

Keyboard cdev The control panel device that allows you to select certain options on your keyboard, such as the Key Repeat Rate.

keyboard characters, *table 92–3*

keyboard command → keyboard equivalent.

keyboard equivalent/command/shortcut A command made via the keyboard rather than by the mouse, as distinct from a menu command ("equivalent" meaning equivalent to the menu). Typical keyboard equivalents, or keyboard combinations, are command-O for Open, command-S for Save, command-P for Print, etc.

keyboard event The action generated by pressing a key on your keyboard. This action will occur either at the moment you press down the key ("key down") or when you release it ("key up"). If you hold down a key so that an action is repeated, it is called an "auto-key event."

keyboarding *(typ.)* A term referring to the first procedure in typesetting, that of inputting copy. 118

keyboard shortcut → keyboard equivalent.

keyboard special character → special character.

Key Caps The Apple-supplied desk accessory that allows you to preview the entire character set of a font.

key combination → keyboard equivalent.

key letters/numbers Letters or numbers forming a reference link between elements of an illustration and their description in a caption.

keyline (1) An outline draw-

ing on artwork, that may or may not form part of the artwork, indicating an area that is to be filled by a mechanical tint. **(2)** A line drawing or a page layout indicating the size and position of an illustration or halftone. **(3)** The outline on artwork that, when transferred to a printing plate, will provide a guide for the register of other colors.

keyline view/preview In some graphics applications, the facility to view an outline of an item without showing any fills that may have been applied.

keypad → numeric keypad.

key plate *(pri.)* The plate that prints black ink in four-color process printing.

Key Repeat Rate The speed at which a character is repeated if you hold down a key.

keystroke The action of pressing a key, or group of keys, at a single time, whether or not it generates a character.

kilobit 1,024 bits.

kilobyte (K, Kb, Kbyte) A unit of measurement representing 1,024 bytes, which is used to describe the amount of memory a computer or disk may have. Since one byte represents a single character, one kilobyte is roughly equivalent to 170 words.

knockout *(rep.)* The term describing an area of background color that has been overlaid, or "knocked out" by a foreground object, and therefore does not print.

Kodak 'Prophecy' system *125*

L

Label menu The menu where you can assign colors and short phrases (labels) to icons. Labels and colors can be modified via the Labels control panel.

LAN *abb:* → local area network.

landscape/horizontal format An image or page format in which the width is greater than the height.

lap *abb:* overlap, of two colors to avoid registration problems. → choke; fatty; spread; trapping.

laptop computer A small,

...ortable computer.

larger Print Area An option (File menu - Page Setup - Options), in many applications, to increase the print area of a page printed on a LaserWriter – but at the expense of the number of fonts that can be used.

large-screen emulation A feature of certain utilities to provide a larger screen size than you may already have – when the pointer reaches the edge of the screen, the screen automatically scrolls.

laser The acronym for light amplification by stimulated emission of radiation, meaning an intense, fine beam of highly integrated light, sometimes generated with considerable energy. It is used widely in computer hardware such as printers and scanners, and for various commercial printing activities such as platemaking and engraving.

laser font A scalable outline font.

laser imagesetter *90*

LaserPrep The file that provides a data link between a PostScript laser printer and your Mac's QuickDraw language.

laser printer A printer that uses a laser to prepare computer output data for printing onto paper. A laser printer may or may not be PostScript compatible, and if not, uses your Mac's QuickDraw language for scaling bitmapped fonts. *39–42, 127*

LaserWriter Apple Computer's own, widely used, model of laser printer.

lasso The lasso-shaped tool used by many drawing applications to select an item by holding down the mouse button and drawing around the item.

latency time → access time.

lateral reverse The transposing of an image from left to right, as in a mirror reflection. → flop.

Latin (1) The standard alphabet used in most European languages, consisting of the upper- and lower-case characters from A to Z. The exceptions are Greek and Cyrillic (Russian, etc.). Oriental languages, includ-

ing Arabic and Hebrew, are usually classified as "exotics." **(2)** A term sometimes given to typefaces derived from letterforms common to western European countries, especially those with heavy, wedge-shaped serifs.

launch To open, or start, a software application. You do this normally by double-clicking on the application's icon, by highlighting the icon and choosing Open from the File menu, or by using either of these techniques to open a document created in that application.

layer In some applications, a level to which you can consign an element of the design you are working on.

layout Visualization which gives the general appearance of a design, indicating, for instance, the relationship between text and illustrations. The term is more properly used in the context of preparing a design for reproduction. Also called tissues, deriving from the transparent paper often used for drawing layouts.

lc; l/c *abb:* → lower case.

LCD/lcd (1) *abb:* liquid crystal display. An electronic method of display commonly seen on calculators, clocks, and computer displays, particularly on portables and laptops. **(2)** *abb:* lowest common denominator, meaning the most basic level that is common to all concerned.

lead(ing) Space between lines of type, originating from days when strips of lead were placed between lines of type to increase the space. In some applications, leading can be specified as: "absolute," meaning the specific value given to spaces between lines of text; "auto," the value given to automatic line spacing by means of a user-definable preference; or "incremental," a value given to line spacing totaling the largest character on the line plus or minus a user-defined value.

leaded Type which is set with space, or leads, between the lines.

leader A row of dots (usually) or dashes, used to guide the eye across a space

to other relevant matter. In some applications, leaders are specified as a "fill" between tab stops in text, and may be any character that you want.

leader line/rule A line on an image, usually keying elements of that image to annotation.

lean matter → fat matter.

left-aligned/justified Ranged left. → ranged left/right.

left indent → indent.

legend The descriptive text printed below an illustration, more often called a caption.

LetraStudio *(app.) 73, 74*

letterhead(ing) Strictly speaking, the heading – a name, address and telephone number of a business or individual – on any item of stationery, but sometimes used to describe the item of stationery specifically used for writing letters.

letterpress *(pri.)* The original relief method printing process, whereby the surface of a raised, or relief, image or piece of type is inked and then pressed onto paper or other surface.

letterspace/letterfit The adjustment of space between type characters from that allocated by the font designer, by kerning or by increasing or decreasing the tracking. → character space; kerning; tracking. *86–90*

lhp *abb:* left-hand page.

library A feature of some applications to provide a facility for storing frequently used items or attributes (such as colors) that you have created so that you can access them immediately from within any document.

lifted matter *(typ./pri.)* Text, already typeset, that is taken from one job to be used in another.

ligature Two or three type characters tied, or joined together, to make a single type character, as in fi, fl, ff, ffl and ffi. *96*

light, light face Type with an inconspicuous light appearance. It is based on the same design as medium, or roman, weight type in the same type family. The opposite of bold face.

lightfast/colorfast *(pri.)* A

term describing ink or other material whose color is not affected by its exposure to light, atmosphere or chemicals.

LightForge (app.) 71

lightness → HSB.

Lightspeed CLS (app.) 58–9, 135

light table/box A table or box with a translucent glass top lit from below, giving a color-balanced light suitable for viewing color transparencies and for color-matching transparencies to proofs.

Limitcheck error An error you may encounter when printing a complex document, caused by an illustration containing too many line segments for PostScript to handle. Some applications may allow you to reduce the number of line segments (→ flatness) in an illustration for printing purposes.

line → rule.

line and halftone → combination line and halftone.

line art(work) Artwork or camera-ready copy consisting only of black on white, with no intermediate tones and thus not requiring halftone reproduction.

line conversion The photographic or electronic method of eliminating the middle tones from a continuous tone original so that it can be treated as line artwork.

line copy → line art(work).

line gauge → type scale.

line increment The smallest allowable increase in the basic measure between typeset lines.

line original → line art(work).

line pattern The sequence of dots, dashes and spaces in a rule.

line tool In graphics applications, the tool that you use to draw lines and rules. If the tool can only draw horizontal and vertical rules it will usually be called an "orthogonal" line tool.

line up The arrangement of two lines of type, two illustrations, or a line of type and an illustration, to touch the same imaginary horizontal line.

line weight The thickness of a line or rule.

lines per inch (lpi, although often described as, say, "150 line") The measurement used to describe the resolution, or coarseness, of a halftone, being the number of rows of dots to each inch. The range in common use varies between around 85lpi for halftones printed on newsprint, to 150lpi or more on art papers. The default setting on laser printers is usually around 60lpi.

lining figures/numerals A set of numerals aligned at top and bottom. Sometimes called "modern" numerals. 96

lining up/lineup table (rep.) A table used for preparing and checking paste-up, flats, etc. It will generally be comprised of a gridded, illuminated surface with movable scales.

linking In some frame-based page layout applications, the facility for connecting two or more text boxes so that text flows from one box to another.

Linotype Hell A German type foundry and manufacturer of typesetting equipment (such as the Linotronic series imagesetters), supplying PostScript and TrueType fonts. The original Linotype machine was the first keyboard-operated composing machine to employ the principle of a "matrix," and cast type in solid lines, or "slugs." It was invented by the German-born American engineer Ottmar Mergenthaler and patented in 1884. The Monotype machine was invented almost simultaneously, in 1885. 90

list box The scrolling box in standard directory dialog boxes that lists the contents of the disk or folder displayed above it.

literal → typo.

lith (rep.) A high contrast and high quality photographic emulsion used in graphic reproduction.

lithography (pri.) A printing process, invented in 1798 by the German Aloys Senefelder, that produces an image from a dampened, flat surface, using greasy ink, based on the principle of the mutual repulsion of oil and water. → offset lithography.

local area network (LAN) A network of hardware devices confined to a small ("local") area – one room, say – using appropriate connections and software. At its simplest, a LAN may be set up so that several Macs have access to a single printer or a centralized hard disk.

LocalTalk The hardware connections used for AppleTalk networks.

lock In some applications, the facility for securing, or anchoring, an item so that it cannot be moved or modified.

locked file A file that will not permit changes to be saved. You can lock and unlock a file by using the "locked" checkbox in the Get Info window (File menu) for that file.

locked floppy disk A floppy disk which is write-protected.

logic board → board.

logical volume A volume created by software, as distinct from a physical volume such as a disk.

logo/logotype Traditionally, any group of type characters (other than ligatures) such as company names or emblems cast together on one metal body. The term is now used to describe any design or symbol for a corporation or organization which forms the centerpiece of its corporate identity.

log on To connect to, or announce your presence on, a network.

long page A page with the type area extended by one or two lines to avoid an inconvenient break.

look-/see-/show-through (pap.) The term used when describing the opacity of a paper, as indicated by the degree to which an image or type on one side of the sheet may be visible on the other.

lookup field A field in a database file that shows the same information as in a specified field in another file.

low-profile SIMM → SIMM.

lower case Description of the small letters in a type font, as distinct from capitals, which are called

pper case.

minance A term used to
describe the strength of a
grayscale video signal.

M

1 abb: → magenta.
1, MB, Mb, Mbyte abb:
→ megabyte.
MacBinary A file transfer
protocol that enables
Macintosh files to be properly transferred to non-Mac
computers.
MacDraw Pro (app.) 61,
2–3, 64
machine code The lowest
level of programming lan-
guage. It is the least like
English, but it is the most
efficient, as a computer
finds it the easiest to understand.
machine proof (pri.) A final
proof made on a machine
similar to the one on which
it will be printed (if not that
actual machine).
Macintosh, the box 26–7
and designers 50–1
models and properties 30–1
organizing work 119–21
set up 105, 106–7
typesetting with 90
MacMoney/InvoiceIt
(app.) 78
**Macintosh Operating
System** The basic software
and firmware in your Mac,
combining disk- and ROM-
based routines that handle
very basic tasks such as
startup, input and output to
peripheral devices, and the
management of RAM space.
→ operating system.
Mac RenderMan (app.) 70,
71
Macintosh User Groups
(MUGs) 52
macro Literally, macro
deriving from the Greek
"makros" = long, large)
means large or large-scale,
prolonging. Macroscopic
means large units as distinct
from microscopic, which
means small. Thus, when
applied to computers, a
macro refers to a single
command which contains
several other commands –
one large unit made up of
smaller units. A macro program is a small application
with which you can build or
record a sequence of
actions, carried out on your
Mac, into a single keyboard
equivalent.

MacroMind Director
(app.) 75
MacWrite (app.) 75
magenta (M) The special
shade of red that is one of
the four process colors used
in four-color printing, sometimes called process red.
Theoretically, magenta contains no blue (cyan) or yellow.
magnetic disk → disk.
magnetic ink characters
Characters printed using a
magnetized ink which are
readable both by humans
and by appropriate
machines, using a process
called MICR (magnetic ink
character recognition).
magnetic media/storage
Any material coated with a
magnetic oxide and used for
storing computer data, such
as disks, tapes, cards, etc.
36–9
**magnifying glass, mag-
nify tool** A tool in many
applications that will
enlarge a document, usually
when (having selected the
tool) you click anywhere in
the screen (the place where
you click will become the
center of the enlarged view),
or by "drawing" a "mar-
quee" (box) around the portion that you want to
enlarge.
main exposure (rep.) The
first exposure in the conventional processing of a
halftone image.
main memory Installed
memory (usually RAM), as
distinct from virtual memory.
→ RAM.
make ready → making
ready.
make-up (1) The sheet indicating the positions of various items on a page. →
layout. **(2** rep.) The final preprint assembly, whether it
be on paper, film or on a
computer, of all items to be
printed. 56–7
making ready (pri.) The
term describing the process
of preparing a printing press
before a new run, to establish register, evenness of
impression, size, etc.
Manual Feed button The
option in LaserWriter Print
dialog boxes (File menu)
that, when checked, will
only print the paper in the
special single-sheet manual
feed guide on top of the

paper cassette of your
printer. (If you put a sheet of
paper into the manual feed
guide, but forget to check
Manual Feed, it will print on
that sheet anyway.)
manual font downloading
→ font downloading.
manuals, for the Mac 52
manuscript (MS/MSS) An
author's text submitted for
publication.
margins The blank areas of
a printed page which sur-
round text or illustrations.
margin guides In some
applications, nonprinting
guides used to indicate the
edges of a predefined text or
image area.
marked proof (typ.) A proof
that has any necessary corrections marked on it before
it is given to the author.
mark-up (1) To specify, to
anyone in the reproduction
process, every detail of a job
that the person may require
to carry out the job properly.
(2) The actual item produced
to put (1) into effect.
marquee In some applications, a moving dotted line
drawn using the pointer or
some other tool, to select
the area within it.
mask (1) A material used to
block out part of an image in
photomechanical reproduc-
tion, photography, illustration or layout. **(2** rep.) A
photographic image modi-
fied in tone or color.
masking (1 pho./rep.)
Blocking out part of an
image with opaque material
to prevent reproduction or to
allow for alterations. **(2** rep.)
A technical method of
adjusting the values of color
and tone in photomechanical
reproduction.
(3) A protective layer applied
to an illustration to cover an
area while other parts are
painted or airbrushed.
master directory block
The block on a disk that contains the disk directory,
which is put into RAM when
you start or insert the disk.
→ directory.
MasterJuggler (util.) 98
master page In some applications, the page to which
certain attributes, such as
the number of text columns,
page numbers, type style,
etc., can be given, which can
then be applied to any other

page in a document.

master proof *(typ.)* A marked proof with client's, editor's and author's comments combined.

mat(rix) *(typ.)* Traditionally, the name for the copper mold from which hot metal type was cast; the term was later applied to the photographic negative on phototypesetting machines from which type characters are generated. 90

math coprocessor
→ coprocessor.

mathematical signs/ symbols Type symbols used as a shorthand for mathematical concepts and processes, i.e. + (add), ÷ (divide), √ (radical, or square root).

matter Traditionally, manuscript or copy to be printed, or type that has been set.

Mbit *abb:* → megabit.

Mbps *abb:* megabits per second, a measure of the speed of data transfer.

mean line The imaginary line showing the top of the x-height of lower case letters. → x-height.

measure The length of a typeset line, used to indicate the width of a text column, usually measured in picas or points, and sometimes in inches or millimeters.

measurements window/ palette A window giving information about various items, such as the position of the pointer, size of box, type attributes, etc., in the document you are working on, depending on which item is selected and the application you are using.
→ palette.

mechanical → camera-ready art(work); paste-up.

mechanical tint The term used to describe a tint, usually flat color, consisting of a line or dot pattern that can be laid down during conventional reproduction or by applying a percentage tint to a selection in some graphics applications.

media (1) A plural term, now accepted as a singular, used to describe any information or communications medium such as television, radio, newspapers, etc. **(2)** A plural term generally accepted as a singular, used

to describe to the actual item on which computer data is stored, such as a floppy, hard, or optical disk, as distinct from the devices in which they are used.
→ disk.

medium (1) A synonym for a catchline. **(2)** The substance which binds the pigment of paint or ink, also called the "vehicle." Printing ink medium is usually linseed oil. **(3** *pri.)* A standard size of printing paper, 18 x 23in. **(4)** A weight of typeface halfway between light and bold, often being the roman version.

meg *abb:* → megabyte.

megabit (Mbit) 1,024 kilobits, or 1,048,576 bits.

megabyte (M, Mbyte, MB, meg) 1,024 kilobytes, or 1,048,576 bytes, or roughly 175,000 words.

megahertz (MHz) One million cycles, or occurrences, or instructions per second, generally used to describe the speed of a computer's central processing unit, or its "clock speed."

memory The faculty of a computer to recall data and remember it, as distinct from storing the data, for which you use media such as disks. Your Mac has two types of memory: RAM, which memorizes the activities that take place on screen until they are written to disk, and which only exists as long as your computer is switched on; and ROM, which is a memory chip that permanently stores data vital to your computer's operation.
→ RAM; ROM; SIMM. 23–4, 28–9

memory allocation
→ application heap; heap; RAM cache; system heap.

memory-management coprocessor → PMMU.

memory, *problems* 140

memory upgrade To increase the RAM of your computer. → SIMM.

menu A list of commands available to you, depending on the application you are using. 18, 20–1

menu bar The horizontal strip across the top of your screen containing the titles of menus.

Menu Blinking A setting in the General section of the

Control Panel that allows you to change the number of times a menu "blinks," or flashes, before it executes the command.

menu box A box, usually with a drop-shadow, and containing a menu title, that displays a menu when you click on it.

menu command A command made via a menu, as distinct from one made via the keyboard.

menu indicator Symbols in a menu that give information regarding menu commands. An ellipsis (...) means selection of that command will display a dialog box before the command can be executed; a check-mark indicates a command is active; right-pointing triangle indicates a submenu; and a down-pointing triangle indicates more to come.

menu item Any of the choices in a menu.

Menu Manager The part of the System Toolbox that handles the setting up and use of menus. → hierarchical menu.

menu title The title of a menu, as displayed in the menu bar or in a menu box.

merge A facility in some applications to combine data from two documents.

message box An unprompted dialog box, giving information. → alert (box).

Metamorphosis *(app.)* 74

metrics Font information, such as character width, kerning, ascent and descent

MFS *abb:* Macintosh file system. The original method of file organization, now superseded by the hierarchical menu system.

MICR *abb:* magnetic ink character recognition.
→ magnetic ink characters.

microchip → chip.

microfloppy A term used to describe 3¼in. floppy disks to distinguish them from 5¼in. floppies.

microphone input port 32

microprocessor → CPU; coprocessor; 68000 series chip. 27

MIDI *abb:* musical instrument digital interface, a communication standard used by computers to control musical sound.

illisecond (ms) One thousandth of a second.

inifloppy A term used to scribe 5¼in. (134mm) ppy disks to distinguish em from 3½in. (90mm) ppies.

inuscules An alternative rm for lower-case letters.

inus leading/linespac-g → negative leading.

ips abb: million instructions per second.

irror-image backup → backup, mirror-image.

ock-up A visualization of publication or pack design owing its size, shape, pe, color, etc.

odal dialog box A dialog ox that will not allow any ctivity to take place other an that within its box. ven desk accessories are ndered inaccessible until e dialog box is closed.

ModelShop (app.) 65

odem abb: modulatoremulator. A device for ansferring data from one omputer to another across lephone lines, using appropriate software. 46–7, 17–18

odern face A typeface haracterized by vertical tress, strong stroke conast, and thin, unbracketed, erifs.

odern numerals → lining gures/numerals.

odifier key Any key that, vhen pressed in combination with a character key, hanges the typed character. ressing Option-Z produces . Other modifier keys are ontrol, Shift, Command and aps Lock.

odular Mac Any Macintosh computer that oes not incorporate the onitor in its case.

odule A self-contained lement of a program that onnects with other elents.

oiré (rep.) An aberration ccuring in halftone reprouction when two or more olors are printed, giving a alftone image an appearnce rather like that of vatered silk. This is caused y two or more dot screens eing positioned at the vrong angles or, sometimes, y the re-screening of an mage to which a halftone creen has already been

applied. The angle at which screens should be positioned depends upon the number of colors being printed, but the norm for four-color process printing, and thus the default setting for most Mac applications that support four-color separation, is: cyan 105°; magenta 75°; yellow 90°; black 45°. 136

monetary symbol A symbol denoting a unit of currency. There are four currency symbols available on Apple keyboards, but the keys you press to get them depend upon which nationality version of the System you are using. The symbols are: $ (Shift-4); ¢ (Option-4); £ (Option-3); ¥ (Option-Y).

monitor The screen on which you view what you do on your computer. A monitor may be able to display in color, grayscale or monochrome, and is either built into the same case as the computer, as with compact Macs, or is a separate unit. Monitors are available in a variety of sizes from 9in. (229mm) (measured diagonally) to 21in. (534mm) or more. Although most monitors use cathode ray tubes some contain liquid crystal displays, particularly portables and laptops. Monitors are variously called "screens," "displays," "VDUs" and "VDTs." 32–6, 106–7

Monitors cdev The control panel device that – depending on what monitor you have – allows you to select the number of grays or colors, check the convergence pattern (to make sure that the red, green and blue beams of light are suitably adjusted), and, if you have more than one monitor connected to your Mac, to adjust their physical positions in relation to each other.

monochrome (1) Any image or reproduction made in a single color. (2) Of monitors, description of those which display pixels only as either black or white, as distinct from grayscale monitors, which display pixels in a range of grays.

monospaced Description of typewriter-like fonts in

which all the characters are of equal width, as distinct from the more usual proportionally spaced fonts.

Monotype A type foundry and manufacturer of typesetting equipment, supplying PostScript and TrueType fonts. The original Monotype process, invented in 1885 by Tolbert Lanston of Ohio (only a year after the invention of the Linotype machine), employed a keyboard-operated composing machine to cast type as individual letters, using large numbers of matrices (which was only feasible due to the invention, by L.B. Benton, of a mechanical punch cutter).

montage The assembly of several images, or portions of them, to form a single original. → photomontage.

motherboard → board.

mount To establish the presence, on the desktop, of a volume or disk so that it can be accessed. 90

mouse The mechanical device that sits on your desk which you manipulate to navigate the pointer on your screen. 48, 106–7

mouse button → button (2).

Mouse cdev The control panel device that allows you to select the tracking speed and clicking rate of your mouse.

mouse event The action generated by pressing the button on your mouse. This action will occur either at the moment you press down the button ("mouse-down") or when you release it ("mouse-up").

Mouse Keys → Easy Access.

mouse pad/mat A small mat specially designed to help your mouse move efficiently. By being easy to clean, it also helps to keep bits of grit out of your mouse.

ms abb: → (1) millisecond. (2) manuscript.

MS-DOS abb: Microsoft disk operating system. An operating system used on non-Mac personal computers, sometimes called PC-DOS. 117

MS(S) abb: → manuscript.

MUG abb: Macintosh user group. → user group.

Multi-Ad Creator (app.) 70

MultiFinder A pre-System 7 Apple-supplied application that allows you to run more than one application, including the Finder, at the same time and to switch between them at will. The limit on the number of applications you can actually run is determined by the size of the applications and by how much RAM you have installed in your Mac.

multimedia The activity of integrating text, graphics, sound and video for (mostly) presentation purposes, and the applications that enable you to do this with a Mac. 74–5

multiple screens The attachment to a Mac of two or more screens. Their relative positions can be modified via the Monitors program in the Control Panels folder (● menu).

multiple-selected items In some applications, the selection of two or more items, so that they can be modified or moved as one.

multitasking The facility to run two or more applications at the same time, when the central processing unit will appear to work on them simultaneously by switching very rapidly from one to the other (sometimes called "time-slicing").

multi-user (**1**) Description of any hardware or software that can be accessed by more than one person at the same time. (**2**) Of software licences, those which permit copying and use by more than one user, usually with a predefined limit.

music font A font which is used for musical notation, sometimes exclusively within music programs.

music program Any application by which music can be composed and played, either with or without a musical keyboard or other audio equipment.

N

Namer The Apple-supplied utility that enables you to give a name to (or change the name of) your LaserWriter or any others on a network – naming printers on a network is important; otherwise, you may not know to which device your work is being output.

naming files 119, 121

nanosecond (ns) A measure of speed, being one billionth of a second – the fewer ns, the faster.

native file format → file format.

neg(ative) (**1** *pho./rep.*) A photographic film or paper in which all the dark areas appear light and vice versa. Negatives are used extensively in the reproduction process and are either made direct from originals or from a positive, or produced by an imagesetter. (**2**) The facility (sometimes called "inverting"), in many applications, to reverse the screen bit map so that the black pixels appear white and vice versa.

negative leading/line spacing In text, a line interval smaller than the point size of the type.

nested folder A folder that is placed inside another folder, in which case, it may be described as being "two layers deep."

network The interconnection of two or more computers and peripheral devices, and the hardware and software used to connect them. → local area network. 105, 108, 109

new line character In some applications, a character that you can insert (by pressing Shift-Return) to start a new line without starting a new paragraph.

NFNT *abb:* new font numbering table → font ID conflict.

nibble/nybble Half a byte (four bits).

Nisus (*app.*) 75

NLQ *abb:* near letter quality, describing a type of low-quality printer.

node Any network device.

noise A term used to describe undesirable fluctuations or interference in a transmitted signal.

nonbreaking space → hard space.

noncontiguous selection The facility, in some word-processing applications, to select unlimited disconnected pieces of text.

nonimpact printing Print work produced without a plate or cylinder, i.e. by the writing head of a plotter.

nonlining figures/numerals A set of old-style numerals designed with descenders (3, 4, 7, 9) and ascenders (6, 8), therefore not of a standard height and alignment, as are lining figures.

nonprinting characters → invisible character/invisibles.

Norton Utilities (*util.*) 79

np *abb:* new paragraph. A mark used in editing and proof correction.

ns *abb:* → nanosecond.

NuBus The bus "architecture" used in the Macintosh II family, designed to a specification created by Texas Instruments. → bus.

NuBus slot The expansion slots in the Macintosh II family to which expansion cards, or boards, can be added to enhance performance such as do accelerators, to run peripheral devices such as monitors, or to act as network interfaces. 29, 32

nudge A facility of some applications to move items, usually in increments of one pixel or one point (or even a fraction of a point), by using a keyboard command. Even if the application you are using does not have a nudge command, you can invoke one by using Easy Access's Mouse Keys feature.

null modem cable A communications link between two computers, usually over a short distance, without using a modem (null = nonexistent).

numbering format A term generally used to describe the style of numbering used for page numbers: 1, 2, 3; I, II, III; etc.

numerals, *table 96*

numeric coprocessor → coprocessor.

numeric keypad The cluster of number keys with a few calculator functions situated (normally) to the right of the keyboard.

O

Oasis (*app.*) 65

object color A colored foreground item that is printed against a background color.

object-oriented Of

aphics applications, those
at allow the selection and
anipulation of individual,
t self-contained, portions
an illustration or design,
distinct from bitmapped
aphics which are edited by
odifying pixels or turning
em on or off. An object-ori-
ted application uses math-
natical points, based on
ctors (information giving
th magnitude and direc-
on), to define lines and
apes. Strictly speaking,
ese points are the
bjects" referred to here
s distinct from an illustra-
ork but not actually done
on, or graphic, as an object)
an object in computer pro-
amming is a database of
athematical formulae. The
ta for each shape is stored
these points, each one a
atabase, which in turn pass
formation from one to the
her on how the paths
tween them should be
escribed – as straight lines,
cs or Bézier curves. This
eans that the quality of the
e between each point is
etermined entirely by the
solution of the output
evice – a line produced by
n imagesetter will be very
uch smoother than the
ame line output on a
aserWriter. 60

CR abb: → optical charac-
r recognition.

EM abb: original equip-
ent manufacturer. The
anufacturer of an item
hich may form part of
nother piece of equipment
nd is marketed under a dif-
erent name, as happens
ith generic disk drives.

ff-line Work done in rela-
on to a computer or net-
ork but not actually done
n the computer or while
onnected to the network.
he opposite of on-line.

ffset lithography (pri.) A
ethod of lithography,
eveloped separately in the
.S. in the early 1900s by Ira
ubel, Alex Sherwood and
he Harris brothers, in which
he image is printed indi-
ectly by "offsetting" it first
nto a rubber-covered cylin-
er, called a "blanket," from
which the image is printed.
is the most widely used
ommercial printing process
nd is sometimes called
hotolithography. This book

was printed by the offset
lithography process.

OK press → pass for press.

old face/style A typeface
characterized by diagonal
stress and sloped, bracketed
serifs. Garamond is an
example of an old face.

OmniPage (app.) 78, 117

one-and-a-half-up Artwork
prepared at one-and-a-half
times the size at which it
will eventually be repro-
duced. It will need to be
reduced by one third or to 66
percent, to be the correct
size.

on-line Work done on a
computer or while connected
to a network.

on-line help In some applications, a file that gives help
and advice, which is always
available while that application is open.

Open A command (File
menu) that enables you to
reveal the contents of a file
or folder or to launch an
application.

open architecture The provision, in the design of a
computer, for modification
and improvement of that
computer and its system.

Open button The button in
the Open dialog box that
opens the highlighted file or
folder in the directory list.
Double-clicking on that file
or folder, or (sometimes)
double-clicking on the icon
of the file or folder while you
are in the Finder, achieves
the same result.

Open dialog box The
Standard File dialog box that
appears when the Open
command is invoked.

open/standing time
Unused production time due
to a break in the schedule.

operating system The software and firmware that
provides the environment
within which a computer
user operates. In the case of
the Macintosh, this environment is made up of the
Operating System ROMs,
System file, Finder, and
related system software.

optical alignment An
arrangement of (usually
curved or pointed) characters
allowing a degree of projec-
tion beyond the margin
when vertically aligned, to
give an overall appearance
of alignment between the

main strokes.
Horizontal optical alignment
is normally already designed
into a typeface.

optical center A point
within a rectangle, slightly
higher than the actual geometric center, at which an
object or image appears to
be centrally placed.

**optical character recog-
nition** (OCR) A means of
inputting copy, without the
need to key it in, by using
software which, when used
with a scanner, converts
typescript into editable computer text. 78, 116–17

optical disk/media A
medium for storing digitized
data by means of minute pits
(the size of which represents
a 1 or a 0) imbedded into the
disk. They are "read" by an
optical pickup using a laser
which is reflected off the
disk's surface by a shiny
metallic layer. Usually
referred to as CDs (compact
disks), optical disks are
widely used for audio and
video recording and com-
puter data storage, and are
capable of holding huge
amounts of data. CDs are
more resilient to damage
than magnetic media, but
are also much slower.
→ CD-I; CD-ROM;
CD-ROM-XA. 39

optical(ly) even spacing
The adjustment of the
spaces between characters
to create an even appear-
ance to a line of type.

optical type font A font
used in optical character
recognition.

option Any button, checkbox, menu, or command that
allows you an alternative
choice.

Option key A keyboard
modifier key which, when
used in conjunction with
another key, provides a special character or a shortcut
to menu commands, or car-
ries out some other action,
depending upon the application or utility you are using.

origin The fixed, or zero,
point of horizontal and vertical axes or of the rulers displayed in some applications,
from which measurements
can be made.

original Any image, artwork

or text matter intended for reproduction.

origination *(rep.)* A term used to describe any or all of the reproduction processes that may occur between design and printing. *108, 124–37*

ornament → dingbat.

orphan A short line, usually the first line of a paragraph, that falls at the top or bottom of a page or column. → club line; widow.

ortho(chromatic) *(rep.)* Photographic emulsion used extensively in conventional reproduction, being sensitive to all colors except red.

orthogonal line tool → line tool.

outline font A typeface formed from an outline which can be scaled or rotated to any size or resolution. Outline fonts, often called printer fonts or laser fonts, are generally used for printing by laser printers and imagesetters, but both PostScript and TrueType font outlines can also be used for screen display. As distinct from bitmapped fonts which are comprised of dots.

outline letter A type design in which the character is formed of outlines rather than a solid shape.

outliner A word-processing application used for organizing headings and text.

out-of-memory message Any message which tells you that there is not enough memory available to perform the task that you require.

out of register → fit (2); register.

output device Any hardware device capable of displaying or producing data from a computer in a visible form, such as a monitor, printer, plotter, imagesetter, etc.

output resolution *126*

overflow In some applications, the term given to excess text when it will not all fit into its allocated space. Traditionally called "overmatter."

overhead A term describing space in a document that is occupied by formatting data rather than by the actual content you have created or need to access.

overhead projector A presentation device for projecting onto a flat surface images that have been created or output on transparent cellulose acetate .

overlay (**1**) A transparent sheet used for preparing multicolor artwork. (**2**) A translucent sheet covering a piece of original artwork on which you write instructions for reproduction.

overmatter *(typ.)* The traditional term for typeset matter which will not fit within the space allocated for it. → overflow.

overprint (**1** *pri.*) To make a second printing, or "pass" (not always in an additional color) on a previously printed sheet. (**2** *pri.*) To print two or more colors so that they overlap, thus producing more colors. The opposite of "knockout."

overrun The term describing words that move from one line to the next, possibly for several successive lines, as a result of a text insertion or correction. The opposite of run back.

overs *(pri.)* The term describing printed copies beyond the number ordered. This is normally deliberate to allow for copies that may be ruined during finishing or lost or damaged during shipping.

Ozalid *(rep./pri.)* A brand-name name describing a copy made by the diazo process and often used to refer to the prepress proofs of an imposed publication. → blues; diazo.

P

p, pp *abb:* page, pages.

page A contiguous segment of memory.

page break In continuous text, the place between two lines where the text is interrupted so that it fits on a page.

page description language (PDL) A type of programming language used to describe image and font data to a printer so that the printer can construct and print the data to your specifications. PostScript is the most widely used PDL. *41, 90*

paged memory manage-

ment unit → PMMU.

page guides In some applications, nonprinting guides that show you the width of margins, position of columns, etc.

page layout → layout.

page layout/makeup application Any application that assists you to carry out all (and more) of the functions normally associated with layout and make-up.

PageMaker *(app.)* *55, 111, 113*

page make-up → make-up

page makeup applications *54–5, 58–9*

page preview A facility to view a page before it is printed, necessary in some applications such as word processors and databases, .

page proofs *(rep./pri.)* Proofs of pages which have been paginated. Traditionally, the term refers to the secondary stage in proofing, after galley proofs and before machine proofs, although there may be other stages of proofing both before and after page proofs, such as the "blues" used to check imposition.

Page Setup A dialog box (File menu) in which you can select various options for printing, such as paper size, enlargement or reduction, paper orientation, inversion etc. The options actually offered depend on the printer you are using, as selected in the Chooser (● menu).

pages to view Refers to the number of pages visible on one side of a sheet that will be, or has been, printed on both sides.

pagination *(rep./pri.)* Strictly speaking, the term given to the numbering of book pages, but also commonly used to describe make-up of material into pages after typesetting and origination.

paint (PNT(G)) A standard bitmapped graphics file format, sometimes called a MacPaint format. PNTG files will only support an image resolution of 72dpi. → EPS; PICT; TIFF. *128*

Painter *(app.)* *65, 66–7*

paint(ing) application/ program Painting applications can be defined as

ose which use bitmaps as
stinct from drawing appli-
ations which tend to be
bject-oriented, although
ome applications combine
oth. → bitmapped; object-
iented. 61, 64–5, 66–7

alette A window, often
ovable, or "floating," that
ontains features such as
ols or patterns which you
elect, or measurements
hich you modify, during the
ourse of your work within
n application.

ANTONE Pantone, Inc.'s
neck-standard trademark
r color standards, control
nd quality requirements. It
s a system in which each
olor bears a description of
s formulation (in percent-
jes) for subsequent use by
ne printer. It is also a sys-
m that is used throughout
ne world, so that colors
pecified by any designer
an be matched exactly by
ny printer. Computer VDU
mulations, supported by
ome graphics applications,
re unlikely to match
ANTONE-identified solid
olor standards, and you
nould always use current
ANTONE color reference
nanuals to match colors
ccurately. Pantone, Inc.,
re, quite rightly, extremely
gilant about protecting
neir system, and conditions
r specification and reprouction are very stringent –
ou must, for instance, fol-
w their rules and regula-
ons before using PANTONE
entification numbers in,
ay, a corporate identity
nanual. They will not permit
ne use of their trademark
MS, the initials of
ANTONE MATCHING
YSTEM, and note that in all
ne references contained in
nis book the word
ANTONE appears in capi-
als – this is another require-
nent. If you have any doubts
bout the way in which you
vant to specify colors – par-
icularly if you are actually
eproducing a reference to a
ANTONE color – fax the
rademark Control
Department at Pantone, Inc.
n 201-896-0242. 59, 65, 67,
9, 129

aper size 41
aragraph format
→ format (4).

paragraph mark → blind P.
parallel interface A computer interface, not found on
Macs, in which eight bits (or
more) of data are transmitted simultaneously in the
same direction along a single cable. As distinct from
serial interface.
parameter RAM (PRAM)
The area in your Mac's RAM
which maintains Control
Panel (● menu) settings,
such as time and date and
startup volume, when your
Mac is switched off. The
PRAM chip is provided with
a continuous power supply
from its own lithium battery
so these settings (with the
exception of the desktop
pattern) do not change if you
startup from another disk. 25
parity bit An extra bit added
to a unit of communications
data, used to verify that the
bits received by one device
match those transmitted by
another.
parked Description of a
drive's read/write heads
when they are at rest,
enabling you to move the
drive or to remove a disk
without damage to disk or
head.
partition(ing) To divide up a
hard disk into smaller volumes, each one treated as if
it were a separate disk and
represented on the desktop
by its own icon. Partitioning
is particularly useful if you
have a very high capacity
hard disk, since, among
other things, you only need
to regularly back up the volumes that you use fre-
quently. There are two kinds
of file partitions – SCSI (real
partitions) and file partitions,
the latter being large files
rather than proper mount-
able volumes.
Pascal Programming language commonly used for
compiling Mac applications.
pass for press (rep./pri.)
Endorsement that a job has
had all corrections made and
is ready for press. Also
called "OK press."
Paste (Edit menu,
Command-V) The command
that copies an item on the
Clipboard and places it in a
document. → Clipboard.
pasteboard In some applications, the nonprinting area
around the page on which

items can be stored or modified. 55
paste-up A layout of a page
or pages incorporating all
the design elements such as
text, illustrations and rules.
A paste-up may be either
"rough," in which case,
while including all the design elements, it will not be
used for final reproduction
(except, perhaps, as a
guide), or it may be "camera-
ready" (also called "mechanicals"), in which case it will
be photographed to make
negatives or positives for
reproduction. → camera-
ready art(work).
patch A piece of program
code used to upgrade software or fix bugs. Patch code
is also used in System
upgrades for overriding
some ROM routines.
path (1) The hierarchical
trail from a file, through folders, to a disk. (2) A line, or
segment of a line, drawn in
an object-oriented
application.
pathname The name given
to identify the path taken by
a file to a disk, such as
jobdisk:jobfolder:jobfile (the
file named "jobfile" is inside
the folder named "jobfolder"
which is on the disk called
"jobdisk"). Note that colons
are used to separate each
name in the path, which is
why you cannot use colons
to name files.
patterned fill/line In some
applications, the facility to
select a pattern from a
palette and use it to fill a
shape or rule.
PC abb: personal computer,
usually used to describe IBM
PCs and other personal computers that are IBM-
compatible.
PC board abb: printed circuit board → board.
PD abb: → public domain.
PDL abb: → page description language.
PDS abb: → processor
direct slot.
peculiars → special sorts.
peer-to-peer A network
system in which data is
spread around different
users, who access it directly
from each other, rather than
from a central "client-
server."
peripheral (device) Any
item of hardware that is

connected to a computer, such as a printer, scanner, hard disk drive.

peripheral cable A cable for connecting a peripheral device to your Mac. → SCSI chain

permanent font An "official" term, although a misnomer, for fonts that are manually downloaded to a printer – they are only permanent until you switch off your printer, meaning you have to download them again when you switch on. As distinct from a "transient," or automatically downloaded, font, which only lasts in memory while a document is being printed.

perspective The art of describing three-dimensional objects on a two-dimensional plane, giving the same impression of their relative positions and size as when viewed from a particular point.

Persuasion (app.) 78
phonogram A symbol designed as the written equivalent of a spoken sound, which may or may not correspond to the International Phonetic Alphabet (IPA).

phosphor The coating on the inside surface of cathode ray tubes, and thus computer monitors, which glows briefly when hit by a bombardment of electrons, thus creating an image.

photocomposition → phototypesetting.

photogravure (pri.) An intaglio printing process in which a photomechanically prepared surface holds ink in recessed cells. Widely used for long runs like magazines.

photolithography → offset lithography.

photomechanical (1 pri.) A method of making printing plates that involves photographic techniques. (**2**) The full version of the term "mechanical" → art(work); camera-ready art(work); paste-up.

photomechanical transfer (PMT) (rep./pri.) A method of photographically transferring images onto paper, film or metal litho plates. An image produced by this method is commonly called a PMT.

Also called diffusion, or chemical transfer, or "velox."

photomontage The use of images from different photographs combined to produce a new, composite image. → montage.

PhotoShop (app.) 65, 68–9
phototypesetting/photocomposition (typ.) Strictly speaking, typesetting produced on photographic paper or film from a film matrix, but now extended to include, by virtue of the output medium being photographically based, computer typesetting produced on an imagesetter.

pica A unit of typographic measurement, one pica comprises 12 points, and, in true typesetting values, one inch comprises 6.0225 picas or 72.27 points. However, computer applications use the PostScript value of exactly six picas, or 72 points, to the inch. → point.

pi character → special sorts.

PICT abb: picture. A standard file format for storing object-oriented images. The PICT format uses QuickDraw routines and thus will support bitmapped images, since QuickDraw routines are what your Mac uses to draw on its screen, and is supported by virtually all graphics applications. Originally PICT only accepted eight colors, but now, as PICT2, it will support 32-bit color, and is thus unlimited. → EPS; paint; TIFF. 128

pictogram/pictograph A simplified, pictorial symbol representing an object or concept.

picture → PICT.
picture box In frame-based applications, a box created for a picture, as distinct from a text box.

picture skew → skew.
pixel abb: picture element. An individual dot of light on your monitor which contributes to forming an image. The more pixels there are per inch, the higher the resolution of your monitor (the Mac standard is 72dpi). In its simplest form (monochrome), one pixel corresponds to a single bit in RAM: 0 = off, or white, and 1 = on, or black.

On color or grayscale monitors, one pixel may correspond to several bits; i.e., an 8-bit pixel can be displayed in any of 256 colors (the total number of different configurations that can be achieved by eight 0s and 1s *33, 34, 42–3*

pixel depth A term used to describe the number of colors or grays a single pixel can display. This is determined by the number of bits used to display a pixel. Thus 1-bit equals 1 color (black), 4-bits (any permutation of four 1s and 0s, i.e. 0011 or 1001) equals 16 colors or grays, and so on, up to 24-bits which can produce 16.7 million combinations of twenty-four 0s and 1s, thus 16.7 million colors.

pixellization A term used to describe the effect of an image that has been broken up into square blocks, resembling pixels, to give it a "digitized" look.

PixelPaint Professional (app.) 65, 66–7
Place The command used by some applications to import an image file.

planographic (pri.) Any method of printing from a flat surface, such as lithography.

plate (1 pri.) A sheet of metal (usually), plastic or paper from which an image is printed (or transferred, in offset litho to a blanket and then printed). (**2**) Strictly speaking, a book illustration printed separately from the text and then tipped or bound into the book, but sometimes erroneously used to describe a full-page illustration printed in a book. (**3** pho.) A size of photographic film, a whole plate measuring 6½ x 8½in. and a half plate measuring 4 x 6½in.

platter A circular, rigid disk which is incorporated, either singly or severally, into a hard disk drive.

plotter An output device that uses an inked pen, or assembly of pens, to produce large format prints. Plotters are used mostly in the CAD/CAM industries.

PMMU abb: paged memory management unit. A microchip which enables the

se of virtual memory, among other things. 27

MS → PANTONE.

MT *abb:* → photomechanical transfer

NT(G) → paint.

oint The basic unit of the nglo-American typographic easurement system. istorically, printing has ways been an inexact science and no two printers uld agree on a standard ystem of type measurement, which meant that type ast in one foundry was compatible with that cast another. In the mid 18th entury, the French typographer Pierre Simon Fournier roposed a standard unit hich he called a "point," hich was further developed y Firmin Didot into a uropean standard which, though their systems were ased upon it, was not dopted by Britain or the .S. The Anglo-American ystem is based on the division of one inch into 72 arts, called points; mathematically, one point should qual 0.013889in. but, in ct, it equals 0.013837in., eaning that 72 points only ake 0.996264in. The uropean didot point equals 0148in. and 12 of these rm a unit measuring 1776in. There is no relationship between the Anglo-merican point and the didot oint, and neither of them late to metric measurement. On the Mac one point easures 0.013889in., and 2 points really do equal one ch. It is no coincidence at the basic Mac screen solution is 72dpi. → pica. 5–6

ointer A general term that fers to any of the many hapes of marker on your onitor which identifies the rrent screen location of ur mouse, your current osition in a piece of text, or at your Mac is undertaking particular activity. Typical inter shapes are the arrow inter, vertical bar, I-beam, ossbar or crosshair, and ristwatch. Sometimes alled a "cursor." 18

ointing interface → GUI.

olygon tool A tool in some pplications with which you n draw polygonal, to

which text, pictures or fills may be applied.

pop-up menu A menu in a dialog box or palette that appears when you click on it. Pop-up menus are usually identifiable as a rectangle with a drop shadow.

port Sockets in a Mac, or peripheral device, into which other devices are plugged. Typical ports on a Mac are the ADB, SCSI and serial ports. 30–2

portrait monitor A monitor with a screen in an upright format, as distinct from the more usual landscape format. The Radius "Pivot" monitor is rotatable to portrait or landscape formats.

portrait/upright Description of an image or page in a vertical format.

posterize To divide a continuous tone image into a predefined or arbitrary number of flat tones.

postlims → end matter.

PostScript Adobe Systems Inc.'s page description language for image output to laser printers and high-resolution imagesetters. → page description language. 40–1, 74, 78, 90–4, 95, 97, 128

PostScript dictionary A file, such as LaserPrep and Aldus Prep, containing definitions of PostScript terms, for use by the printer.

PostScript font → outline font

PostScript interpreter The built-in code that printing devices use to understand PostScript commands.

PostScript printer Any printing device using Adobe-licensed PostScript page description language.

PowerPoint *(app.)* 78

PPC *abb:* program-to-program communication. → IAC.

PPI *abb:* pixels per inch.

PRAM *abb:* → parameter RAM.

PRAM chip → parameter RAM.

precautions, *on machines* 137–8

prepress → origination.

preferences An option in many applications to enable or disable features of the application (such as the unit of measurement) and to modify the program default

settings. Preferences can be modified for a single document or, sometimes, all documents – if none are open when you make the modifications. → default; preset defaults.

prefs file An application file that records your preference settings so that when you reopen a document you don't have to reset the preferences.

prelims, preliminary matter → front matter.

PRES → Chooser documents.

presentation visual → comp (2); dummy (2); mock up.

preset defaults Preprogrammed settings of an application that remain in use until you change them. → preferences.

press proof → machine proof.

pretzel/cloverleaf/propellor symbol → command key.

preview → keyline view.

primary colors Pure colors from which theoretically, although not in practice, all other colors can be mixed. In printing these are the so-called "subtractive" primaries: cyan, magenta and yellow. The primary colors of light, or "additive" primaries, are red, green and blue.

Print A command (File menu) that, when selected, displays the Print dialog box.

print buffer A hardware device that intercepts data on its way to be printed and stores it until the printer is available, thus allowing you to continue working. As distinct from a print spooler.

Print dialog box The dialog box, invoked by the Print command, in which you select the options offered by the application you are working in. The most basic Print dialog box will allow you to select the number of copies you require and which pages.

printed circuit board (PC board) → board.

printer *(rep./pri.)* The film or plate of a single color produced for four-color process printing.

printer driver → driver.

printer file A file containing a font that can be

downloaded to a printer.

printer font A font used for printing, as distinct from a font used for screen display. → font downloading.

printer port A serial port via which you can connect your Mac to a printer, network or modem.

printer resolution *41*

printers, *in set-up* *106–7*

printers, *problems* *140*

printing film, *density* *132*

printing-in-progress Printing activity as described in a dialog box. In addition to advising you of the printing status of a document, this normally allows you, by providing a Cancel button, to cancel printing.

PrintMonitor The Apple-supplied print spooling application that allows you to print while you carry on working. → background printing; print spooler.

print origination → origination.

print spooler Software that intercepts data on its way to be printed and diverts it to disk until the printer is available, thus allowing you to carry on working. Apple's PrintMonitor is a print spooler. As distinct from a print buffer.

problems, *on machines* *137–40*

process blue → cyan.

process color → CMYK.

process color printing *(rep./pri.)* The printing that uses the four process color inks – cyan, magenta, yellow and black – to recreate full-color images. Halftone screens are used to break up continuous tone images into tiny dots which, when printed in each of the process inks overlap to form most colors, although by no means all.

processor chip → central processing unit; coprocessor.

processor direct slot (PDS) The slot for expansion cards included on a Mac SE or SE/30, although a card for one model cannot be used in the other.

process red → magenta.

process yellow (Y) The special shade of yellow which is one of the four process colors used in four-color printing.

program A set of coded instructions that controls the operation of a computer. → application; software.

program defaults → default; preferences; preset defaults.

programmer Someone who writes computer programs, as distinct from someone who uses them.

programmer's switch A plastic switch included with some Macs (although you may have to attach it yourself), having two buttons: a reset button (the frontmost) that does the same thing as the Restart command (Special menu), and the interrupt button (rearmost) which is used by programmers for accessing various programming and debugging software.

→ interrupt button; reset button.

programming language A specially devised vocabulary used to write computer programs. Programming languages are either "high-level," which are based as closely as possible on English, or "machine code," the lowest level, being the least like English but the easiest for a computer to understand. The languages most frequently used for writing Mac software are BASIC, C++, FORTRAN and Pascal.

→ compiler; computer languages; interpreter.

progressive proofs *(rep.)* Proofs used in color printing to show all colors both separately and in combination.

PROM *abb:* programmable ROM.

prompt In some applications or in special circumstances, a symbol, i.e. >, indicating that the computer is waiting for you to enter an instruction.

proof *(typ./rep./pri.)* A representation on paper, taken from a laser printer or imagesetter, inked plate, stone, screen, block or type, in order to check the progress and accuracy of the work. Also called a "pull."

proof correction marks A standard set of signs and symbols commonly understood by all those involved in preparing copy for

publication.

proofreader A person who reads proofs for corrections and who marks them accordingly.

Prophecy system *(Kodak)* 125

proportional spacing A method of spacing characters so that letters and numbers occupy an appropriate amount of space for their design, to accommodate, for example, the difference in width between m and i.

protocol A set of mutually agreed rules that hardware and software must observe in order to communicate with one another.

public domain (PD) Description of any item of "intellectual property" that is free of all copyrights, thus freeing it for use by anyone for any purpose, either because its copyright period has lapsed or because, as is sometimes the case with computer software, its creator has deemed it so.

publish and subscribe A Mac system facility, supported by some applications to automatically update a document ("subscriber") with information created or modified in another ("publisher").

pull → proof.

pull-/pop-/drop-down menu The menu that appears when you click on a menu title in the menu bar along the top of your screen.

push button A round-cornered rectangular button in a dialog box by which, when you click on it, you invoke the command specified on the button. If the button rectangle has a thick rule around it, this means that it is the default button and will respond to the Return or Enter keys being pressed. → button.

Put Away (File menu) The command that you use to return a file or folder on the desktop (or in the trash) to whence it came.

Pyro *(util.)* 79

Q

quad *(typ.)* In conventional typesetting, a space whose width is normally that of its height, thus "to quad," or "quadding," is to fill out a

ne with quad spaces.

QuarkXPress *(app.)* 55, 6–7, 90, 96, 111, 113, 115, 23, 129, 135

QuickDraw The part of the Mac system that performs all display operations on our screen.

Quicken *(app.)* 78

QuicKeys *(util.)* 78

Quit (File menu) The command by which you "shut down" an application and return to the Finder, as distinct from closing a document within the application, in which case the application remains open. Pressing Command-Q usually achieves the same thing.

Quoin *(app.)* 58, 91

qwerty The standard typewriter-based keyboard layout used by most, although not all, devices that require the use of a keyboard. The name derives from the arrangement of the first six characters of the top row of letter keys. → Dvorak keyboard.

® The mark attached to a trade mark indicating that it is registered and cannot be used by any other person or organization.

A paper sizes *(pap.)* The designation of untrimmed paper sizes in the ISO A series of international paper sizes. → SRA paper sizes.

radial fill A fill pattern made up of concentric circles of gradated tints.

radiation shield A wire mesh or glass filter that fits over your monitor screen to reduce the level of emanating radiation. → ELF.

ragged left/right → ranged left/right.

raised cap(ital) A bold-face capital that projects above the line of type. Also called "cocked up initial."

raised point/dot A full point (period) printed at half the height of capitals rather than on the baseline.

RAM *abb:* random access memory. The working space instantly available to you very time you use your Mac. When you launch an application or open a document, it is loaded into RAM and stored there while you work with it. However, an

item only stays in RAM for as long as your Mac is on (→ dynamic RAM) or until you write, or "save" it to disk. To carry out even basic graphic design work efficiently, you will need at least 4MB RAM, but you'll probably find you need more, especially if you work with scanned images. → SIMM. 23, 24, 25, 28–9, 36

RAM cache A piece of RAM that you set aside (via the General icon in the Control Panel) which stores the most recent actions you have carried out so that when you need them again, they do not have to be retrieved from disk.

RAM chip → SIMM.

RAM disk A part of RAM that is temporarily "tricked," by certain utility software, into thinking that that particular portion is a disk drive. Because the process of retrieving data from RAM is so much faster than from disk, operations performed by items stored in a RAM "disk" will speed up. This "disk" is represented on the desktop by its own icon, which is erased when you switch off.

ranged left/right A style of typesetting in which lines of unequal length line up on either the left or right of a column of text so that they are vertically flush with each other, leaving the opposite ends of the lines uneven or "ragged."

ranging figures → lining figures/numerals.

raster The method of display (and of creating images → RIP (**1**)) used on video screens, and thus monitors, whereby the screen image is made up of a pattern of several hundred parallel lines created by an electron beam "raking" the screen from top to bottom at a speed of about one sixtieth of a second ("raster" comes from the Latin word rastrum, meaning "rake"). An image is created by the varying intensity of brightness of the beam at successive points along the raster. The speed at which a complete screen image, or frame, is created is called the "frame" or "refresh" rate. → refresh rate. *127*

raster image processor → RIP.

Ray Dream Designer *(app.)* 70, 71

RDEV → Chooser documents.

Read Me A file that accompanies many programs, giving important information or revisions to printed documentation. The files will usually be in TeachText format or in a popular word-processing format such as Word or MacWrite.

read only Of disks, memory and documents, those that can only be read from, and not written to.

read-only memory → ROM.

read/write head The part of a disk drive that extracts (reads) data from, and deposits (writes) data to, a disk. One read/write head is positioned above each side of every disk platter (a hard drive may consist of several platters). These move, on rails, over the surface of the platter while the platter rotates at speed. Also called a "disk drive head."

real time The term used to describe the actual time in which events occur, thus on your computer, an event that corresponds to reality. For example, at its very simplest, a character appearing on screen the moment you type it, is said to be real-time, as is a video sequence that corresponds to actual clock time.

reboot To restart your Mac. → boot; cold boot; restart; warm boot.

rebuild desktop To renew the desktop file in order to speed up Finder operations. The desktop file records not only new files, but deleted ones as well, so the more files you add and delete, the more the desktop file keeps growing. Rebuilding it gets rid of obsolete information. You rebuild the desktop by holding down Option-Command while you restart the computer.

record A total set of related fields in a database, comprising an individual entry.

rectangle tool → square-corner tool.

recto The right-hand page of a book.

redraw rate The speed at which an application renders an image on screen after a change has been made. Sometimes erroneously confused with refresh rate. → refresh rate.

reduction glass/tool → magnifying glass.

reflection copy *(rep.)* Any flat item which is reproduced by photographic means, using light reflected from its surface. → camera-ready art(work).

reflection tool In some applications, a tool by which you transform an element into its mirror image, or make a mirror-image copy of an element.

reflow The term describing the automatic repositioning of running text as a result of editing.

refresh rate The frequency, measured in hertz, with which a screen image, or "frame" (a single pass of an electron beam which "rakes" the screen several hundred times from top to bottom) is redrawn. A refresh rate of 71.3Hz means that the image is "refreshed" 71.3 times every second. A screen with a slow refresh rate may produce unacceptable flicker. → raster. *36*

register *(rep./pri.)* The correct positioning of one color on top of another or of the pages on one side of a sheet relative to the other (called "backing up") during printing. As distinct from "fit."

register/registration mark *(rep./pri.)* The marks used on artwork, film and printing plates which are superimposed during printing to make sure that the work is in register.

relational database A database program which allows different files to exchange data with one another, as distinct from a flat-file database in which files are self-contained and cannot exchange data.

release version The version of a program that is released for general sale, following the alpha and beta tested versions.

relief printing *(pri.)* Printing from a raised surface, as in letterpress printing.

removable hard disk
→ disk; hard disk drive.

rendering *65, 70–1*

repro(duction) *(rep.)* The entire printing process from the completion of artwork or imagesetter output to printing. Also called origination. *133–7*

reproduction copy → camera-ready art(work).

ResEdit An Apple-supplied resource editing application, used for modifying any Mac program, system or otherwise.

reset button One of two buttons on the programmer's switch, the reset button is the frontmost and is an alternative way of restarting your Mac, more particularly after bombs. → interrupt button; programmer's switch.

resident font A font stored in ROM (usually in the printer ROM).

resolution The degree of precision – the quality, definition, or clarity – with which an image is represented or displayed, such as by a scanner, monitor, printer or other output device. → pixel.

resolution, *and imagesetters 127, 129*
and laser printers 40
and monitors 32–3, 34–5
and reproduction 126
of scanners 43–4, 136

resource The term describing a system file that provides information to the central processing unit so that it can communicate with a peripheral device.

resource fork The part of a Macintosh application file that contains resources, that is, the information it uses for menus, fonts and icons, as distinct from the data fork which contains data generated by you.

Restart A command (Special menu) that enables you to reboot your Mac without switching it off (shutting down) and switching on again.

Restart button The rarely invokable button that appears in some bomb alert boxes. → bomb.

restart To reload your Mac's operating system from disk, but without switching it off (shutting down) and switching it on again. You restart

your Mac if you have installed or removed certain system files (such as inits and cdevs) so that they may be activated or flushed out of the system, or after it has "bombed." Any work that you have not saved will be lost when you restart.

rest in pro(portion) → RIP (2).

restore To return backed-up files to disk if the originals are damaged or deleted.

result code Macspeak for "error code." → error/result code.

Resume button A button that sometimes appears in bomb dialog boxes, but which very rarely works.

retouching *(pho./rep.)* Altering or correcting an image, artwork or film by hand to make modifications or remove imperfections. Scanned images are usually retouched electronically using appropriate software. *65, 68–9*

Return key The key that operates much like a typewriter "carriage return" key in that it moves the text insertion point to the beginning of the next line, usually creating a new paragraph as it does so. In most applications and dialog boxes, it also duplicates the actions of the Enter key.

reverse b to w *abb:* reverse black to white. Instruction to reverse out an image or type. → reverse out.

reverse indent → hanging indent.

reverse l to r Instruction to reverse an image from left to right. → flop; lateral reversal.

reverse out *(rep.)* To reverse the tones of an image or type so that it appears white (or another color) in a black or colored background. Also called "drop-out," "save out."

reverse P → blind P.

reverse reading → wrong reading.

reversed type → reverse out.

RGB *abb:* red, green, blue. → additive colors; color model.

rich text format → RTF.

RIFF *abb:* raster image file format, Letraset's brandname file format for storing images. *128*

right-aligned/justified Ranged right. → ranged left/right.

right reading *(rep.)* Description of positive or negative paper or film on which the text, if any, can be read as normal, that is, from left to right.

right-reading, emulsion-side-down *(rep.)* Description of negative film on which the text, if any, can be read as normal, i.e. from left to right, and in which the photographic emulsion is on the underside.

RIP (1) *abb:* raster image processor, a device that converts a page description language such as PostScript into a form which can be output by a high-resolution imagesetter. → raster. *127*

2) *abb:* rest in pro(portion), an instruction to reproduce an image or artwork, giving only one dimension – the rest to be reduced or enlarged in proportion.

RISC *abb:* reduced instruction set computing. A microprocessor that provides high-speed processing by accepting only a limited number of commands, without – due to advances in memory technology – loss of efficiency.

river An aberration in typeset text, in which a series of word spaces form a linked or continuous stream of white space down a page. Often caused by badly justified type.

ROM *abb:* read-only memory, memory which can only be read from, and not written to. ROM resides in a chip on the Mac's motherboard and is where the "firmware" part (meaning software that's permanently built in and cannot be changed) of the operating system is kept. The data stored in ROM can only be updated by changing the ROM chip, which is why the constantly changing part of the operating system is provided as disk-based software. *23, 24*

roman The standard characters of a font in which the characters are upright, as distinct from italic.

root directory/level The term that describes the first level at which files and folders are placed, represented by the window that appears when you double-click (open) on a disk icon.

rotation tool In some graphics applications, a tool which, when selected, enables you to rotate an item around a fixed point.

rough A preliminary drawing showing a proposed design. Also called a "scamp." *114–15*

round-corner tool In most graphics applications, the tool that, when selected, enables you to draw a rectangular box or shape with rounded corners. You may or may not be able to modify the corner radius.

router → gateway.

routine A piece of programming code designed to perform a specific task.

RS *abb:* receive-send, a standard laid down by the U.S. Electronic Industries Association (EIA) for data transfer connections between computers or devices. The letters prefix a number, as in the RS-422 printer and modem port on Macs.

RTF *abb:* rich text format, a Microsoft file format for transferring formatted text documents. *128*

rule A line. The term derives from the Latin *regula* meaning "straight stick" and was used to describe the metal strips, of type height, in various widths, lengths and styles, which were used by traditional typesetters for printing lines. *94–5*

ruler In some applications, the feature of a calibrated ruler, in your preferred unit of measure, at the edges of a document window.

ruler guide In some applications, a nonprinting guide which you obtain by clicking on the ruler and dragging to the desired position.

ruler origin → origin.

runaround Text that fits around a shape, like an illustration. Also called "text wrap."

run back The term describing words that move back from one line to the previous line, as a result of a text deletion or correction. The opposite of overrun.

run-in → run on.

running text The main body of a text which runs from page to page, although it may be broken up by illustrations or other matter.

run-in heading A heading leading into the text starting on the same line, as distinct from a heading placed above the text.

run on (1 *pri.)* Sheets printed in addition to the specified quantity. **(2** *typ.)* An instruction that two paragraphs are to be set as one as indicated.

run ragged Ragged right. → ranged left/right.

S

sad Mac icon The unhappy fellow who appears in place of the smiling icon at startup, indicating that something has gone wrong during the internal diagnostic tests that your Mac performs during startup. The sad Mac icon is accompanied by various sounds (or a number, depending on your model of Mac) which are different from the normal startup chord, and which indicate (to a trained ear) the nature of the problem.

SAM *(util.)* 79

same disk backup → backup, same disk.

sampler A device that digitizes sound so that it can be manipulated by computers.

sans serif Description of a generic type style without serifs and usually without stroke contrast.

saturation → HSB.

Save (File menu) The command that writes data from RAM to disk, thus ensuring that your work is preserved. Get into the habit of saving your work as frequently as possible – all you have to do is press Command-S. *138, 140*

Save As... (File menu) The command with which you can save a document under another name in the same or another location (or it can have the same name if it's in another location). Some applications will also let you save a document in another file format.

Save dialog box The dialog box that appears the first time that you save a document, asking you what you

want to call it and where you want to put it.

save out → reverse out.

sc, s caps *abb:* → small caps.

scale/scaling To determine the degree of enlargement or reduction required to obtain the desired reproduction size of an image.

scaling text → horizontal scaling.

scamp → rough.

scanned image *(rep.)* An image that has been converted by a scanner to a suitable file format that you can import into an application. To designers, the size of the file is important, since a single high resolution four-color scan for high quality reproduction may create a file of many megabytes, thus reducing the practicality of working with any quantity of scanned images. On jobs containing multiple images, it is more usual for designers to work with low resolution scans and use them for position only. → scanner.

scanner *(rep.)* An electronic device which converts artwork and transparencies into digital form so that they can be manipulated by a computer and/or output to separated film. A scanner may be a relatively simple "desktop" flatbed type or a very sophisticated reprographic device used for high-quality color separation. *42–6, 106–7, 133–4*

scatter proof *(rep.)* A proof of illustrations in which all the images are positioned at random and as closely packed as possible, without reference to their final page position. This is done in order to cut proofing costs, particularly when large numbers of illustrations are involved, such as in illustrated book work.

Scenebuilder *(app.) 71*

Scitex "IPSO" system *125*

Scitex Response system *136*

Scitex Visionary *(app.) 91, 135–6*

Scrapbook An Apple-supplied desk accessory where you can permanently store text or images, as distinct from the Clipboard which only holds items temporarily. To use the Scrapbook, you

select an item you are working on, copy or cut it, open the Clipboard and then select Paste from the Edit menu. The item will automatically appear on its own "page" in the Scrapbook.

Scrap Manager The part of the Toolbox that handles copying and pasting between applications and/or desk accessories.

scratch A term describing disk space that you may not need for normal Mac use, but which you have set aside by creating a partition, in case a non-Mac (or Mac) application requests it for temporary storage.

screen (1) → monitor.
(2) → halftone screen.
(3) → radiation shield.

screen angle *(rep.)* A term referring to the angle at which halftone screens of images printing in two or more colors are positioned, to minimize undesirable dot patterns when they are printed. The angle at which screens should be positioned depends upon the number of colors being printed, but the norm for four-color process printing, and thus the default setting for most Mac applications that support four-color separation, is: cyan 105°; magenta 75°; yellow 90°; black 45°.
→ halftone screen; moiré.

screen clash → moiré.

screen dump → screen shot.

screen filter → radiation shield.

screen font A file containing a bitmapped font that your Mac uses to render a typeface on your screen – or at least, that was how a Mac originally displayed a font on screen. Graphic design on the Mac was once a very frustrating occupation because of the vagaries of the bitmapped on-screen display of type – the notorious "jaggies." Fortunately, the advent of outline font technology has made it possible for screen rendering of typefaces to be much more accurate – the outline printer font can be "borrowed" for screen display. Unless you are using TrueType fonts, you will need Adobe Type Manager

to make this work with PostScript fonts. Even with ATM, you still need to install at least one size of the bitmapped screen font – so that its name appears in menus. Screen fonts are installed by using Apple's Font/DA Mover (unnecessary with System 7) or by using a font management utility such as Suitcase II or MasterJuggler.

screen printing *(pri.)* Also known as "silkscreen" printing, a printing process whereby ink is forced through a fine mesh stretched across a frame. The image is formed by means of a hand-cut or photographically generated stencil, which is bonded to the screen. Commercially, screen printing is generally used for printing onto difficult surfaces, for display work and small print runs.

screen resolution
(1) → pixel; resolution.
(2 *rep.)* Of halftone screens, the number of lines, or rows of dots, per inch. The greater the number of lines per inch, the finer the resolution – until the dots start filling in (which is dependent on the printing process and on the quality of paper). → halftone screen.

screen ruling → halftone screen; screen resolution (2)

screen saver, blanker A utility program (usually a control panel device) for preserving the phosphor coating on monitors by dimming the screen image, or by putting up a moving pattern, after a preset (by you) time of inactivity. *79*

screen shot/grab/dump/ capture A "snapshot" of part or all of the current screen image. Several utility programs are available for this purpose.

screen size (1) → monitor.
(2) → screen resolution.

screen tester *(rep.)* A device used for identifying the screen resolution of a printed halftone image.

screen type *(rep.)* Of a halftone screen, its pattern, such as dot, line, etc.

script The name given to programming languages that certain applications, such as HyperCard, allow you

o write.

scroll, scrolling To move the contents of a window (or directory listing) up or down, or sideways, so that you can view a part of a document that was hidden beyond the edges of the window. You do this by means of scroll bars, scroll boxes and scroll arrows.

scroll arrow The arrows at each end of a scroll bar that, when you click on one, move the contents of the window up, down, or sideways.

scroll bar The bars on the sides and/or (usually) bottom of a window (or directory listing) in which sits the scroll box. If the bar contains a gray fill, it indicates that there are portions of the document that go beyond what is displayed in the window.

scroll box The box that sits within the scroll bar of a window (or directory listing). It can be moved either by using the scroll arrows, or by clicking on it and dragging it up or down (or sideways) along the scroll bar. The position of the window image in relation to the whole document is indicated by the relative position of the scroll box to the scroll bar (if the scroll box is halfway up the scroll bar, the part of the document displayed in the window is halfway through the document).

SCSI (pron: skuzzy) *abb:* small computer system interface. A computer industry standard for interconnecting peripheral devices such as hard disk drives and scanners. The internal hard disk drive in your Mac is also a SCSI device. *30*

SCSI bus A term sometimes used to describe a chain of devices linked to a Mac SCSI port.

SCSI (daisy-)chain The linking, in sequence, of several peripheral devices to a SCSI port. There are various factors to bear in mind when setting up a SCSI chain: the maximum number of devices you can add to those already there (your internal drive and the Central Processing unit) is six; the total combined length of cabling between

all the devices must not exceed 23 feet (7 meters), but an upper limit of 16 to 20 feet (5 or 6 meters) is safer; no two devices should have the same ID number (→ SCSI ID number); there must be no more than two terminators in the entire chain (→ SCSI terminator); the actual position of a device, or order of devices, in the chain relative to other devices may be important – refer to the manufacturer's instructions.

SCSI device A peripheral device that attaches, or is attached, to a computer by means of a SCSI connection.

SCSI device, *problems 138*

SCSI ID number The number, or "address," assigned to each SCSI device connected to a Mac. There are eight numbers, from 0–7, numbers 0 and 7 being pre-assigned to your internal drive (if you have one) and your Mac's Central Processing unit respectively. The remaining six numbers are available to any other device in the chain, but each device must have a unique number. The numbering order of devices is arbitrary, but the device with the highest number takes priority if a situation demands it. The method of changing the number of a device varies; it may be by means of a "push-wheel" button, a dial, software, or it may even be preset internally.

SCSI partition → partition.

SCSI port The point where a SCSI cable connects to a SCSI device, using one of two varieties of SCSI connectors – 25-pin or 50-pin. Permutations of cable connections depend not only on the number of pins in the connector, but also on whether it is male or female. The SCSI port on your Mac is a 25-pin female bus.

SCSI Probe *(util.) 140*

SCSI terminator A device that protects a SCSI cable from "signal echo." A terminator may be internal within a device, or it may be a plug, resembling a SCSI connector, which you fit to the SCSI port of a device. On some devices, termination may be turned on or off by means of

switches. Internal drives are already terminated, but if you add another device, that too must be terminated – the first and last devices in a chain must be terminated and your internal drive, if you have one, counts as the first (physically the first, regardless of SCSI ID number). If you don't have an internal drive, the first and last external devices in a chain must be terminated. The last device in a SCSI chain connected to a Macintosh IIfx must use a special Apple terminator.

search path The route taken by your Mac when it looks for a file. → path (1).

SE Bus The data path from the expansion slot to the Central Processing unit, unique to the Macintosh SE (but not the SE/30, which has its own, called the "Direct Slot"). → bus; expansion slot.

secondary color A color obtained when two primary colors are mixed.

sector A segment of a track on a disk, containing space for 512 consecutive bytes of data, and being the smallest contiguous space in which data can be stored. → cylinder; track (2).

sector interleave factor → interleave ratio.

seek time → access time.

see-through → look-/see-/show-through.

segment A portion of an application. An application may be made up of several segments, not all of which need to be in RAM at the same time.

Select All (Edit menu) A command by which you can, in the Finder, select the entire contents of a window. It is also a command in some applications which enables you to select the entire contents of a document, page or an active box.

select(ing) To choose a thing (such as an icon or a piece of text) so that you can do something to or with it. To alter the state of any item, it must first be made active, or selected. If nothing within a window is active, but the window itself is, it may be understood by some applications that the entire

document is selected; i.e., a spelling check may be applied to a portion of text if that is selected, or to the whole document or text chain if it is not. You select something by clicking on it or dragging across it, depending on the current circumstances.

selection rectangle/box A dotted line forming a rectangle, drawn using the pointer or a "selection" tool, and which either disappears once the desired selection is made, or becomes a marquee. → marquee.

separation → color separation.

separation artwork Artwork in which a separate layer is created for each color to be printed.

serial interface A computer interface which transmits data bits sequentially, one at a time, in the same direction along a single wire or channel inside a cable. As distinct from a parallel interface.

serial ports The sockets on your Mac where you plug in devices which use a serial interface, such as printers and modems. *30*

serif The small terminal counterstroke at the end of the main strokes of a type character.

server → file server.

set In traditional type design, the width of an individual character. The width, or set, of the widest character (an em) is measured in points and subdivided into units, the set of each other character being a multiple of these units.

service agreement *109*

service bureau A company that provides general computer services from disk conversion to color scanning. The main use of a bureau by designers is for high resolution imagesetting – typesetting to bromide or film from your disk. *123, 129, 131–3*

set solid A term describing type set on its own body size without any leading: 10pt on 10pt.

Set Startup *(Sys.6)* The command (Special menu) that, when invoked, displays a dialog box in which you

can turn MultiFinder on or off. You can also choose whether you want certain applications, desk accessories or documents to open automatically on startup.

set-up *105–9*

set-up, *case studies 110–13*

set-up, *cost 108–9*

SGML *abb:* standard generalized markup language, a mark-up coding structure suitable for converting PC word-processor documents to conventional (non-Mac) computer typesetting systems.

shaded letter (1) → shadow font. **(2)** A letterform filled with hatched lines rather than solid tone.

shadow font Letterforms given a three-dimensional appearance by heavy shadows beside the main strokes.

shared disk A hard disk, attached to a networked computer, which can be accessed by other computers on the network.

shareware The term describing software that is freely available through user groups, bulletin boards, etc., and which you pay for only if you decide to continue using it. Unlike public-domain software, shareware is protected by copyright (not to be confused with "copy protected" – shareware, by its nature, is never copy-protected). *78*

shift-clicking To make multiple selections by holding down the Shift key while you click on the item.

Shift key The modifier key used to generate capital letters and other characters displayed on the keyboard. It can also be used for a variety of specific functions (→ shift-clicking) as well as serving as a general modifier key.

short page A page containing text to a length shorter than the usual length on other pages, adjusted to improve the layout or accommodate a break.

Show Clipboard A command in most applications enabling you to view the contents of the Clipboard, or in other words, to see the last item that you cut or copied.

show-through → look-/see-/show-through.

shuffling In some page make-up applications, a term describing the re-ordering of the pages of a document while retaining a logical numbering sequence.

Shut Down (Special menu) The command that enables you to turn off your Mac "safely" – that is, by first saving open documents, and ejecting any inserted disks. On the Macintosh II series, using Shut Down also turns off power to the Mac.

shut down To turn off your Mac or a peripheral device, having saved and closed all open documents and ejected all disks.

sidebar → box feature/story.

side bearing The letterspace assigned to each side of a PostScript type character that, if an application permits, can be adjusted to provide greater or less kerning.

SIG *abb:* special interest group.

signature (1) → Creator. **(2** *fin.)* The consecutive number, letter or other mark at the tail of each section in a book, which serves as a guide for binding. **(3** *fin.)* A numbered section prior to binding.

SIMM *abb:* single in-line memory module, a small plug-in board containing eight (sometimes nine) of the chips your computer uses for RAM. SIMMs are available in densities (capacity) of 256K, 1MB, 4MB and 16MB. A minimum of four SIMM's (two on some models) of equal density must be used. SIMMs may be either low- or high-profile (referring to physical height), depending on the model of Mac. *28, 29*

single-sided floppy disk → disk.

68000 series chip The series of microprocessor chips made by Motorola that encompasses all the processing chips used in Macs, including central processing units i.e. 68040, coprocessors i.e. 68882, and paged memory management units i.e. 68851.

size/sizing up

scale/scaling.

ze box The box in the wer right-hand corner of a indow that enables you, by icking on it and dragging, alter the size of the indow.

ze, *of monitor 33*

f type 85–6

kew, skewing In some plications, a feature nabling you to slant an em, such as a picture or ord.

lab/square serif Descrip- on of typefaces with quare serifs of almost the ame thickness as the prights, used in most egyptian typefaces.

lash → solidus.

lide presentation soft- vare 78

lip-sheeting → interleav- ng (1).

loped roman A term escribing an italic version f a font that is an optically r digitally distorted version f the roman design, as dis- nct from a separate, pecially-designed italic.

lot → expansion slot.

mall capitals/caps (sc, caps) Capital letters which re smaller than the stan- ard size, usually being bout the size of the x- eight. Traditionally, small aps were a specially esigned and cut font, rather han just being a smaller ze of type. However, on the Mac, small caps are gener- ted by scaling a single out- ne printer font, resulting in mall caps that are lighter in reight than the capitals and ower case. More and more onts are becoming available which have a specially esigned version for provid- ng small caps, giving a nuch more even "color" to ext setting. 96

mall computer system nterface → SCSI.

mall icon → by Small con.

mart quotes The term ometimes given to the facil- ty provided by some appli- ations to convert quotation marks from straight "pecks") to typesetting, or "curly" nes ("" '').

moothing A term describ- ng the refinement of itmapped images by round- ng off the corners of the

square dots, or pixels.

snap to A facility provided by some applications to exercise a sort of "magnetic pull" on items by guides and rulers, thus making position- ing of items more accurate.

softback → paperback.

soft copy (1) A copy of a file or document supplied on a disk, as distinct from a "hard" copy of the file or document as a printout on paper. (2) Text matter appearing on a computer monitor. (3 *typ.*) Typeset copy used for checking a text before camera-ready art is produced.

soft dot *(rep.)* A halftone dot on film that is less dense at the edge than at the center and is thus easier to etch for correction purposes.

software The term used to describe specially written collections of data, called programs, that make it pos- sible for a computer or any other item of computer- related hardware to perform its tasks. 50–83

software, *for graphic designers 76–7, 111, 113*
for set-up 100
toolbox 80–3
training 52–3
upgrading 53–4

solidus A type character in the form of an oblique stroke, used as a fraction slash (/) and generated on a Mac keyboard by pressing Shift-Option-1.

sort (1 *typ.*) A single charac- ter of type. (2) A feature pro- vided by some applications to arrange data in any cho- sen order.

Sound The Apple control panel device that allows you to choose a sound for alerts and to modify its volume. 30

Sound Manager The Macintosh device driver that generates sound.

source (1) Used of files, folders, and disks to mean the original being copied, as distinct from the copy, or duplicate. (2) Used of files, folders, and disks to mean the one something came from, as distinct from the target, the one it is going to.

source document A docu- ment from which items have been copied, as distinct from the document an item is being copied to – the

"target," or destination document.

source volume Used of files, folders, disks and devices to mean the place you are copying something from, as distinct from the "destination" – the place it is going to.

space An invisible, graded unit for spacing out a line of text.

Spacebar The key for creat- ing spaces between type characters.

spec(ification) A detailed description of the compo- nents, characteristics and procedures of a particular job, product or activity.

special character A type character supplied as part of a font, or character set, but generated by pressing modi- fier keys.

special effects 65, 70–1

Special menu One of the standard Finder menus, con- taining commands for such things as emptying the Trash and shutting down.

special sorts Type charac- ters not normally included in a font, or character set, such as fractions, musical nota- tions, etc. Also called "pecu- liars" or "pi characters." 96

specimen page A proof of a page as an example of a proposed style of design, paper quality, printing, etc.

speed, *of computers 27–8*
of modems 46–7

spelling checker A means of checking a document for spelling errors by way of a special dictionary, built in to most word-processing appli- cations, but also available as stand-alone utilities. Spelling checkers may be of batch or interactive mode varieties.

SPH *abb:* sheets per hour.

spike suppressor → surge suppressor.

spine *(fin.)* The center of the case of a book, which runs down the back of the book when it is cased in. Also called a "backbone."

split dash/rule A rule used as a traditional decoration. It is a rule that is thick at its center and tapered toward the ends, and which is split at the center by a bullet, star or other ornament.

spooler → print spooler.

spot color *(rep./pri.)* The

term used to describe any printing color that is a special mix of colors, and not one of the four process colors.

spread (**1**) In general usage, two facing pages of a document or publication. Technically, a double truck or double-page spread occurs when matter crosses the gutter to occupy the two center pages of a section. Otherwise it is a "false double." (**2**) → trapping.

spreadsheet An application that, using a grid system of rows and columns which create interacting rectangles, called "cells," makes it possible to carry out complex calculations. 75, 78

square-corner/rectangle tool In most graphics applications, the tool that enables you to draw a rectangular box or shape.

squared(-up) (**halftone**) (rep.) A halftone image that has been trimmed to a square or rectangular shape.

squares (fin.) The portion of the inside of a case which projects beyond the cut edges of a book.

square serif → slab serif.

SRA paper sizes (pap.) The designation of untrimmed paper for bled work in the series of international paper sizes.
→ international paper sizes; RA paper sizes.

s/s abb: same size, an instruction to reproduce an item at its original size.

stacking order In graphics applications, the position of an item relative to other items in front of or behind it.

staircasing → jaggie.

standard character set → character set.

Standard File dialog box The dialog box you get when you select Open or Save As from the File menu, or when you open or save documents within an application. Also called directory dialog box.

Standard File Package The routines for providing the standard Macintosh user interface when a file is opened or closed.

standard generalized markup language → SGML.

standard menu One of three menus (Apple, File and Edit) that appear as standard in almost all applications.

standing time → open time.

starburst (**1** pho.) A photographic effect of radiating lines from a highlight, provided by a filter that diffuses light from a strong, concentrated source. (**2**) In some applications, the name given to the shape that the pointer assumes when certain transformation tools are selected.

star network A network configuration in which the the central processing unit node has a number of other nodes radiating from it in a star shape.

start bit A bit used in data communication to indicate the start of data transmission. → asynchronous communication; stop bit

start(ing)/startup → boot(ing) up.

startup application (Sys.6) The application which is opened first when you start up your Mac – the Finder or MultiFinder.

startup disk/device Any disk – internal or external, hard or floppy – that contains, at the very least, the System and Finder files which your Mac needs in order to boot up. 138

startup document/file → init.

startup errors 140

startup sheet The printed test sheet that a LaserWriter produces each time it is switched on, telling you, among other things, how many sheets have been printed on that particular printer.

startup-screen file The image displayed at startup. The design must be in a special startup screen format, must be called StartupScreen and must be in the system folder to work.

static RAM → dynamic RAM.

stationery A document which serves as a template – when opened, it is automatically duplicated, leaving the original intact.

stem The most distinctive vertical stroke, or that closest to vertical, in a type character.

step and repeat To produce multiple copies of an image at different sizes in defined increments.

stet A Latin word meaning "let it stand." It is used when marking up copy and correcting proofs to cancel previous instruction or correction.

Sticky Keys → Easy Access.

stop bit A bit used in data communication to indicate the end of one byte. → asynchronous communication; start bit.

storage The term used to describe data that is preserved for future use or modification, as distinct from memory, in which data is merely "in transit." → disk. 24, 25, 29–30

storage media 36

straight matter A body of text without break for headings, illustrations, etc.

StrataVision 3d (app.) 65, 70–1

stress The apparent direction of a letterform, given emphasis by the heaviest part of a curved stroke.

string A given sequence of characters, including spaces and special characters.

stripping (**1** rep.) Assembling two or more images to produce a composite for making final film in photomechanical reproduction. (**2** typ.) To insert a typeset correction in film or on camera-ready art. (**3** fin.) To glue a strip of cloth or paper to the back of a paperback book or pad as a reinforcement.

stripping up as one (rep.) Assembling two or more images or items of film to combine them as a single piece of film in photomechanical reproduction.

strobe → flicker.

stroke (**1**) The outline of an shape or type character, as distinct from the inside area called the "fill." (**2** typ.) A straight, diagonal part of a type character.

Studio 32 (app.) 65

StuffIt Deluxe (util.) 79

Style (**sheets**) In some applications, the facility for applying a range of frequently used attributes, such as typographic and paragraph formats, to elements in a document by using specially assigned

...mmands. *116*

...yle The term used to ...scribe a stylistic modifica- ...n of a font, such as italic, ...adow, outline, etc.

...bdirectory Any directory ...her than the root directory.

...bhead(ing) Any heading ...r the division of a chapter.

...bject *(rep.)* The term used ... describe any single image ...hich is to be reproduced or ...iginated.

...bmenu A menu attached ... a main menu item, which ...ppears as the result of ...lecting that item. It is nor- ...ally indicated by a (▶).

...bscriber → publish and ...bscribe.

...bscript → inferior char- ...cter.

...bsidiaries → end matter.

...btractive colors The pri- ...ary colors used in printing ...cyan, magenta and yellow.
→ primary colors; process ...olor.

...uggested Memory Size ...formation provided via the ...et Info dialog box (File ...enu) regarding the mini- ...um amount of memory that ...n application needs to be ...ble to run, as suggested by ...s author or producer. This ... the portion of RAM that ...ill be set aside for use ...xclusively by that applica- ...on. A box is provided for ...ou to modify the amount of ...emory allocated to the ...pplication, and you may ...eed to increase it if you are ...orking on very long, com- ...lex or graphics-intensive ...ocuments. To alter the ...emory size, you must first ...uit the application.
→ Application Memory Size.

...uitcase (file) A file, repre- ...ented by an icon of a suit- ...ase – thence its name – ...which may be either a desk ...ccessory or a screen font.

...uitcase II *(util.)* 78, 89, 98

...UM II *(util.)* 79

...uperDrive → floppy disk ...rive.

...uperior The term used to ...escribe figures or letters ...hat are smaller than text ...ize, the top of which is ...ligned with the cap height ...f the text as in (²), as dis- ...'nct from superscript, which ...ppears above the cap ...eight.

...uperscript The term used ... describe figures or letters

that are smaller than text size, and which are raised above the cap height as in (²), as distinct from superior.

Super 3D *(app.)* 65

support The term used to describe after-sales help, provided by the producer of a product or by its sales rep- resentative.

surface mapping → tex- ture/surface mapping.

surface mount SIMM Alternative term for a "low- profile" SIMM.

surge suppressor An essential item for protecting hardware from damaging fluctuations in power supply. Various forms are available, such as in-line units or power strips. Also called "spike suppressors" and "power cleaners."

swatch A color sample.

surprinting → overprint.

swelled dash/rule A rule that prints as a thick line in the center, tapering at both ends.

switch-launching *(Sys.6)* To exchange the current System and Finder (the one that you started up from) for another on a separate disk, without restarting your Mac. You may want to do this to gain access to fonts and desk accessories on another disk or to use a different System version. The icon of the disk whose System and Finder files are currently being used is always at top right of your screen. You can switch-launch by holding down Option-Command while you double-click on the Finder icon on the disk you want to switch to. Alternatively, you can hold down the Option key while double-clicking an applica- tion icon on the disk you want to switch to, although this method is unpredictable. The version number of the Finder on the target disk must be the same as, or later than, the current startup disk. You cannot switch-launch in MultiFinder.

Swivel 3D Professional *(app.)* 65, 70–1

SYLK *abb:* symbolic link, a file format for transferring spreadsheet data between applications. *128*

symbol A letter, figure or

drawn sign that represents or identifies an object, pro- cess or activity, although not necessarily pictorially.

synchronous communica- tion A communications pro- tocol by which data is transmitted, in chunks, between rigid timing signals. As distinct from asyn- chronous communication.

sysop *abb:* system operator, a person who operates a bulletin-board system.

system A complete set of connected things, organized to achieve an objective.

system disk A disk contain- ing (at the very least) a System and Finder file. If you use it when you boot up, it becomes the startup disk.

system error → bomb.

system extension A file, stored in the Extensions folder, that adds enhance- ments to the system soft- ware.

System file The file used to provide, with the Finder and software residing in ROM, the Mac's operating system. The System file also con- tains fonts, sounds and key- board files. *22*

system folder A folder that contains the System and Finder files and any other files that are run as part of the system. It is distinguish- able from other folders by an icon of a Mac on its front. Also called a "blessed folder."

system heap The part of RAM set aside for use by the System. The size of the heap is determined at startup.

system operator → sysop.

system software The term that describes all the pro- grams that contribute toward the operating infras- tructure of your Mac. It includes, in addition to the System and Finder files, all the RAM-based files – con- trol panel devices, inits, desk accessories, utilities, fonts and resources – in your sys- tem folder.

System Tools The name given to describe a collec- tion of concurrent versions of system files.

T

tab-delimit To separate data elements such as records or fields by using

the Tab key.

Tab key The key that moves the insertion point to the next tab stop or, in dialog boxes, databases and spreadsheets comprising fields, from one box (field) to the next.

tablet → digitizing pad/tablet.

tab stop The place at which the text insertion point stops when the Tab key is pressed.

tabular work Type matter set in columns.

tabulate To arrange text or figures in the form of a columnar table, according to fixed measures.

tail The bottom edge of a book.

tail margin The margin at the bottom of a page, also called a "foot margin."

take back (typ.) An instruction, marked on a proof, to take back characters, words or lines to the preceding line, column or page.

take in (typ.) An instruction, marked on a proof, to include extra copy supplied.

take over (typ.) An instruction, marked on a proof, to take over characters, words or lines to the following line, column or page.

tape drives 39

taper Of gradated tones and colors, the progression of one tone or color to the next. Gradations may be in equal increments or may be logarithmic (the increments of tones or colors increase from one end of the gradation to the other).

taper angle The direction of gradated tones or colors.

target Used of files, folders, and disks to mean the one something is going to, as distinct from the source, the one where it came from.

target printer The device that a document is sent to for printing.

TeachText An application that allows you to read "plain text" documents. These are documents that frequently accompany application files to provide instructions for installation, corrections to the documentation, etc.

tear-off menu In some applications, a menu that, when it pops down from the menu bar, can be "torn" off

by dragging it away from the menu bar onto the desktop, where it can be moved around as you need it.

technical support → support.

temp file A temporary file, used by the application that created it.

template (1) A shape, or sheet with cutout shapes, used as a drawing aid. (2) A document or page created with page, paragraph and text formats to be used as a basis for repeated use in other documents.

terminal emulation Software that enables one computer to mimic another by acting as a terminal for its "host."

terminating resistor/terminator → SCSI terminator.

text (1) Information presented as readable characters. (2) Typeset matter forming the main body of a publication.

text box/field (1) In frame-based applications, a box, created with a text tool, for entering and working with text. (2) A field, such as in a dialog box, into which you enter text.

text by modem 117–18

text chain A set of linked text boxes, with text flowing from one to another.

text editor Any program which you use to enter and edit text. → word processor.

text file A file containing only text bits, without any formatting. → ASCII.

text input 116–18

text insertion bar The blinking bar in a text box that indicates the insertion point.

text insertion point The place, indicated by the text insertion bar, where the next character will be positioned.

text marker In word processors, a symbol positioned in the text to provide a reference marker so that you can return to it instantly (by using the Find command). Also called a "wildcard."

text on disk 117

text reflow → reflow.

text tool → I-beam pointer.

text type/matter (typ.) Any typeface of a suitable size for printing a body of text, usually in a range of 8pt to 14pt.

text wrap → runaround.

texture/surface mapping A graphic technique of wrapping a two-dimensional image around a three-dimensional object.

thick (typ.) The term sometimes used to describe a word space measuring one third of an em.

thin (typ.) The term sometimes used to describe a word space measuring one fifth of an em.

third-party A term sometimes used to describe an item, whether hardware or software, not made by the manufacturer of the item it is designed to be used with

three-dimensional modelling 65, 70–1

throughput A unit of time measured as the period elapsing between start and finish of a particular job.

Thumb Design Partnership, case study 110–12

thumbnail (1) Rough, miniature layouts of a proposed design or publication, showing a variety of treatments the order of chapters, etc. (2) In some applications, the facility to view and print pages together on a sheet a reduced size.

tied letter → ligature.

TIFF abb: tagged image file format, a standard and popular graphics file format used for scanned, high-resolution bitmapped images. 128

tight A term referring to a design, or to text, that is very closely-packed and includes little blank space.

tiling (1) The term used to describe copying an item and repeating it in all directions, thus creating a pattern. (2) The term used to describe the method of printing a document page that is too large to fit onto a single sheet by breaking it into overlapping portions which, when assembled, form the whole page.

time-slicing → multitasking.

tint (1) The effect of the admixture of white to a solid color. (2) The effect achieved by breaking up a solid color into dots and allowing white paper to show through. Tint are specified in percentages of the solid color. 129, 130

...sues → layout.

...le bar The bar at the top ...an open window which ...ntains its name and, when ...tive, six horizontal rules. ...e window can be moved ...ound the desktop by click-...g and dragging its title bar. ...e title bar may or may not ...ntain a close box and/or a ...om box.

...le page The page, nor-...ally a right-hand page, at ...e front of a book which ...ars the title, name(s) of ...e author(s), the publisher ...d any other relevant infor-...ation.

...le verso (T/V) The verso ...the title page of a book, ...ually containing copyright ...formation. → verso.

...ggle Of menus and check-...xes, those that turn from ...f to on (or from a positive ...mmand to a negative one), ...vice versa, each time you ...lect or check it.

...nal value The relative ...nsities of tones in an ...age. → color value.

...ne-line process (rep.) A ...chnique of producing line ...t from a continuous tone ...iginal by combining a neg-...ive and positive film ...age.

...ol A feature of most ...aphics applications, con-...sting of a device (tool) ...hich, when selected, turns ...e pointer into a shape rep-...senting that tool, which ...u then use to perform the ...signated task; i.e., you use ...box tool for creating boxes. ...–3

...oolbox The part of the ...ftware written into the ...acintosh ROM that ...ables software developers ... take advantage of the ...ac user interface. The ...olbox Managers handle ...ch things as dialog boxes, ...indows, fonts, mouse, key-...oard, and so on. In fact, it is ...e Toolbox that sets the ...acintosh computer apart ...om other computers. 23

...oolbox Managers ... Toolbox.

...ol palette/box In those ...pplications that feature ...pecial tools, the window, ...sually floating, on which ...ey are displayed for selec-...on. → palette.

...PD abb: → two-page ...splay.

tps abb: → trimmed page size.

track (1 pri.) The printing line from the front edge of a plate to the back. Items imposed in track will all be subject to the same inking adjustments on press. (2) The term describing the con-centric "rings" circumscrib-ing a disk, in which data is stored. Each track is divided into sectors. → disk; sector.

trackball A device for mov-ing the pointer, resembling an upturned mouse – i.e. with the mouse ball on top rather than underneath. You move the pointer by fondling the ball. Because the device remains stationary, it occu-pies less desk space than the conventional mouse.

tracking A term describing the adjustment of space between the characters in a selected piece of text. As distinct from kerning, which only involves pairs of characters.

tracking values, table 102–3

training, in software 52–3

transformation tools The name sometimes given to tools that change the loca-tion or appearance of an item. 82

transient font An automati-cally downloaded font that only lasts in a laser printer's memory until the document currently being printed has finished printing. As distinct from a so-called "perma-nent" font, which lasts in memory until the printer is switched off.

transitional A classification of typefaces that are neither old face nor modern, such as Baskerville and Fournier.

translator The term describ-ing data required by Apple File Exchange so that it can translate a document cre-ated on one operating sys-tem into a document that can be used on another.

transparent A term used to describe any software item that operates without any interaction on your part – apart from installing it in the first place.

transpose To swap the positions of any two items of text, or two images, either by design or because they are wrongly ordered.

trapping (rep./pri.) The slight overlap of two colors to eliminate gaps that may occur between them due to the normal fluctuations of registration during printing. → choke; fatty. 119, 137

Trash The garbage can icon, which performs like a folder, in the bottom right-hand cor-ner of your desktop where you put files as a prelude to deleting them. Dragging the icon of a disk to the Trash both ejects the disk and removes its icon from the desktop.

trim (fin.) To cut printed sheets to the required size.

trim marks → corner marks.

trimmed page size A term used to describe the size of a printed and bound book, referring to the page size rather than the size including the binding.

troubleshooting 137–40

trs abb: → transpose.

TrueType Apple's outline font format produced as an alternative to PostScript. A single TrueType file is used both for printing and for screen rendering – unlike PostScript fonts, which require a screen font file as well as the printer font file. TrueType font files reside in the System suitcase file. → outline font. 41, 74, 95, 97

turning off → shut down.

T/V abb: → title verso.

twenty-four-/24 bit color The allocation of 24 bits of memory to each pixel, giving a possible screen display of 16.7 million colors (a row of 24 bits can be written in 16.7 million different combi-nations of 0s and 1s). → four-bit color; eight-bit color.

twice up Artwork prepared at twice the size at which it will be reproduced.

two-page display (TPD) Name given to a 21in. moni-tor (measured diagonally). → monitor.

Type 1 font The Adobe PostScript outline font for-mat containing hints. Type 1 fonts were formerly encrypt-ed, meaning that you could not alter them, but Adobe has now made the format available to all in response to the introduction of the open format of TrueType.

Type 1 fonts come as two files: an outline printer file and a bitmapped screen file. → Adobe Type Manager; hinting; encryption; outline font. *74, 78, 91*

Type 3 font A PostScript font format which, not being encrypted, was introduced as an alternative to the encrypted Type 1 font format. Type 3 fonts do not contain hints and, in any case, are now virtually obsolete. → hinting; encryption. *74, 91*

TypeAlign *(app.) 73, 74*

type area The area of a page designed to contain the main body of text, thus creating margins.

type design, *and the computer 71–9*
software 72–3

type effect The modification of type characters to create a special effect, such as outline, zoom, etc.

typeface The term describing a type design, including variations on that design such as italic and bold, but excluding all the other related designs, as distinct from type family.

type family A term describing all the variations related to a basic type design, such as Goudy Old Style, Goudy Catalogue, Goudy Handtooled, etc., as distinct from a typeface.

type mark-up → mark-up.
type measurements *85–7*
type scale/gauge A rule marked with a scale of line measurements in varying increments of point size.
type series → font series.
typesetting (**1** *typ.*) The process of converting text into a recognized font and producing it in a form suitable for printing. (**2** *typ.*) The text item produced by (**1**).
typesetting, *by computer 124–5*

type specifications The characteristics of type used in a design, such as font, size, measure, etc. → mark-up.
type style → style.
TypeStyler *(app.) 73, 74*
type synopsis/specimen sheet A printed sample of a font showing the full character set.
typo *(typ.) abb:* typographic error. An error occuring

during typesetting, such as the wrong font or size, as distinct from a literal, such as a spelling mistake, which may also be an error in a manuscript.

typographer (**1**) A person whose occupation is typography. (**2**) → compositor.
typography The art, and arrangement, of type. *84–104*

typography, *and the imagesetter 129, 131*
horizontal scaling 104
justification methods 100–1
special sorts 96
tracking values 102–3

U

UC *abb:* → upper case.
UCR *abb:* → under-color removal.
u/lc *abb:* upper and lower case, an instruction for type to be set in both upper and lower case, as appropriate.
umlaut → accent.
under-color removal (UCR) *(rep.)* The technique of removing unwanted color from scanned color separations either to reduce the amount of ink or because the colors cancel each other out, such as removing the magenta and yellow dots when there is enough black and cyan to cover.
underline/underscore A rule printed beneath a word or portion of text.
Undo (Edit menu) A standard command, found in most applications, that allows you to revert to the last text or format change. Some applications allow several levels of "Undo."
ungroup To "Undo" a group.
unit system A system of type design in which character widths conform to unit measurements associated with the set of the character. → set.
Universal Copyright Convention An international assembly that, in 1952, agreed protection for the originator of an "intellectual work" – a text, photograph, illustration, etc. – to prevent the use of that work without permission from its creator or copyright owner. The work must carry the copyright mark ©, the name of the owner of the copyright and the date of its first

publication. → copyright.
Universal Product Code (UPC) → bar code.
UNIX The AT&T operating system devised to be multi tasking, and portable from one computer type to another. Apple's UNIX system is called A/UX.
unjustified Lines of type which do not align with both left and right margins, as does justified type. Unjustified type may be ranged left or right, or it may be centered. The appearance of unjustified type is also called free line fall.
unlock → lock; locked file; write-protect.
unmount To remove a volume from the desktop or eject a disk.
unsharp masking The technique of enhancing the details in a scanned image by exaggerating the density of pixels at the edges of a color change (the image is first blurred, hence the term "unsharp").
upgrade (**1**) To modify or enhance a computer. You can upgrade your Mac by changing the logic board to one that gives the Mac greater capabilities, by adding a chip such as a PMMU, or by simply installing a later version of the system software. (**2**) A newer, enhanced (often merely by debugging it) issue of a program, sometimes in the form of a "patch," and as distinct from a completely new version. Upgrades can be identified by a decimalized figure – 1 being the original, 1.2 and 1.3 being upgrades and 2.0 being a rewrite, or new version. *53–4*
upload To send data to a distant computer. Opposite of download.
upper case The capital letters of a type font.
upright → portrait.
user A person who uses hardware and software, as distinct from someone who makes or writes it.
user group A group of people who share experiences, knowledge, problems, software, etc., relating to a specific type of computer. A Macintosh user group can often be recognized by the

tials MUG as part of its me.

er interface → GUI; erface.

er-specified defaults gram defaults that have en specified or modified the user.

ility A program that hances or supports the e of your Mac generally, applications specifically. pical utilities are backup grams, font management grams, file-finding pro- ams, defragmentation pro- ams, file recovery grams, etc. 78–9

lue → color value; tonal ue.

OU/VDT abb: visual dis- ay unit/terminal. monitor.

ctor → object-oriented.

lox → photomechanical nsfer.

ntura Publisher (app.)

rification A term used to scribe the process of test- g the integrity of the data cks on a disk drive by iting and reading data hich is checked against nes for accuracy.

rso The left-hand page of book or, more precisely, e other side of a leaf from recto (right-hand page).

rtical alignment The acement of lines of text in lation to the top and bot- m of a page, column or x.

rtical bar pointer I-beam pointer.

rtical blanking interval blanking interval.

rtical justification The acing out of a block of text that it vertically fills a ge, column or box.

ry low frequency (VLF) ELF.

deo A Latin term meaning see," now used in refer- ce to all television-based oducts.

deo card A plug-in board at controls an external onitor. → board. 35–6

deo digitizer → digitizer.

deoPaint (app.) 65

deo port 30, 32

deo RAM The portion of AM reserved for monitor splay. → RAM.

ew The Finder menu that

allows you to choose your preferred form of viewing the contents of a window, such as by Label, by Date, by Icon.

virtual Computer jargon for "imaginary" or "conceptual," or something that seems as though it exists, but really it doesn't – or at least it does, but only until the software that created it doesn't! So "virtual reality" is an imag- ined reality, indistinguish- able from real life provided the environment that created it is in operation. "Virtual memory" is a technique of making memory seem larger than it really is by using whatever memory space, other than in its own RAM, may be available elsewhere for holding data, such as on a hard disk, and loading it into main memory in such a way that it appears as if it were in main memory all the time. This means that you can work with as much memory as you have disk space, but the price you pay for this luxury is speed – vir- tual memory is only as fast as the access time of your disk, although if you have plenty of RAM, the memory exchanges between RAM and disk should be almost transparent. To take advan- tage of virtual memory in System 7, you must have a "paged memory manage- ment unit" (PMMU) installed in your Mac, since it is this memory manager that manu- factures and controls the vir- tual memory. 25, 27, 28

virus A computer program that is deliberately written to alter the normal operation of a computer. These virus programs are spread from computer to computer across networks or when disks are copied in one and used in another. Viruses may infect some files, but not others (say, applications, but not documents), and they mani- fest themselves in different ways, sometimes by crash- ing your computer, or by sim- ply beeping, displaying a message, or causing strange behavior such as bouncing the pointer around the screen or altering font styles. Although very few viruses cause malicious

damage, some may create serious problems. In any event, all Macs should have virus protection software installed. 78–9, 138

virus protection program A utility program designed, at least, to alert you to the fact that a disk or file is infected and, at best, to eradicate the virus and pre- vent any other possible infections. There are many such utilities available, both commercial and shareware.

visual → rough.

visual interface → GUI.

VLF abb: very low frequency → ELF.

volume A device or a parti- tion where data is stored. → disk; partitioning.

volume bitmap A record of the used (represented by an "on" bit) and unused (off) blocks on a volume.

volume directory → directory.

W

Walkthrough (app.) 78

WAN abb: wide area net- work. A network spread over a large area and which may use satellite or land-based telecommunications links. As distinct from a local area network (LAN), two or more of which may connected to each other by a WAN.

warm boot To restart your Mac without recourse to the power switch. You can reboot your Mac by selecting the Restart command (Special menu) or by using the reset button on the pro- grammer's switch.

weight The degree of bold- ness of a typeface.

w.f. (typ.) abb: wrong font, a mark used in proof correc- tion to indicate type set in a different font from the one specified.

white line A space between lines of type equiv- alent to the type size, includ- ing leading.

white space Page areas with no text or images. → working white.

wide area network → WAN.

widget A colloquial term for any unspecified device.

widow Strictly speaking, a short line at the end of a paragraph that falls at the top of a column or page, but

the term is often used to describe a single word at the end of any paragraph.

wildcard → text marker.

WIMPs abb: Windows, icon, mouse (or menus) and pointer – the acronym for the graphical user interface of the Mac. *17, 19*

window An area on the screen that displays the contents of a disk, folder or document. Windows can be opened or closed, moved around the desktop, and you can sometimes change their size or scroll through them. *18–19, 20–1*

Windows The Microsoft PC application that partially emulates the Macintosh user interface.

Wingz *(app.) 75, 78*

word A term used to describe a given number of bits.

Word *(app.) 75*

word break → hyphenation.

WordPerfect *(app.) 75*

word processor An application that provides text editing features such as spelling checkers, indexing, sorting, etc. *75*

word space The space between whole words, based on the width of characters of the typeset size.

word underline → underline.

word wrap The automatic flow of text from one line to the next as you enter it, without the need to press the Return key.

working methods, *case study 112*

working white (ww) A term describing white space in a design or layout which contains no text or images, but which forms an integral part of the design.

worksheet A term sometimes used to describe a spreadsheet template.

workstation A term used to describe the physical location and immediate environment of computer input – in other words, the place where you work on your computer.

WORM abb: write once read many, a large-capacity data storage device utilizing optical disks onto which data can be written only once and which can then never be erased. *39*

wristwatch pointer The shape the pointer usually assumes to advise you that data is being processed. → pointer.

write-enable The opposite of write-protect.

WriteNow *(app.) 75*

write once read many → WORM.

write-protect To protect a disk from erasure, accidental or otherwise, or from contamination by viruses, by preventing any data from being written to it or deleted from it, although the contents can still be read.

writing head → read/write head.

wrong reading *(rep./pri.)* The term used to describe copy or film that reads backwards when viewed with the emulsion on the desired side.

ww abb: → working white.

WYSIWYG (pron: wizzywig) An acronym for "what you see is what you get," referring to the accuracy of on-screen rendering relative to printed output. *40*

X

XCMD abb: → external command.

x-height The height, or "mean-line," of a lower case letter, without ascenders or descenders.

xerography A dry copying process in which electrostatically charged powder is bonded to paper.

XFCN abb: → external function.

XON/XOFF A "handshaking" protocol used by computer when communicating via modems.

YZ

Y abb: yellow → process yellow.

zapping the PRAM The term used to describe the setting of a Mac's parameter RAM to its original default settings, if and when it becomes corrupted. You do this by holding down the Option-Command-P-R keys while restarting your computer, or *(Sys.6)*, selecting the Apple menu and then holding down Shift-Option-Command while you select the Control Panel (the new settings take effect after you restart your computer). Date and time settings will not be affected.

zero point → origin.

zone One part of two or more connected networks.

zoom box The box at the right of some window title bars that, when clicked, expands the window to display all of its contents (if possible). Clicking it again reduces it to its original size.

CREDITS

p.68: (top) Adobe Systems Inc; p.69: Quarto (photographer Anthony Blake); p.110: British Petroleum; p.111: Bank of Scotland; p.112: Business Design Center; p.113: from *The Real World*, Marshall Editions Developments 1991; p.134: (top) Quarto (photographer David Burch). I would like to thank the following for supplying software used in the preparation of this book: **Adobe Systems UK** (Illustrator, PhotoShop); **Aldus UK Ltd** (Digital Darkroom, PageMaker); **Amtech International Ltd** (Disk Doubler, J.A.G., Ray Dream Designer); **Claris UK** (MacDraw Pro); **Crosfield UK** (Lightspeed CLS); **Electronic Arts** (Studio/32); **Gomark Ltd** (ModelShop II, Swivel 3D Professional, StrataVision 3d); **Letraset UK** (ColorStudio, DesignStudio, FontMonger, FontStudio, ImageStudio, LetraStudio, Painter); **SuperMac Technology** (PixelPaint Professional).

YOU'VE READ THE BOOK.
NOW SPIN THE DISK.

An expanded version of the Glossary section in *The MacDesigner's Handbook* is available on floppy disk. On the disk is a file containing explanations of more than 2,500 commonly used computer and design terms. The file is easy to use and you can keep it in your Apple Menu, making it readily accessible. The disk comes with full instructions on how to install and use the file.

The price* of the disk is $18.00 (U.S.), or $20.00 (overseas), which includes postage by U.S. Mail.

YOU WILL NEED:

1. A 1.44Mb floppy disk drive.
2. The application HyperCard®, version 2.1 or later.